MILTON
AND
THE MARTIAL MUSE

MILTON
AND
THE MARTIAL MUSE
PARADISE LOST
 AND EUROPEAN
TRADITIONS
OF WAR

JAMES A. FREEMAN

PRINCETON UNIVERSITY PRESS
PRINCETON, NEW JERSEY

Copyright © 1980 by Princeton University Press
Published by Princeton University Press, Princeton, New Jersey
In the United Kingdom: Princeton University Press,
Guildford, Surrey

All Rights Reserved
Library of Congress Cataloging in Publication Data will be
found on the last printed page of this book

Publication of this book has been aided by a grant
from The Andrew W. Mellon Foundation.

This book has been composed in VIP Aldus

Clothbound editions of Princeton University Press books
are printed on acid-free paper, and binding materials are
chosen for strength and durability

Printed in the United States of America by
Princeton University Press, Princeton, New Jersey

For Matt, Eric, and Margaret

Quid sit cum Marte poetae?
(What does a poet have to do with Mars?)
Ovid, *Fasti*

The late times of *Civil War*, and *confusion* to
make recompense for their infinite calamities,
brought this advantage with them, that they stirr'd
up mens minds from *long ease*, and a *lazy rest*, and
made them *active, industrious* and *inquisitive*. . . .
But now since the *Kings* return, the blindness of
the former *Ages*, and the miseries of this last, are
vanish'd away: now men are generally weary of the
Relicks of *Antiquity*. . . . Now there is a universal
desire, and *appetite* after *knowledge*, after the
peaceable, the fruitful, the nourishing *Knowledge*.

Thomas Sprat, *The History of
The Royal Society of London*

CONTENTS

LIST OF ILLUSTRATIONS

Figures 1, 5, 6, 7, 9, 10, 15, 16, 17, 22, and 26 are used by courtesy of Fratelli Alinari; figures 2, 11, 14, 19, and 24 by permission of The Huntington Library, San Marino, California; figure 4 by courtesy of the Museum of Fine Arts, Boston, Maria T. B. Hopkins Fund; figure 8 by permission of the British Library; figures 12 and 18 by courtesy of the Library of Congress, Washington, D. C.; figures 23 and 25 by courtesy of the National Portrait Gallery, London; figure 27 by courtesy of the Folger Shakespeare Library, Washington, D. C.; and figure 13 by courtesy of Columbia University, Rare Book and Manuscript Library, Gonzalez Lodge Collection.

ACKNOWLEDGMENTS

No Milton scholar works alone. Even during those hours when I seemed to be by myself, exploring how *Paradise Lost* both reflects and rejects popular ideas about war, a group of extraordinary individuals accompanied me. A brief mention cannot repay them for their varied kindnesses. Yet each of the following helped me, and I am happy to thank the Graduate Research Council of the University of Massachusetts for awarding me study grants in 1977 and 1978; the editor of *Milton Quarterly* Roy Flannagan and the editor of *Comparative Literature* Steven F. Rendall, for allowing me to summarize material that I originally presented in their journals; the interlibrary loan coordinators at the University of Massachusetts, Edla Holm and Ute Bargmann, for locating many vital books; Joseph Frank, for reading and praising an early draft; Ernest Gallo, for sharing his knowledge of medieval matters; William B. Hunter, Jr., for offering humane support; Vincent J. Di Marco, for supplying Leo the Emperor's book on war as well as solutions to several medieval problems; Paul L. Mariani, for civilizing some barbarities in my style; Richard Noland, for encouraging research during his time as English Department Chairman and Dean of Humanities; John T. Shawcross, for supplying facts and correcting errors, with authority and warmth; Sara and Anna Volterra, for providing such gracious assistance in Florence; my sons, Matt and Eric, for offering playful alternatives to war; my wife, Margaret, for editing, enduring, and being.

A NOTE ABOUT REFERENCES

In the following pages, I usually translate classical passages from standard Oxford or Teubner texts. Sometime I use the readily available Loeb translations. In both cases, the reference is in parentheses immediately following the quotation. Patristic and medieval churchmen are usually translated directly from *Patrologiae Cursus Completus . . . sive Latinorum sive Graecorum*, ed. J.-P. Migne, 387 vols. (Paris, 1844-66). Biblical quotations come from the King James version. Renaissance and modern works are identified in the footnotes. Since I draw upon certain Renaissance books more than once, those frequently used are cited in an initial footnote and thereafter identified by a short title in parentheses after the quotation.

ABBREVIATIONS OF MILTON'S WORKS

Britain	*The History of Britain* (1670)
CD	*De Doctrina Christiana* (*On Christian Doctrine.* Completed c. 1658)
C. E.	Columbia Edition of *The Works of John Milton*, 23 vols., ed. Frank Allen Patterson (1931-40)
Def. 1	*Defensio pro Populo Anglicano* (*Defence of the English People.* 1651)
Def. 2	*Defensio Secunda* (*Second Defence.* 1654)
Ed	*Of Education* (1644)
Eikon	*Eikonoklastes* (1649)
El	*Elegies* 1-7 (1626-30)
Ely	"In obitum Praesulis Eliensis" ("On the Death of the Bishop of Ely." 1627)
Fam Let	Familiar Letters (various dates)
Manso	Latin poem to Giovanni Baptista Manso (written c. 1638)
Nat	"Naturam non pati senium" ("Nature is not Subject to Old Age." 1628)
Il P	*Il Pensoroso* (written c. 1631)
PL	*Paradise Lost* (rev. ed., 1674)
PR	*Paradise Regained* (1671)
Pro	*Prolusions* 1-7 (1674)
RCG	*The Reason of Church Government Urged against Prelatry* (1642)
Sonn	*Sonnets* 1-23 (various dates)
TKM	*The Tenure of Kings and Magistrates* (1649)

MILTON
AND
THE MARTIAL MUSE

INTRODUCTION

In 1638, the very year Milton reached Florence, Peter Paul Rubens sent a large painting to the grand duke of Tuscany. No one today knows what the Medicis thought about *The Consequences of War* (Figure 1). They were, after all, descended from a famous mercenary and had commissioned other artists to celebrate their military victories. Yet the letter that accompanied Rubens' brilliant allegory left no doubt concerning his distaste for combat:

> The Principal figure is Mars who . . . rushes forth with shield and bloodstained sword, threatening the people with great disaster. He pays little heed to Venus, his mistress, who . . . strives with caresses and embraces to hold him. . . . Nearby are monsters personifying Pestilence and Famine, those inseparable partners of War. . . . You will find under the feet of Mars a book as well as a drawing on paper, to imply that he treads underfoot all the arts and letters. . . . The grief-stricken woman clothed in black, with torn veil, robbed of all her jewels and other ornaments, is the unfortunate Europe who, for so many years now, has suffered plunder, outrage and misery.[1]

Rubens' canvas illustrates how Milton dealt with war, especially in *Paradise Lost*. The energy both artists display typifies innumerable other treatments of the topic. Greek vases, Roman tombs, and Renaissance walls strain the limits of plastic art

[1] Rubens to Justus Sustermans, quoted in *The World of Rubens, 1577-1640* by C. V. Wedgwood (New York, 1967), pp. 168-69. Rubens' *War* is now in the Pitti Palace, Florence. I assume that Milton saw it in the Uffizi, however; John Zoffany's souvenir painting *The Tribuna of the Uffizi* (c. 1775) shows *War* in the center as well as other works similarly removed to the Pitti, Raphael's *Madonna of the Chair* and *The Four Philosophers*. There is a sad historical irony in Rubens' earlier *Peace and War*. Now in the National Gallery, London, it was inspired by his visit to England in 1629 and dedicated to the monarch who had brought such tranquility, Charles I.

when they try to translate war's passion into visual images; written works as dissimilar as epic and epitaph also show how men long to discover symbols that will communicate the extraordinary significance of human conflict. Yahweh's fire, Mars' sword, and God's iron rod bring divine power into the realm of mortals, elating some with a victory that apparently defends truth or punishes crime, and crushing others who have somehow broken a universal law. Even when campaigns end, men relive them in order to form their chaotic immediacy into rational narratives. Like other historical events that challenge human understanding (Jesus' Crucifixion, for example), wars traditionally inspire their witnesses with remarkable vigor.

Although any contemporary who viewed Rubens' work or read Milton's epic would have recognized their intensity, he might have felt uncomfortable with their statements about war. Both artifacts condemn it, thus displaying an antipathy unusual in the Renaissance and largely absent from previous ages. Here and there someone had mentioned the prosperity that peace brings or the misery of noncombatants or the danger of a standing army. But these humane concerns were, regrettably, mere divergences from the broad highway of Western thought. The road inexorably led to war. Most of its major signposts agreed that men's most strenuous efforts should end in a holy war or, at least, a just war. Only a few thinkers ever stepped aside to suggest alternate direction for our frenzies.

The painting and the poem communicate their hostility to war in different ways. *The Consequences of War* urges itself on viewers; they need little thought in order to appreciate how line, form, and color work together to deprecate combat. Rubens' pyrotechnic symbols speak loudly to almost everyone, but Milton reached out with many subtle devices to those who honored war. He wanted his finest work to reprove a generation that believed even the most injurious war gave scope for true nobility. In other works he linked the word "war" with negative words such as "ravages," "mischiefs," "burden," "abominate thoughts," "raging confusions," "fatal," "fires," and "hazards."[2] But *Paradise Lost* launched Milton's supreme attack on the notion of desirable conflict. Since he faced overwhelming opposition when he expressed his novel ideas on real valor, he carefully constructed the poem so it both satisfies conventional expectations and yet criticizes those war myths he felt were untenable. Thus any modern reader who wishes to experience the epic needs to understand those specialized terms evolved by classical and Renaissance commentators on warfare. Far from being pictorial appliqué, traditional ideas concerning soldiers, generals, drilling, haranguing, advising, scouting, and fighting serve as essential (and almost forgotten) passwords into *Paradise Lost*.[3]

[2] *Index to the Columbia Edition of the Works of John Milton*, ed. Frank Allen Patterson (New York, 1940), *s.v.* War. This Columbia edition is used for the prose in citations below and indicated as C.E. For poetry I use Merritt Y. Hughes' edition of *John Milton: Complete Poems and Major Prose* (New York, 1957).

[3] An early study in James Holly Hanford's "Milton and the Art of War," *SP*, 18 (1921), 232-66. Some other articles treat military topics (mainly the war in Heaven): H. H. Scudder, "Satan's Artillery," *N & Q*, 195 (1950), 334-47; Arnold Stein, "Milton's War in Heaven: An Extended Metaphor," in *Answerable Style* (Minneapolis, 1953); Everett H. Emerson, "Milton's War in Heaven: Some Problems," *MLN*, 69 (1954), 339-402; J. H. Adamson, "The War in Heaven: Milton's Version of the *Merkabah*," *JEGP*, 57 (1958), 690-703; Edgar F. Daniels, "Milton's 'Doubtful Conflict' and the Seventeenth-Century Tradition," *N & Q*, 206 (1961), 430-32; Priscilla P. St. George, "Psychomachia in Books V and VI of *Paradise Lost*," *MLQ*, 27 (1966), 185-96; Stella P. Revard, "Milton's Critique of Heroic Warfare in *Paradise Lost* V and VI," *SEL*, 7 (1967), 119-39; Edward Weismiller, "Materials Dark and Crude: A Partial Genealogy for Milton's Satan" *HLQ*, 31 (1967), 75-93; William B. Hunter, Jr., "Milton on the Exaltation of the Son: The War in Heaven in *Paradise Lost*," *ELH*, 36 (1969), 215-31; Frank S. Kastor, "By Force or Guile Eternal War: *Paradise Lost*, IV 776-1015," *JEGP*, 70 (1971), 269-78; Geoffrey Ridden, "*Paradise Lost, IX*. 119-22," *MQ*, 7 (1973), 109-10; Boyd M. Berry, "Puritan Soldiers in *Paradise Lost V, VI*: The War in Heaven," *SP*, 71 (1974), 89-104; Stella P. Revard, "The Warring Saints and the Dragon: A Commentary Upon Revelation 12:7-9 and Milton's War in Heaven," *PQ*, 53 (1974), 181-94; James A. Winn, "Milton on Heroic Warfare," *Yale Review*, 66 (1976), 70-86.

Three unpublished works define special aspects of Milton and war: Donald C. Dorian, *A Study of Milton's Ideas of War* (Columbia M.A. Thesis, 1929);

Milton's dislike of war inspired a sustained, learned, and sophisticated poem to degrade systematic hostility. Contentious by nature, Milton was not one to only stand and wait when convinced by a righteous cause. He habitually used all the resources of his mind to overwhelm an opponent. One example of Milton's personal belligerency, this one literary, may indicate why *Paradise Lost* attacks war on so many levels. He knew that his beloved Virgil had promised to write a magnificent epic in honor of Caesar. The speaker of the third *Georgic* vows to

> try out a pathway by which I too can rise from earth and fly as a conqueror on men's lips (*victorque virum volitare per ora*). First I will lead back with me (if only life is granted) the Muses, bringing them back to my homeland in triumph from their Aonian summit (*Aonio . . . vertice*). First I will bring back to you, O Mantua, palms from Idumaea. On the blooming meadow I will set up a marble temple beside the water. (*Georgics* 3. 8-13)

Here Virgil challenges his own predecessors: he boldly alludes to the famous epitaph of Ennius (*volito vivos per ora virum*) in order to exceed it—the new speaker will fly as a victor. The twice repeated "first" looks like a gauntlet thrown in front of another exemplar: Hesiod uses many words referring to first acts to begin his *Theogony*. Also, Virgil goes beyond Pindar by using the temple near water to symbolize an heroic poem—as the Greek had almost done—and he boldly combines it with a Roman triumph.

The way in which Milton confronts this passage from Virgil, a writer whom he revered from the early 1620s, helps us understand the complex way in which *Paradise Lost* attacks war. Cer-

---

Stella Hill Purce, *The War in Heaven: A Study of the Tradition and Paradise Lost* (Yale Dissertation, 1960); Robert Thomas Fallon, *Milton's Military Imagery: Its Growth and Function in his Art* (Columbia Dissertation, 1964).

I relegate more general studies of art, war, philosophy, and history to the Bibliography. Since scholars resemble Hansel and Gretel entering the dark wood, I now cite only those works I use directly so that footnotes do not unduly litter our path.

tainly Milton's epic begins with one of literature's most ringing declarations of war. In the course of a mere twenty-six lines, the speaker vows "to soar / Above th' *Aonian* Mount," that is, to surpass the achievement of his classical models. Prompted by a Spirit that prefers "Before all Temples th' upright heart and pure," his poem simultaneously recalls and rejects the pagan *templum* of Virgil. "The Lady of Christ's" (as Milton's Cambridge classmates called him) here snubs "Parthenias" (the maiden, Virgil's decorous sobriquet). Similarly, the Christian narrator can deal more authoritatively with primary matters ("First Disobedience . . . first taught . . . In the Beginning . . . from the first") since he looks from Mount Sinai, not the diminished "Olympian Hill" (7. 3). The Renaissance habit of *retractatio*, or perfective imitation, aids Milton's relentless questioning of every tradition during this poetic parricide. Just as Virgil freely stamped his models with a unique hallmark, so Milton energetically refashions those expressions that praise war.

Milton's retractation of war *topoi* is subtle not only because he had enormous literary ambition. His prodigious reading convinced him that war had a dangerously bivalent identity as both tool and master, vital for national survival yet heartless to individuals, a necessary gamble when advancing high ideals but certain to educe base conduct, logical and heroic in reflection although insane in execution. For Milton, as for Tennyson, there loomed that ambiguous specter, "the blood-red blossom of war with a heart of fire" (*Maud* 3. 6. 5). War was like those honeycombs that Xenophon's hungry Greek soldiers found in an obscure Asian village:

Those who tasted the combs went quite out of their heads. . . . A small dose made them act drunk, a large one prompted fits of near madness or death-like torpor. . . . There was wide-spread depression, but no one died. The next day they recovered those senses which they had lost almost at the same hour they had first been afflicted. (*Anabasis* 4. 8. 20-21)

Milton carefully compounds his greatest work to cure the intoxication that reduced his fellow men into worshippers of battle.

The double goal of *Paradise Lost*—to captivate a learned audience and to correct its attitude—springs from one fact Milton knew about his contemporaries: almost everybody approved of war. The sermons they applauded and epics they praised, even the mathematical texts they studied, assumed that readers had given prior assent to the premises and the practices of armed conflict. An astonishing number of seventeenth-century Europeans had either served on active duty or, at the very least, had seen armies, read treatises on soldiering, and heard reports about current battles. Englishmen had been involved with the high-handed rule of Charles in the 1630s, Civil War in the forties and crisis in the fifties of "Swordsmen and Decimators— Cromwell's Major-Generals."[4] Milton understood that both Royalists and Roundheads valued military knowledge. "King and Protector alike," reminds a modern historian, "had to study matters of external defence and internal security and each dreamed of 'a perfect militia.' " In order to lure others from the road to destruction, Milton had to prove that he knew more about the ideas he attacked than experts who sponsored them.

The following pages deal with the sources of Milton's military references and the complex way in which he manipulates traditional notions. Chapter I outlines the common ideas about war that were his unwelcome but inescapable heritage. These concepts glow less fervidly today since we no longer have universal conscription and antiwar sentiment has grown. Also, long-range weapons remove the experience of combat from the lives of most men. We can escape, but Milton had few alternatives. Public and personal pressures force him to confront many war commonplaces in *Paradise Lost*. When he dramatizes the conclusions about combat to which his cultural and private awarenesses lead him, he speaks with an energetic subtlety that

---

[4] An article with this title by Ivan Roots appears in *The English Civil War and After: 1642-1658*, ed. R. H. Parry (Berkeley, 1970). The following quotation is on p. 79.

exceeds the flamboyant simplicity of an artist like Rubens. Chapter II studies Satan's army; Chapter III analyzes their general, Satan. Chapter IV supposes we have stepped over that line in history's dust dividing the mass of Europeans who praise war from those few who detest it. From this new vantage point such topics as bees and pastoralism are examined to show how military references enliven them.

Along the way lurk many war allusions that are simultaneously accurate in denotation but pejorative in intention. Initially, Satan and his troops appear to be faultless soldiers who satisfy the dreams of innumerable war books for a perfect militia. Yet close reading reveals shortcomings that disqualify the fallen for consideration as ideal warriors or, finally, as acceptable creatures in God's universe. Their failure as fighters also helps to impugn the entire notion of virtuous militarism. Milton diagnoses the sickness of Satan by theological and martial standards. These two canons cooperate to educate any reader who has given unqualified praise to perfect armies. Turning his back to the pervasive assumption that one who wishes to "put on the whole armor of God" must be a soldier, Milton encourages us to reject stock opinions about military affairs. His epic succeeds if we notice how often martial practices clash with ethical theory. Repeatedly, we receive information that seems acceptable by the rules of war. Yet such soldierly facts often turn against themselves when their full meaning is understood. We ourselves are obliged to remain on guard while reading *Paradise Lost* since our habitual response to particular war matters proves to be inadequate or perverse.

Readers who are most interested in modern criticism will recognize that I accept without recapitulation several familiar theories. Milton repeatedly fools us, probably to chastise our infected intelligence. In addition, he progressively strips evil of its glamor. He also assumes we know as much as he does (a rather intimidating expectation) and will respond to his allusions. Next, he consciously writes on several levels simultaneously, composing a palimpsest for study rather than versifying hastily on a *tabula rasa*. Finally (at least for the major premises I endorse), Milton gives us a fair chance to understand his epic since he deals with significant traditions, especially those concerning war.

I willingly share a good deal of historical information (in the text, when possible) to prove how obsessively Europeans talked of soldiering and how brilliantly Milton exploits the preoccupation. An allusion to combat may hide behind even the plainest epic statement. We moderns should imitate late Renaissance men (the sheer mass of military documents warrants such normative beings). They heeded an ancient warning here articulated by Cyprian but often repeated in Milton's day:

> The Lord has commanded us to exercise prudence, and has instructed us to watch with thoughtful anxiety, lest an Adversary, who is ever watchful, and ever on the alert to ensnare, after having stolen entrance into the breast, out of sparks kindle flame. . . . For this cause, dearest brethern, we must be keeping sentry, and toil with all our might, . . . against a raging enemy, who is directing his darts against all parts of our body. . . . Wherefore, dearest brethern, the mind ought to be standing in its array and armed, equally whether against the treacherous plots or the open threats of the Devil. (*Treatises* 12. 1. 2)

In short, evaluating military allusions is not just an activity for Projectors in some Swiftean academy; rather, recognizing the traditions of war trains our souls to fight evil in all its manifestations and informs our minds about central questions in Milton's epic.

Just as Milton was goaded by discussions of war that he felt were defective, so I began this study since no one else had clarified the military vocabulary in *Paradise Lost*. That harmless lexical drudgery was, however, only the first step in comprehending how relentlessly Milton attacks war and how little his assaults have been explored. Most critical comments teased rather than satisfied my curiosity about his achievement. Miltonists tend to be prodigious collectors of other men's opinions, yet the few statements on military matters helped only in a negative way. Alastair Fowler rightly says in his edition of the epic that we should "note how much of the imagery is drawn from military contexts, in passages concerned with evil agents."[5] But much of the specific noting, I concluded, must be my responsibility.

Even a list of basic war words demonstrates how carefully Milton manipulates them. Consider what Adam says to comfort Eve when they are about to retire:

> Millions of spiritual Creatures walk the Earth
> Unseen, both when we wake, and when we sleep:
> All these with ceaseless praise his works behold
> Both day and night: how often from the steep
> Of echoing Hill or Thicket have we heard
> Celestial voices to the midnight air,
> Sole, or responsive each to other's note
> Singing thir great Creator: oft in bands
> While they keep watch, or nightly rounding walk,
> With Heav'nly touch of instrumental sounds
> In full harmonic number join'd, thir songs
> Divide the night, and lift our thoughts to Heaven.
>
> (4. 677-88)

Most of us recognize that Adam deals with her anxiety by making references to music ("voices . . . note/ Singing . . . instrumental sounds," etc.); but we should also hear how accurately Adam uses soldiers' words to characterize these guardian angels. Their "bands . . . keep watch" and "Divide the night" in Paradise just as (according to a military historian) "the Romans diuided the whole night into foure watches, . . . and these watches were distinguished by seuerall notes & sound of cornets or trumpets."[6] Some of Milton's vocabulary may refer

---

[5] This important footnote is on p. 942 in *The Poems of John Milton*, ed. John Carey and Alastair Fowler (London, 1968).

[6] Clement Edmunds, *Observations Upon the First Five Books of Caesars Commentaries* (London, 1604), p. 16. Cited as *Observations 1604*. There are several editions of this standard work. I also quote from the complete edition of London, 1600 (cited as *Observations 1600* although a second title page, which introduces the study of Caesar's *Commentaries* 6 and 7, is dated 1604). The 1609 edition had commendatory verses by Joshua Sylvester and Ben Jonson.

Milton's vision of good angels who both sing and guard is not unusual. John

equally to music or to army motions ("join'd . . . Divide"). Yet he arranges the passage so that we see more than a choir of wandering minstrels. He specifies duties for two classes of sentries: some "keep watch"; others, presumably their officers, "nightly rounding walk" in conformity to the common military requirement that a superior "him selfe shall rounde by night tyme to discover[,] redress and reprehende the faultes and negligences of the . . . cinteries."⁷ Adam is correct when he soothes Eve with the information about "troops making patrols ('rounds' we call them)"—Roger Williams had supplied this terminology in his history of war in Holland.⁸ But our Father does not realize that Satan too has vowed, "I must walk round / This Garden, and no corner leave unspi'd" (4. 528-29). The Fiend destroys harmony in the Garden by his warlike actions ("I have walkt thee round," he admits to the innocent couple. 9. 114), and he demonstrates how ambiguously "round" functions in *Paradise Lost*. When God superintends the activity, it enhances life. We will later hear,

> There is a Cave
> Within the Mount of God, fast by his Throne,
> Where light and darkness in perpetual round
> Lodge and dislodge by turns, which makes through Heav'n
> Grateful vicissitude, like Day and Night.
>
> (6. 4-8)

Davies of Hereford invited the "Angels which (in Soule inchaunting Quires) / Do celebrate your Souveraignes holy praise" to "descend" so they might protect James I and his Danish visitors: "Then, come (Celestial Soldiers) make a Ring, / About the Kings." *Bien Venu* (London, 1606), Sig. A3ʳ·ᵛ.

For these and subsequent Renaissance works, I silently bring titles (except of some sermons in III.1) into conformity with modern typography by capitalizing and tranforming the letters u, v, and vv into their current equivalents: v, u and w. I also eliminate idiosyncratic italicization. The quotations, however, are left unaltered: original spelling and punctuation often give valuable clues to phrasing.

⁷ Gerat Barry, *A Discourse of Military Discipline* (Bruxells, 1634), p. 49.

⁸ *The Actions of the Low Countries* (London, 1618), ed. Davies, p. 46.

This statement is completely military ("Lodge and dislodge" appear in innumerable war texts), but here "round" communicates benign alternation, not mischievous revolution. Anyone who recognizes the traditional words associated with guard duty can appreciate how Milton varies them in these excerpts, whereas ignorance of war words and images allows major ideas in *Paradise Lost* to escape.

Certainly other critics talk of war in the poem. One of these, Hippolyte Taine, is so much a prisoner of nineteenth-century satanolatry that he misreads egregiously. After praising Satan as the brave ruler of a realm that may be dreary but is free, Taine attacks God and Heaven. Satan, he admits later,

talks like a drill-sergeant. "Vanguard, to right and left the front unfold." He makes quips as clumsy as those of Harrison, the former butcher turned officer. What a heaven! It is enough to disgust one with Paradise; one would rather enter Charles I's troop of lackeys, or Cromwell's Ironsides. We have orders of the day, a hierarchy, exact submission, extra-duties, disputes, regulated ceremonials, prostrations, etiquette, furbished arms, arsenals, depots of chariots and ammunition. Was it worthwhile leaving earth to find in heaven carriage-works, buildings, artillery, a manual of tactics?[9]

Although Hell is more like a camp than Heaven, Taine at least senses the vulgarity of military activities.

More provocative than the French savant, R. C. Jebb, the great Greek scholar, quotes lines from *Paradise Lost* to distinguish between the styles of primary and secondary epic. Milton says that "never since created man, / Met such imbodied force" as Satan's army (1. 571-87). Nowhere in human history had there been regiments that could compare with the devil's, not the pygmies warring against cranes, giants against Olympians, Thebans or Trojans against enemies, nor even the notable bands

[9] H. A. Taine, *History of English Literature*, tr. H. Van Laun (New York, 1872), 1: 449-50.

of Arthur or Charlemagne. Starting from this martial simile, Jebb comments, with serene assurance,

> We begin to be aware that, in these splendid verses, the poet is exhibiting his erudition. But this characteristic of the literary epic,—its proneness to employ the resources of learning for the production of a cumulative effect,—is only one of the traits which is exemplified by the passage. Homer would not have said, as Milton does, that, in comparison with the exiled Spirits, all the chivalry of human story was no better than *"that small infantry warred on by cranes"*; Homer would have said that it was no better than the Pygmies. Homer says plainly and directly what he means; the literary epic likes to say it allusively.[10]

To be sure, learning is one of Milton's characteristics. Yet he uses his knowledge of famous armies as a sculptor uses his mallet, not to call attention to the act of creation, but to bring his private concept into public notice. By sliding over Milton's "cumulative effect," Jebb illustrates the Victorian tendency to neglect structure in order to concentrate on golden moments.

Instead of castigating a fine (albeit timebound) scholar, I feel it more important to prove that Milton's references implement a plan. Here they assert that the perfect militia in every human era, whether that of Rome, Great Britain, or France, failed to equal the infernal army. Even the metamorphosis of Homeric pygmies into Miltonic "small infantry" is not the cheap magic of some pedant in love with any learning, no matter how tangential. Rather, the allusion doughtily supports that cumulative effect of the other references: "small infantry" (as Addison suspected)[11] is a two-layer phrase, at once historical and rhetor-

---

[10] *Homer* (London, 1887), p. 17.

[11] *Spectator*, No. 297 (9 February 1712). Addison feels the simile detracts: it is one of several "defective" passages "that degenerate even into Punns." With his usual critical skill, Richard Bentley admits there is "a Pun, from small *Infants*, as well as *Foot-Soldiers*." Yet he must "take leave to think it spurious; because the *Pygmees* must have been call'd not *Infantry*, but *Cavalry*; since they fought not on Foot, but riding upon *Rams* and *Goats*." *Milton's Paradise Lost. A New Edition* (London, 1732), *ad loc*.

ical, helping us know that war involves foot soldiers and (in Milton's view) immature humans. Compared to Satan's volunteers, even the most renowned earthly army is a childish parody, a bit of infantile imitation. In the larger scheme of the poem, this simile restates what we shall often hear: a system operates in Heaven, Hell, and Earth whose premises are completely military. Out of small words like "infantry," Milton builds a coherent poem whose most humble allusion reduplicates the large assertion that war is hellish.

Before we can appreciate how Milton marshals his forces to make readers withdraw their reflexive support for militarism, we should turn to the cultural matrix from which grew his ideas about "impious War" (*Paradise Lost* 1. 43). Combat notions so permeated the Renaissance that Milton often summons up a platoon of soldierly premises with one word or phrase. Perhaps he begins his survey of notable human armies with pygmies and cranes because the only English translation of the best known war text, Vegetius' *De Re Militari* prominently pictured a pygmy strangling a crane (Figure 2).[12] If so, then the suggestions made on a structural and semantic level gain an added historical dimension. The emblem of some mannikin throttling a bird may repulse our civilized imaginations since it suggests reduced humanity and recurrent enmity. Yet this same emblem further undercuts the notion of valorous war if it indeed refers to the most famous book about Mars' art. Whether Milton is as blatant as Rubens or as cunning as here, his epic contradicts most previous opinions concerning war.

[12] *The Foure Bookes of Flavius Vegetius Renatus*. Tr. John Sadler (London, 1572). The engraving is on Sigs. *4ᵛ, ***2ᵛ and D1ᵛ. According to St[ephan] Bateman, *The Doome, Warning All Men* (London, 1582), p. 9, pygmies live a perversely accelerated life: they give birth at five and die at eight.

I

PUBLIC AND PERSONAL RESPONSES TO WAR

Public Approval of War

Throughout his life Milton heard respectable authorities from almost every age, tongue, and genre proclaim that war is noble and mere study a detriment to kingdoms. He felt that combat debases human beings since it involves a "waste of wealth and loss of blood" (*Sonn* 12. 14), but his typical contemporary agreed with Francis Bacon: "the Principal Point of *Greatness* in any *State*, is to have a Race of Military Men."[1] Most ancient and modern authorities approved of war or found strong reasons to excuse it. Occasionally, some raised their voices against various abuses such as killing non-combatants or taxing citizens to support permanent armies. Cyrenaics, Epicureans, Seneca, and Marcus Aurelius briefly lamented the beastliness of conflict in the ancient world; during the Renaissance, a tiny group of men like Erasmus, John Colet, George Herbert, and James I echoed their pacific notions. But when Milton examined the major traditions of Western thought in order to support his view that battle actualizes the most odious elements of human potential, he stood nearly alone.

Understandably, pagan literature makes extravagant claims for combat. Originating from and harking back to a heroic age, epics like the *Iliad* assume conflict presents men with a chance for some *aristeia* that will earn fame before black death snatches them from our bright world. Even though the tableau on Achilles' shield concerns peacetime activities, the gorgeous artifact itself has, like the poem, been necessitated by war. Virgil also

---

[1] Essay No. 29. In Francis Bacon, *Essays*, ed. W. A. Wright (London, 1862), p. 121.

tries to find a place in his imaginative world for the viciousness of battle. His *Aeneid* deplores death for young or innocent victims, yet he accepts it as a tool by which wise *fatum* manipulates history. Only after crushing the arrogant in battle, predicts Anchises, will Romans accomplish their unique goal of furnishing law to all humans. Statius, Lucan, Silius, even Petronius, sweep their strings more loudly when discussing war. Excepting only elegists like Tibullus and Propertius, who carried on a foppish duel with soldier-rivals, and atypical protestors like Euripides in *The Trojan Women*, most ancients probably approved of Epaminondas' truculent boast. When Pelopidas, who had a worthless son, scolded Epaminondas for not siring children, the great general replied haughtily: "I do have a son—the battle of Leuctra. Unlike your useless boy, my victory will live after me and make me immortal" (Cornelius Nepos, "Epaminondas" 10).

Early Christian writers disappointed Milton even more than heathen since their authority persisted through the Renaissance and they conspicuously drew their ideas from the Bible. Yet they too accepted war. "The idea of original sin," notes Momigliano, "made war appear even more inevitable and natural" to Milton's spiritual antecedents than to his secular predecessors.[2] The interval between Rome's fall and London's rise hardened Christianity so that it both tolerated and advocated bloodshed. One and one-half millennia produced few bans on war. Some practical measures like the Truce and Peace of God were enacted, some praises like Boniface's "Aenigmata de Virtutibus," applauding *Pax vere Christiana* along with faith, hope, truth, pity, patience, humility, and virginity, were written, and some questions were raised about the possible conflict between warring well and obeying the commandments. Few statements, however, encouraged the average seventeenth-century believer to reject warfare.

Whatever vision of universal harmony these may have in-

---

[2] Arnaldo Momigliano, "Some Observations on Causes of War in Ancient Historiography." In his *Studies in Historiography* (New York, 1966), p. 123.

spired, the early church soon blurred. Tertullian bravely attempts to explain away the many biblical accounts of war by claiming that weapons and booty are mentioned figuratively: "Who can use the sword and not contradict justice?" The most powerful two-edged sword that a Christian should wield is the Bible with its Old and New Testaments (*Adversus Judaeos* 9). Yet other early thinkers busily laid the foundation for a militant church. Lactantius scolds the Stoics for failing to distinguish just wrath from unjust. The former should be allowed in order to correct human depravity (*De Ira Dei* 12). We shall often meet the idea of legitimate force, even in *Paradise Lost*. Here it is enough to note that as the church gained power, it required excuses to use that power. Like Tertullian, Lactantius finally pulls back from involvement with real campaigns: he defends "Thou shalt not kill" since "God wished man to be a sacred creature" (*Divine Institutes* 6. 20).

After Constantine adopted Christianity as the official faith, the theoretical tolerance for excusable conflict grew. Observers like Ambrose look on a world reeling with visible and invisible contentions. Chiunni, Alans, Goths, and Sarmatians struggle physically while Christians fight spiritual foes such as avarice, lust, anger, and ambition (*Expositio in Lucam* 10. 10-11). Ambrose's pupil Augustine similarly accepts strife as one constant in a universe that includes material as well as supernatural opponents. He scatters apologies for earthly war throughout his writings. Miserable as it is—even when just—human wrongdoing causes it (*The City of God* 19. 7). Moreover, both bad and good men will have to participate in war. Only their attitude distinguishes them: impious men call belligerence "joy" while decent men term it "necessity" (*The City of God* 4. 15. Hincmar of Rheims considers this and other Augustinean maxims in *Explanatio in Ferculum Salmonis* 1. 7-11). Augustine further insists that when God orders a conflict, there can be no imputation of sin, even if the soldier kills (*De Doctrina Christiana* 1. 17, 26). Quite early in the church's history, *justum bellum* managed to smother "*non occides.*"

Later authorities offered little more support to Milton. Raban

Maur unabashedly prefers the contemplative life: "A true soldier of Christ strips his mind of worldly quarrels" (*Expositio super Jeremiam* 19). He diligently lists the names of army offices and weapons, noting that the church also has deacons, but religious *deacani* lead men, not hurt them (*De Universo* 16. 3). Still, Maur admits that Jesus was right when he did not abolish war: it is not necessarily *iniquum* and it teaches obedience (*Commentario in Librum Judicum* 1. 8). Other writers in the late Middle Ages speak longingly of tranquility, but acknowledge war's ascendency. Barely three centuries separate Smaragdus from St. Ivo of Chartres, although their perceptions of allowable conduct seem light years apart. It may have been simple to say in the ninth century, as Smaragdus does, "If we wish to be God's children, we must be peaceful: humble, gentle, openhearted and pure in speech" (*Diadema Monachorum* 12); it certainly was natural to say what Ivo did while the Crusades approached: kings may declare war without sin; soldiers may kill without sin; kings or soldiers who die in a just war go directly to heaven (*Panormia* 8. 15-60). The monastic ideal of harmony on any large scale apparently even embarrassed St. Bruno, who recalls with rectitude that Christ, the Prince of Peace, holds no attraction for ill-natured men or animals. But instead of listing the horrors of war, Bruno drifts into a self-indulgent speculation: did the animals on Noah's ark fight immediately after the Flood? He concludes that the survivors' descendants began to fight (*Sententiae* 2. 7). Less speculative opinions from the high Middle Ages are delivered by Philip of Harveng. He urges that Cain's fratricide should be censured, but, with greater fervor, he urges that spilling the blood of "barbarians" should never give us pause: God enjoins all holding public office to execute both domestic and foreign malefactors (*De Institutione Clericorum* 5. 38). Philip's sentiment follows those of many previous clerics who list admirable killers like Abraham, Moses, Ehud, and David. St. Bernard extends the possibility of virtuous extermination to his own day when, stung by information that Abelard has enlisted supporters, he reminds us how worthy were the persecutors of heretics like

Arians, Manicheans, Nestorians, and Marcionites (*Epistle* 193). Ironically but clearly, Bernard signals that where war was concerned, his thousand-year-old church returned for inspiration to a philosophy more consistent with Homer than with Tertullian and Lactantius. This reversion may be symbolized by one detail from the Legend of the True Cross: after Helena discovered Jesus' cross and the instruments of his passion, she ordered the nails to be melted and refashioned into weapons.

Renaissance and Reformation authorities continued to support war. They not only accepted its utility, but searched for ways to make it more productive. Pagan and Christian works were reread for technical advice. One author studies Julius Caesar *"for the better direction of our moderne Warrs"* (Edmunds, *Observations 1604*, Title Page) while another reinterprets the Bible *"For the rightly wageing of warre according to Holy Writ."*[3] Mature readers no doubt agreed with Erasmus' *Querela Pacis* or shuddered at Philip Vincent's *Lamentations of Germany*: the first reasoned that war is man's most illogical and sinful act; the second pictured atrocities like cannibalism. Anyone with eyes must have wept at Jacques Callot's grotesque series, *Les Grandes Misères de la Guerre*.[4] Alexander Leighton begins *Speculum Belli Sacri* with a sustained blast against "The Evill of Warre": "for war is the fruit of sin, the wages of sin, and the cause of sin; yea evē on the one part it is sin it selfe."[5] Theology aside, "The world for the proofe of this affoords a world of woefull experience, both from sacred and profane Writ. . . . let us look upon the latest warres in France,

---

[3] Ric[hard] Bernard, *The Bible-Battells. Or the Sacred Art Military* (London, 1629), title page.

[4] (Basel, 1517). William James Hirten's *The Complaint of Peace By Erasmus* (New York, 1946) conveniently reproduces the 1559 translation by Thomas Paynell, adds a modernized version and furnishes an illuminating Introduction. A worthy companion study is Robert P. Adams, *The Better Part of Valor: More, Erasmus, Colet, and Vives, on Humanism, War, and Peace* (Seattle, 1962). Vincent includes savage pictures of mothers eating children and torturers calmly mutilating victims in *The Lamentations of Germany* (London, 1638). Callot's engravings were published at Paris in 1633.

[5] *Speculum Belli Sacri* (n.p., 1624), p. 1.

Bohemia, and the Palatinate" (p. 3). Yet Leighton proceeds to deny his premise. Diametrically opposed to Milton's method, Leighton's first condemns what he plans to support. He justifies his more than three hundred pages by chastising any "frantic" Anabaptists who might agree with sentimental pacifists like Vives: "Notwithstanding of all this, that hath been said of war; yet Warre vvell undertaken is not onely lawfull but also necessary" (p. 6). Although Leighton was a clergyman, few readers would have been surprised by his truculence. Divines from all sects supported belligerence. Luther calls war a "scourge" in his table talk, but the Augsburg Confession (1530) clearly obliges Christians to fight in just campaigns: "Docent quod Christianis liceat jure bellare (Article 16, the Gospels teach that Christians may participate in a just war). Catholics after Trent accept without complaint Aquinas' defense of war making, which is itself largely indebted to Aristotle and Augustine (Summa Theologica 2. 2. 40, 108). John Calvin gives aid and comfort to most Protestants when he argues persuasively,

> But if it is objected, that in the New Testament there is no passage or example teaching that war is lawful for Christians, I answer, first, that the reason for carrying on war, which anciently existed, still exists in the present day, and that, on the other hand, there is no ground for debarring magistrates from the defence of those under them; and, secondly, that in the Apostolic writings we are not to look for a distinct exposition of those matters, their object being not to form a civil polity, but to establish the spiritual kingdom of Christ; lastly, that there also it is indicated, in passing, that our Saviour, by his advent, made no change in this respect.[6]

[6] John Calvin, Institutes of the Christian Religion 4. 20. 12. Tr. Henry Beveridge (Edinburgh, 1846), 3: 534. Theologians did not hesitate to call the killing that war necessitated "murder." Yet they offered pat excuses:

Defensiue murthers, whether they be of one or of many, priuate or publicke, be separate from the kynde of unlawfull murthers. And to this sort belong the murthers of warres, which be not then unlawfull when they be

Not only theologians speak for war: wherever Milton turns, experts assure him that "the Profession of a Souldier is allowed to be lawful by the Word of God."[7] Furthermore,

It is needelesse . . . to dispute, whether it be lawfull, either for Christian Princes to make warres, or for christians to serue in warres. Those that thinke it unlawfull, as men de-uoyd of iudgement in religion and state, are declared long since to be both heretical, and phrenetical persons.[8]

Even the deity, Milton's great taskmaster, was routinely militarized. Clement of Alexandria adumbrates a Renaissance rationale when he envisions God as "our Great General, the Word, Commander-in-Chief of the universe."[9] He is as modern as Henry Lawrence, who reminds his readers in 1649 that "Iesus Christ" is "The great Generall of all his people."[10] The first commandment may have prohibited images of God, but writers in the early seventeenth century often called him a military leader. In *Pallas Armata*, Thomas Kellie heaps up Biblical phrases to prove his point that "*The fountaine of all Artes and Sciences, The Eternal Himselfe is a Souldier as the* . . . *Scrip-*

---

excused both by the necessitie of defence, and also by the duetie of the magistrate.

(from Wolfgangus Musculus, *Common Places of Christian Religion*, tr. John Man [London, 1578], p. 189).

[7] George [Monk], Duke of Albemarle, *Observations Upon Military & Political Affairs* (London, 1671), p. 1.

[8] Matthew Sutcliffe, *The Practice, Proceedings, and Lawes of Armes* (London, 1593), p. 1. In her informative "*No Standing Armies!*" *The Antiarmy Ideology in Seventeenth-Century England* (Baltimore, 1974), Lois Schwoerer speculates that the excessive praise for soldiers in the late 1500s and early 1600s resulted partly from their neglected or despised state. Even James I, who disliked war, knew that Britain needed an army.

[9] *Paedagogus* 1. 8. 65. 1. Quoted in *Christian Attitudes Toward War and Peace* by Roland Bainton (New York, 1960), p. 80.

[10] *An History of Angells* (London, 1649), Sig. *2^r. Many expressions in the Bible encouraged the tradition of a warrior god: Ex. 15:3; Ps. 18:34, 144:1; 2 Sam. 22:35.

ture sayeth: The Lord is a Man of Warre."[11] Just as Milton was preparing to travel abroad, in search, perhaps, of support for his decision to be a poet, John Ball issued the third edition of his popular *Treatise of Faith*. Ball reminds any pious quester that "The chiefest strength of souldiers lyeth in their Captaine . . . : but all our strength lyeth in Christ, the Captaine that leadeth us to salvation."[12] Moral analogies such as these deluged Milton, assuring anyone who heard them that the godlike human being strove to become a soldier, not a poet. Lawrence Grimald exhorts his countrymen (including Milton, "the Lady of Christ's") that "Vertue is not a Ladie of solatarie or idle life, but loueth labour, reioyceth, and triumpheth in times of perill."[13]

Perhaps most distressing to Milton, who was neither "frantic" nor "phrenetical," secular thinkers failed to suggest rational alternatives to religion's crusading mentality. The rules of war that theorizers as varied as Plato, Aristotle, Cicero, Gentili, and Grotius promulgated did not presuppose that reason might someday eliminate the need for conflict. Like almost all men, they accepted as their premise the inevitability of war. Milton himself follows in the footsteps of these codifiers by defending immoral but accomplished acts such as rebellion and regicide. He formulates his own requirements for a just war in *De Doctrina Christiana* (2. 17), thus showing he knows as well as they that faith or philosophy cannot avoid battle but must seek to understand it. Along with Castiglione, Milton realizes that in a perfectly logical world, war "is bad in itself"; but on

[11] *Pallas Armata* (Edinburgh, 1627), Sig. ¶4^r.

[12] *Treatise of Faith*, 3rd ed. (London, 1637), p. 294.

[13] *The Counsellor* (London, 1598), p. 117. Compare Samuel Butler's *Hudibras* 1. 1. 911-14:

> Honour is, like a widow, won
> With brisk attempt and putting on;
> With entering manfully and urging,
> Not slow approaches, like a virgin.
> (ed. Alfred Miles
> [London, 1895], p. 28)

our planet, already overpopulated with agitators, it is inescapable. "I hold," says the pragmatic Count Ludovico da Canossa, "that the principle and true profession of the Courtier must be that of arms."[14]

Although personally longing for the time when "no War, or Battle's sound / Was heard the World around" (*Nat* 53. 4), Milton understands how most of his teachers hear a kind of harmony in "the odious din of War" (*Paradise Lost* 6. 408). To Milton's credit he does not again retreat to Horton or "a lodge in some vast wilderness" like the hermitage Cowper was to imagine,

> Where rumour of oppression and deceit,
> Of unsuccessful or successful war,
> Might never reach me more.
> (*The Task*, Book 2. "The Timepiece," 1-5)

Rather he faces up to the combined inheritance of religious and civil opinion. Sadly, but resolutely, he accepts the almost universal truism:

> As the Gouvenour of this World hath apointed Life and Death, Summer and Winter, Day and Night, and almost giuen eurie thing a contrarie, so hath hee made Peace and Warre to haue an interchanging course on the face of this earth.[15]

---

[14] Baldesar Castiglione, *The Book of the Courtier*, tr. Charles S. Singleton (Garden City, N.Y., 1959), p. 312. Ludovico's words are on p. 32.

[15] James Achesone, *The Military Garden, or Instructions for All Young Souldiers* (Edinburg,1629), Sig. *2r. Kellie varies the trope: "A well gouerned Common-wealth in time of Peace, will prepare for Warre, knowing the course of the world, to bee still subject to change and alteration (resembling the ebbing and flowing of the Sea,) & constant in nothing but inconstancie (Pallas Armata* Sig. gg 2r,v). George Monk mixes his metaphors but makes the same point: "Peace, fulness, pride, and War, are the four Fellies, which being let into one another, make the Wheel, that the Times turn on; and after a long Scene of Peace, War ever entreth the Stage" (*Observations*, p. 3). Books as ancient as Judges and *The Peloponnesian War* sponsored a cyclical view of history; Renaissance war books were partial to the comparison of winter and war. The longest and most literate example begins a work Milton knew well, Robert

Milton's refusal to slink out of our human predicament brings him into a curious agreement with military authors. Edw[ard] Davies, for example, repeats the common seasonal analogy:

it is very needfull, and requisite in the Summer of Peace to forecast, and prouide against the Winter of Warres.[16]

Perhaps this common association between a sequence in nature of antithetical seasons and the inevitability of war in human affairs accounts for the way Milton patterns his description of events following the Fall. Soon after Adam and Eve disobey, thereby guaranteeing an end to their idyll, our world alters: "Sun," "Moon," planets, seasons and "Winds," once benign, become hostile. Then, "Discord . . . / Death introduc'd through fierce antipathy: / Beast now with Beast gan War" (*Paradise Lost* 10. 651-714). Immersed in this world of universal conflict, Adam and Milton choose different tactics to console themselves. Our Father seeks "to disburd'n [himself] . . . with sad complain" (10. 719); the poet, however, decides to fight as sanely as he can against fighting.

War Books

Milton confronts battle for some very specific reasons, public and private. He knew that his audience never lost sight of war. Although the English had not engaged in any large-scale operations from the battle of Pinkie (1547) until the Civil War, they had been bombarded for that entire period with information about generals, soldiers, strategies, and campaigns. The most obvious proof of his public's urge to participate in war vicariously is the awesome number of war treatises that they read.[17]

Ward's *Anima'dversions of Warre; or A Militarie Magazine of the Truest Rules, and Ablest Instructions, for the Managing of Warre* (London, 1639), p. 1: "The Winter Solstice must succeed the Summer, and Warre must follow Peace."

[16] *Military Directions, or the Art of Trayning* (London, 1618), Sig. A2^v.

[17] For locating books published before the Civil War, the indispensible guide is *A Bibliography of Military Books up to 1642*, by Maurice J. D. Cockle, 2nd

These many "arts," "principles" and "observations" contain all that a future Alexander has to know. They tell him how to select, train, arrange, discipline, and inspire troops. Further, they discuss tactics, weapons, formations, rules, and commands. Their lessons on surveying, troop disposition, angles of fire, and positions for drill are frequently illustrated to make them clear for the newest recruit. These treatises were so familiar that textbooks dealing with mathematics or fireworks often clarify their instructions by inventing a combat situation.[18] Even sermons and moralizing satires allude to predicaments that spring more from descriptions of military writers than prescriptions of the church fathers. Whether based on pure theory or on personal observation, war books organize the most diverse material into seductively simple systems.

Some *artes* smack more of colleges than campaigns. They dispense rational maxims researched from myth, history, and previous texts, of which there were many. As Byron realized, ancient Greece was the land "where grew the arts of war." Books on martial skills had begun there: Aeneas Tacticus, Polybius, Asclepiodotus, Onasander, and Aelian codified mili-

---

ed. (London, 1957). For locating later works, a useful guide is *Bibliography of British History: Stuart Period, 1603-1714*, ed. Godfrey Davies and Mary Keeler, 2nd ed. (Oxford, 1970), pp. 218-39. Works from mid-century are named in *The English Civil War. A Military History of the Three Civil Wars, 1642-1651*, ed. Peter Young and Richard Holmes (London, 1974), pp. 347-53.

[18] A few examples: Leonard and Thomas Digges, *A Geometrical Practice, Named Pantometria*. 2nd ed. (London, 1591); John Dansie, *A Mathematicall Manuel: Wherein is Handled Arithmeticke, Planimetry, Stereometry, and the Embattelling of Armies* (London, 1627), note especially p. 78: "Now because I honor the pro[f]ession of a souldiour, I will show him some vse of these logs"; John Roberts, *The Compleat Cannoniere: or, the Gunners Guide . . . With Divers Excellent Conclusions, both Arithmeticall and Geometricall belonging thereunto: As also Sundry Serviceable Fireworkes* (London, 1639). A handsome Florentine primer pictures knights clashing on a battlefield littered with weapons, fallen horses, and human dead as it states a problem in arithmetic: "The King of France was routed in battle, with 1/4 of his soldiers killed and 2/5 wounded and 1000 taken prisoner and 6000 escaped." Biblioteca Riccardiana, Florence, MS No. 2669, reproduced in *The Horizon Book of the Renaissance*, ed. Richard M. Ketchum (New York, 1961), p. 135.

tary information that appeared less systematically in writers like Xenophon, Polyaenus, and Arrian. Roman theory was summed up by Frontinus, Modestus, Vegetius, and Leo, who used examples from authors like Caesar, Livy, Sallust, and Tacitus.[19] Surviving into the Renaissance, all these discussions were combed, annotated, translated, and imitated.

Milton's predecessors venerated one text in particular, the *De Re Militari* of Flavius Vegetius Renatus. Although it had been written about A.D. 400 by a researcher who was more antiquary than military, it supplied a paradigm that became almost obligatory for later essays.[20] In addition, contemporary authors

[19] *Don Juan* 3. 1. 3, to be fair, does credit Greece with inventing the art of peace, too. Ancient writers, no matter what their actual era, existed for the Renaissance in an eternal present. The dates of these military authors are instructive, however, since they span nearly eight hundred years of antiquity and demonstrate that war has always been an urgent topic.

Aeneas Tacticus	— mid-4th c. B.C.
Polybius	— 2nd c. B.C.
Asclepiodotus	— 1st c. B.C.
Onasander	— mid-1st c. A.D.
Aelian	— 100 A.D.
Xenophon	— c. 428-354 B.C.
Polyaenus	— mid-2nd c. A.D.
Arrian	— mid-2nd c. A.D.
Frontinus	— c. 30-104 A.D
Vegetius	— c. 400 A.D.
Caesar	— 100-44 B.C.
Livy	— c. 59 B.C. — 17 A.D.
Sallust	— 1st c. B.C.
Tacitus	— late 1st c. B.C.

A glance at Jackson Campbell Boswell, *Milton's Library* (New York, 1975) will show how many of these (and other) authors Milton definitely knew. Military works repeat each other so that reading one often amounts to reading several. My colleague Vincent DiMarco graciously secured a microfilm of the medieval *De Bellico Apparatu Liber* attributed to Leo, Emperor of Byzantium. Although the author remains unknown, *De Bellico Apparatu* is, like Vegetius, a storehouse of commonplaces. Sir John Cheke, whom Milton mentions, translated the book from Greek to Latin at Basle, 1554. It is a relatively rare work, but valuable to show how persistent the basic ideas were.

[20] Henry N. MacCracken, "Vegetius in English: Notes on the Early Transla-

repeatedly pressed Vegetius to provide *sententiae* or historical examples for their essays. Even the worldly Machiavelli based his own examination of war upon Vegetius rather than on his Florentine experiences.[21] Milton himself responded to the theoretical portion of these handbooks: the two passages from Machiavelli that he transferred into his *Commonplace Book* during the early 1640s are of philosophical, not particular, points.[22] However, other Renaissance students valued Vegetius for more practical reasons since, in short compass, he at least mentions most of the problems that any leader must solve in order to win.

Vegetius' first book deals mainly with recruits. If possible, he says, they should be from northern countries: "whom the Sunne burneth not so nere, being more rashe and unaduished, yet a great deale better blouded, are moste ready of all, & desirous of warre" (Sig. A1ʳ). He suggests the merits of citymen or countrymen, young or middle-aged trainees, those who are of a certain physical profile and those with specialized occupations. His sensible discussions encourage a good recruiting officer to search out young outdoorsmen who are strong, even if not tall. Those enlisted should exercise constantly so that activities like marching, running, leaping, and swimming become easy. Also, they should be taught how to handle various kinds of weapons, how to fortify camp and how to maintain proper formations. (This last requirement becomes an obsession with some later writers. They dream up complex formations with little field utility but that are intriguing to describe.) The raw material of Vegetius' army is thus a hardy recruit, willing to enlarge his expertise as huntsman or wood chopper by more specialized drill in weapons.

Vegetius' second book describes how to organize these trained soldiers. As we shall see, all theorists stress the neces-

tions." In *Anniversary Papers by Colleagues and Pupils of George Lyman Kittredge* (Boston, 1918), pp. 389-403.

[21] *Libro dell' Arte della Guerra* (Florence, 1521).

[22] They are listed under Milton's headings, "State" and "King." See Ruth Mohl, *John Milton and His Commonplace Book* (New York, 1969), pp. 160, 189.

sity of organization. Legion, cohort, century—the names of units differ in later accounts, but the idea remains: power can be wielded efficiently only when it is strictly ordered. Vegetius also names officers, defines their areas of responsibility, and assigns them distinctive insignia. Here, too, subsequent teachers modify the names that he conjures up from several periods of Roman history: as Raban Maur knew, "names for these offices and formations change in different languages" (De Universo 16. 3). Yet all readers sensed the rightness of Vegetius' premise that success comes from division of labor. Organization ties together the horizontal duties of infantry, cavalry, and auxiliaries with the vertical duties of subordinates to superiors. Such division also allows for a certain nobility since rewards and punishments are administered publicly, thereby reminding the entire army of its interdependence.

When Vegetius turns to operations in his third book, he assumes that his personnel and equipment are ready for combat. He discusses a wide range of topics, some routine (how to maintain health, food supply, and morale), others more subtle (how to make tired soldiers fight or how to evaluate the enemy's strength). This section is the most heterogeneous Prudential advice—"Manhoode doth more auaile then multitude of men" (Sig. G1ʳ)—complements advice on how to ford rivers or how to build engines of war. (Many later treatises picture these infernal catapults, rams, siege towers, and cannon with varying de grees of artistry.) Despite the piecemeal nature of this third book, it comes nearest to the double face of actual war. On the one side, it rationally teaches that muscle, mind, and machine must cooperate if the commander wishes a better than even chance of victory. On the other side, its randomness hints to the wise that uncertainty always rules a large area. No matter how diligently one has trained for conflict, he must always emulate Michelangelo's wary David and glance over his left shoulder for the approach of fortuna. As "Captaine" Lewes Roberts cautions, "a minute produceth that in the field which an Age hath not seene no nor heard of before."[23]

[23] Warre-Fare Epitomized (London, 1640), Sig. A3ʳ.

With psychological cunning, Vegetius concludes his hand-book by giving concrete details. His fourth book leaves behind the mysterious and talks of mundane matters: how to fortify a city, what siege machines are useful, what methods can be employed to capture a town, even one supplied with food and water, and (in some editions) what ships and tactics prevail at sea. All in all, his epitome of the warrior's craft deserved read-ing. While short on what may be called significant historical or philosophical insight, *De Re Militari* nevertheless supplied a framework that other thinkers, many more wise or experi-enced, could use. Like the Druids' great wicker cages, these edi-tions of Vegetius held much that past wars surrendered to fu-ture campaigners so the latter might ward off defeat.

Most military books read by Milton's audience strive to go beyond Vegetius when they turn to pragmatic matters. Matthew Sutcliffe looks back on his career as both minister and judge marshal when he scolds theoreticians

> which neuer had seene the field; and . . . which spend whole bookes in talking of the diuers formes of battels, some like starres, some like sheares, some like sawes, and some like winde-mill sailes, which neuer haue vse but in mosters; and leaue [out] the most necessary points of warre, in preparing for the warres, choice of souldiors, marching, encamping, fighting, retiring, besieging, or de-fending of townes, ambuscades, stratagemes, and such like. (*Practice*, Sig. A4ᵛ)

Even when texts subordinate imagination to utilitarian con-cerns, they have to consider such abstract topics as what consti-tutes a just war, what personality traits are desirable in soldiers, and what principles have guided successful leaders in the past. Despite their different emphases, both theoretical and practical books often juxtapose the most heterogeneous subjects. Yoked together by violence or necessity, depending upon the author's control, are logical arguments in favor of religion and lessons on geometry, laws to govern an ideal encampment and pictures of actual formations, abstract qualities needed for different ranks and specific tricks used by Joshua, Hannibal, and Scanderbeg.

Whether projectors or pragmatists wrote these *artes militares*, they offered an image of man that pleased Milton's contemporaries but challenged him. The organization and scope of war books, if not their subject matter, seem to assert man's rationality. Their perfect mortal is not Cicero's polymath orator or Paul's imitator of Christ or Erasmus' Christian humanist. Rather, to most Britons, he is a stalwart devotee of *Pallas armata*. A manual with this name published in 1627 pictures on its title page the military ideal: dapperly mustachioed, fashionably dressed, arms flung wide in a Christlike gesture, he wields a pen in his left hand and sword in the right. He bestrides a cross-topped globe flanked by book and helmet, compass and drum—instruments that are proper (as the motto reads) *Marti musisque* (Figure 3).[24] This scholar-soldier furnished the young Milton and his peers a model for their talents. His learning and vigor perhaps did not repair the ruin of our first parents, but worked to tame the insolence of tyrants, greed of conquerors, and heresy of pagans. He perfects his abilities so he may be (as a second motto says) *Pro Principe et Patria in Vtrvmqve Paratvs*.

The learned warrior loomed over the late Renaissance. Sir Philip Sidney epitomizes innumerable other less famous men who tried to develop a personality such as that imputed to Richard Elton. Author of *The Compleat Body of the Art Military*, Elton is said (by one reader of his book) to be a paragon:

> *Who art Proficient both in* Arms *and* Arts!
> Mars *and* Minerva *who are counted two*
> *Divided essences both joyn in* You.[25]

[24] By Sir Thomas Kellie. See footnote 10 above. Mercifully, perhaps, Milton could not see William Faithorne's allegorical engraving of 1658, "The Embleme of Englands Distractions." Now in the Mansell Collection, it shows Oliver Cromwell in armor, serenely looking past his upraised sword as an open book dangles from his left hand. Dora and Erwin Panofsky give a learned pedigree to the sword / book icon in *Pandora's Box*, 2nd ed. (New York, 1962), pp. 40-41.

[25] (London, 1650), Sig. # 3ᵛ. The enthusiastic reader was "a William Short Captain." Half a century earlier, the frontispiece of a Spanish war book illus-

If we ask whether Elton deserved such commendation or whether it was just friendly puffery, we evade the point Milton knew: cultural formulas reveal what certain groups feel obliged to value. *Pietas* and the other Roman virtues celebrated in Horace's odes may not have energized many Augustans, but first-century citizens spoke of them; *sprezzatura* probably did not describe the mien of many sixteenth-century Italians, but they appreciated the ideal. Of course, other societies had honored Mars and Minerva at the same ceremonies.[26] Yet Milton's age elevated the wise warfarer to extraordinary heights. Undoubtedly, the solid majority of seventeenth-century Europeans agreed with General George Monk when he said, "I take the Office of a Chief Commander to be a subject capable of the greatest wisdom that may be apprehended by natural means" (*Observations*, p. 150). Anyone who could put to use all the data in the encyclopedic war books was popularly thought to be a credit to God, king, country, and conscience. No matter what profession individuals followed, they habitually honored as society's most useful contributor not "the Diuine, nor Lawyer, neither . . . the Husbandman[,] Artificer nor Marchant." Rather, primacy

> lyeth & resteth in the strength and valour of them that beare Armes: For when preaching, processe, Plea, nor perswasion, can preuaile, in reforming the abuses of euill disposed persons, then must the sword of violence be put in execution, by them that are able and skilfull, forcing

trated how widespread the ideal was. Don Bernardo de Vargas Machuca anticipates Elton by holding a compass in his right hand (poised over a globe of "America") and caressing his sword hilt with the left hand. Machuca's motto is less than subtle: "To the sword and the compass—more and more and more and more." Reproduced in Geoffrey and Angela Parker, *European Soldiers 1550-1650* (Cambridge, 1977), p. 41. I do not believe *Milicia y descripcion de las Indias* was translated into English. It gives a detailed account of what Machuca's countrymen would later call guerrilla warfare.

[26] See Appian, *Roman History* 8. 20. 133. Minerva is, of course, partially a war goddess. She both benefits men by providing the olive tree and afflicts them by hurling Jupiter's thunderbolt. Her actions illustrate the equivocal nature of wisdom, a problem which exercised Milton.

them to obedience, by abating the fury of the tumultuous
and disordered multitude, or else to cut them off, that
peace, and ciuill justice, may be continued.[27]

This author accepts many paradoxical clichés continuing to gal-
vanize support for soldiers in our own time: only the threat of
war can keep peace; only killing can restore life to beleaguered
states; only strict military order can guarantee license to
"amorous Gentlemen, . . . nice Ladies and mincing Gentle-
women." These commonplaces so permeate late Renaissance
writing that even the most captious hesitated to challenge them.
A satire appended to Dacre's translation of Machiavelli's *Prince*
runs through possible occupations. In answer to the repeated
question about what profession to adopt, the speaker rejects
farmers, merchants, and lawyers with acerbic verse. Turning to
soldiers he asks,

> Shall wee be Souldiers then? but, to what end?
> Vnchristian comfort is the fruit of blood:
> Better keepe inward with a faithfull friend,
> Then purchase foes for any priuate good:
> And better pray that quarrels all may cease,
> And say, God saue the holders vp of peace.[28]

Yet the young Milton (he was about sixteen when this ap-
peared) could hardly have shaped his future conduct from such
a barb: the speaker continues to malign scholars, physicians,
musicians, "alkemists," and others. With some humor he
wonders, "Shall wee turne Poets? proue Satiricall? / And call an
Asse, an Asse, a Hogge, a Hogge?" but concludes, "Oh no, I

[27] Thomas Trussell, *The Souldier, Pleading his Owne Cause* (London, 1626),
pp. 3-4. The "Gentlemen . . . and . . . Ladies" in the next reference appear on p.
22.
[28] The author of these lines is not known. His poem, *Machivells Dogge*, ap-
pears as an appendix to E. D[acres'] translation of *The Prince* (London, 1617),
Fol. 5ʳ. The following lines on "Poets" appear on Fol. 6ᵛ. Henry Cornelius
Agrippa also demolishes soldiers after farmers and before noblemen in *The Van-
ity of Arts and Sciences* (London, 1676), pp. 253-57. In other words, soldiers
were no more foolish than other men.

loue no pleading in such cases," and then demolishes usurers
and ratcatchers.

War books both prompted and reflected the climate of belief
in which Milton spent his life. Most of his contemporaries ap-
parently did not find the mental environment so hostile since
they accepted opinions such as these written by the Earl of Or-
rery three years after Milton's death: *"no Profession in the
World, is more built on true Reason, and sound Judgment,
than the Military is."*[29] While Milton could appreciate certain
martial qualities in individuals, he found much to vex him in
the ubiquitous *artes militares*. War making was not an end in
itself. He praises Fairfax in Sonnet 15 and then admonishes,
"what can War, but endless war still breed." Anyone who as-
saulted popular but incomplete war ideas needed a good deal of
self-confidence. Soldierly authors formed a kind of club openly
touting its own members. A friend of Richard Elton compares
him to established theorists like "Barriff,"

> *Machiauell, Markham, Hexham, Weymouth, Ward,*
> *Aelian, Bingham, Roberts, Cruso, Gerrard,*
> and divers other, *honour'd Sons of War.*
> (*Compleat Body*, Sig. §4ᵛ)

We shall meet most of these men as they discuss "rare
Castra-mentations" and "deep *Stratagemick Demonstrations*"
(*ibid.*). Although Elton's advertisement has a Gilbert and Sulli-
van lilt, it points to material that informed the minds and
roused the patriotism of Milton's countrymen.

War News, Pictures, Propaganda

Milton felt three further public pressures that added their
weight to these reflective treatments of war. The first came
from reports of soldiering on the Continent. Nearly every day,
news journals arrived. Also, veterans eager to recount their

---

[29] Roger Boyle, Earl of Orrery, *A Treatise of the Art of War* (London, 1677),
Sig. b 1ʳ.

foreign adventures made the otherwise quiet island reverberate with talk of big wars and plumed troops. Since England's military techniques had atrophied during the sixteenth century, men of the early seventeenth century paid particular attention to events across the Channel. They relished every anecdote of soldiers who accompanied popular leaders like Maurice of Nassau or Gustavus Adolphus. One anonymous pamphleteer details a battle fought in 1616 between Gustavus and *"Sigismond King of Poland."* The short narrative is based upon a premise we have already heard in books of war theory:

> *To see Kings and Princes sweat in Battailes in these days,*
> *is so rare and unusuall, that this warlike Encounter . . . is*
> *. . . worthy to be engrauen in Tables of brasse.*[30]

These personal reports add a dash of adventure to the expected plea for preparedness. To stay-at-home Britons, the chronicler who actually observed battle supplies facts (thus making Fairfax's reform of the army understandable) as well as immediacy.

Many accounts resemble cool intelligence reports. Thomas

[30] "A Great Man in the State . . . of Sweden," *A Trumpet Call to Souldiers on to Noble Actions* (London, 1627), Sig. A2ʳ. In this section I offer a very few new books, mainly from the 1620s or concerning the Siege of Ostend, a brave action which remained in people's memories long after the Spaniards overcame the Dutch defenders. But reports from overseas had been arriving on the English shore for many years. Some of the more interesting ones from earlier years are· Petrus Frarinus, *Oration Against the Unlawfull Insurrections of the Protestantes of our Time, Under Pretence to Refourme Religion* (Antwerp, 1566); this lurid booklet pictures Calvin and Beza as they order Catholics to be hanged, shot, disembowelled, crucified, and burned; Anonymous, *A Discourse of Such Things as are Happened in the Armie of my Lordes the Princes of Navarre, and of Condey* (London, 1569); [John?] Norris, *A True Discourse of the late Battaile Fought betweene our Englishmen, and the Prince of Parma, on Monday the 15. of November 1585* (London, 1585); Anonymous, "A Briefe Report of the Militarie Services done in the Low Covntries, by the Erle of Leicester" (London, 1587); Anonymous, *A Discourse of all Such Fights . . . which have Happened in France* (London, 1590); Anonymous, *Newes Lately Come on the Last Day of Februarie 1591 from Divers Partes of France, Savoy, and Tripoli in Soria* (London, 1591); Anonymous, *The Destruction and Sacke Cruelly Committed by the Duke of Guyse* (London, 1592). Needless to say, the facts in these accounts often float on surging seas of partisan rhetoric.

Overbury journeys through France with a keen eye since "It is at this day [1609] the greatest united force of Christendom." He dutifully catalogs its military potential:

The weaknesses of it are, First, the want of a sufficient Infantry. . . . Second, is the unproportionable part of the land which the Church holds, all which is likewise dead to military uses. . . . The Third, is the want of a competent number of ships. . . . The Fourth, is the weakness of their frontiers. . . . The Last, is the difference of religion among themselves.[31]

Overbury's dry language recurs when other men tell of adventures that could have called forth more eloquence. Henry Hexham might have bragged a bit more as he recounts that the allies survived a barrage at Ostend in 1602: "the enemy had shot upon and into the town, above 163,200 cannon shot, to beat it about our ears."[32] Or William Dillingham might have spoken more dramatically when he recalls a gory incident:

Not long after [1601], the Lord of Chatillon met with an unhappy mischance. For being upon the high Bulwark of Sand Hill, with Colonel Utenbruch and other Gentlemen and men of Command; he had his head struck off, above the teeth, with a cannon shot; and his brains dashed upon the Colonel's left cheek.[33]

Many other authors pare down emotion when talking of military details since they assume it might interfere with proper evaluation. Years before the Royal Society formulated rules for factual language, Alexander Leighton, who is himself highly articulate, defends this dry style when he claims, "I haue en-

---

[31] *Observations, in His Travels, Upon the State of the Seventeen Provinces . . . 1609* (London, 1626). In *Stuart Tracts: 1603-1693*, ed. C. H. Firth (New York, rpt., 1903), pp. 225-26.

[32] "Account of the Assault on Ostend, 7th January, 1602." In *Stuart Tracts: 1603-1693*, ed. Firth, p. 200.

[33] "Continuation of the Siege of Ostend, from 25 July, 1601, as far as 7 Mar. 1602." In *Stuart Tracts: 1603-1693*, ed. Firth, p. 177.

deavoured *rather with simplicitie of phrase & aptnesse of dictio*
(as becommeth the subiect) to expresse the truth, then to adorn
with colours" (*Speculum*, Sig. C1ʳ).

Not all records available during Milton's youth were so
utilitarian. Many self-advertising heroes offered themselves as
models to young England. A subgenre of highly colored first
person narratives mingled piety and melodrama to show that
glory awaited any boy who kept his wits—and happened to en-
counter pirates or foreign enemies. Several resemble American
dime novels of a later century: the British hero is resourceful,
his foes cowardly or stupid, his battles fierce and the settings
exotic. When Milton was about thirteen, for example, John
Rawlins sailed back to Penzance in command of the same vessel
on which he had been a slave. Immediately after docking, he
wrote *The Famous and Wonderful Recovery of a Ship of Bristol
. . . from the Turkish Pirates of Argier* [Algiers]. Although cap-
tured, Rawlins organizes a shipboard revolt and, crying "For
God, and King James!" slays his infidel captors. His stirring ac-
count openly preaches to young (and older) readers that religion
plus self-reliance produce an admirable citizen:

> I can say no more. The actors in this comic tragedy are
> most of them alive. The Turks are in prison! the ship is to
> be seen! and Rawlins himself dare justify the matter! a
> man not to be dallied withal in these things; nor any way
> to be made partaker of deceit.[34]

Other "penny dreadfuls" recount similar bold deeds. When
Milton was about seventeen he could have read Richard Peeke's
popular pamphlet, *Three to One. Being an English-Spanish
combat performed by a Western Gentleman of Tavistock in
Devonshire, with an English quarterstaff, against three
Spaniards with rapiers and poniards; at Sherries in Spain, the
15th day of November 1625.*[35] Like Rawlins, Peeke is captured,
this time while robbing a Spanish nobleman. His judges allow

---

[34] (London, 1622). In *Stuart Tracts: 1603-1693*, ed. Firth, pp. 272-73.
[35] (London, 1626). In *Stuart Tracts: 1603-1693*, ed. Firth, pp. 275-93.

him to display his mettle by duelling three fierce Spaniards. Predictably, Peeke triumphs and is offered employment by the admiring king. He refuses, with commendable patriotism. *Three to One* vigorously balances personal bravado with biblical maxims, inspires the well-known ballad "Dick of Devonshire," and provides yet another hero to an appreciative country. Also in 1626, Milton could have bought an anonymous pamphlet again proving that one resourceful Briton might, with God's help, defeat awesome odds. The title summarizes the contents: *A True Relation of a Brave English Strategem Practised lately upon a sea town in Galicia* . . . *most valiantly and successfully performed by one English ship alone of thirty tons, with no more than 35 men in her.* Here a Captain Quaile lures Spanish guards from their seaside fort by pretending his vessel is French. After imprisoning them in the cabin, he leads the ship's company to attack the fort and town, "pillaging . . . for eight hours together." Their high jinks do more than furnish excitement to an audience at home: they help to hurt the giant enemy of England. While Spain's vast empire may daunt those of lesser vigor, Quaile's raid proves that "this golden faggot of dominion may have many sticks plucked out of it, if cunning fingers go about to undo the band."[36] How many young contemporaries of Milton actually responded to these news accounts by journeying to the Mediterranean cannot be determined, but their very publication demonstrates that conflict in any good cause received notice.

One final work, more famous than the others, appeared in London during 1630. John Smith's boastful but apparently accurate *True Travels* must have excited and intimidated readers who, like Milton, were entering manhood.[37] Smith has *"Adventures . . . In Europe, Asia, Affrica, and America"* for over thirty years *("from Anno Domini 1593. to 1629,"* says the Title Page). Even before Smith's narrative begins, the printer manipulates an audience by supplying a nine-panel, fold-out il-

---

[36] (London, 1626). In *Stuart Tracts: 1603-1693*, ed. Firth, p. 301.
[37] *The True Travels, Adventures, and Observations* (London, 1630).

lustration of Smith's heroics. He swims from a wreck in one panel, lifts the seige of "Olvmpagh" in another, fights three heathen (labelled with the half moon of Islam), receives the heads of three Turks, and clubs the Bashaw of Nalbrits to death prior to escaping on a spirited horse. Smith triumphs in *The True Travels*, as well as in *The Generall Historie of Virginia*,[38] because he is a professional soldier. His abilities to fight with a variety of weapons, to build suitable fortifications, and to think clearly during emergencies save him from enemies all over the earth. His rescue by Pokahontas, pictured in *The Generall Historie* between pages 58-59, even hints that soldiers appeal to women of all cultures. Although Milton had dedicated his life to literature, he must have known that the stern muse of battle beckoned many of his peers.

These adventures that claimed to have actually happened are mirrored by fictional narratives also stressing the young hero's military prowess. Soon after Milton came of age, Richard Johnson's *Most Pleasant History of Tom ALincolne* appeared. Unlike the poet, this *"Red-Rose Knight"* wins instant fame as *"The Boast of England."* Within a dozen pages, Tom leads his army against the king of "Portingale," defeats him and sets off to *"Fayrie Land"* where he marries the daughter of Prester John (Milton's 1629 Elegies 5 and 6 only dream of girls), and eventually discovers that he is King Arthur's son. There are the usual dragons, hermit, golden tree, night owls, and, somewhat unexpectedly, a treacherous death and burial in a dungheap. The meanderings of this gothic plot help to fill a reader's empty day, but they have certain lessons too. When Johnson describes Tom's army camp, the passage gives substance to military dreams in the same way that other passages had incarnated adolescent fantasies of love and heroism:

his Campe resembled one of the greatest Cities in the world, for all kinds of officers were there found in order: and also a great number of Merchants to furnish it with all

---

[38] *The Generall Historie of Virginia, New-England, and the Summer Isles* (London, 1631), Sig. C2^R.

manner of necessaryes. Hee in no case permitted any rob-
beries, priuy fighting, force, or violence: but with seuerity
punished those that were therein found guiltie. His desire
was, that his Souldiers should glory in nothing so much, as
in Martiall prowess, Vertue, and Wisedome.[39]

Although *Tom ALincoln* makes little claim for veracity, its
army statements might have been found in the most earnest
war book. If Milton read it, his 1632 sonnet "How soon hath
Time" has special poignancy. Tom lived, fully and publicly,
while the young poet feels robbed of twenty-three years. Mil-
ton can point to "no bud or blossom" while Tom vigorously
commands men, defeats enemies, and wins true love.

The combination of cool and impassioned war reports appar-
ently did mould certain characters. The *Short Memorials* of
Thomas, Lord Fairfax[40] show the famous leader acting profes-
sionally in the midst of confusion. At one time he notes unemo-
tionally that a cannon ball killed two "Villains" who earlier had
paused during battle to rob a corpse (pp. 40-41. As long ago as
the time of Emperor Leo, soldiers were warned not to loot
bodies until fighting had finished: "*nullum cadauer ante belli
finem spoliandum.*" De Bellico Apparatu, Sig. Q₄ᵛ). Another
time, after being shot through the wrist, he grasps his reins in
the good hand, spends nearly forty hours on horseback "with-
out any rest or refreshment" and reaches a safe town. There he
tenderly comforts his five-year old daughter who had fallen

---

[39] *The Most Pleasant History of Tom ALincoln* (London, 1631), Sig. C2ᴿ.

[40] Ed. Brian Fairfax (London, 1699). Other soldiers exhibit similar valor. A
dauntless colleague of Robert Monro went on the *Expedition with the Worthy
Scots Regiment . . . 1626* (London, 1637). Although shot in the leg by a cannon
ball, Monro's friend "did call couragiously, go on bravely, Camerades, and I
wish I had a Treene, or a woodden leg for your sakes" (p. 17). The most engag-
ing scene of derring-do is recounted by Francis Vere in *The Commentaries*, ed.
William Dillingham (Cambridge, 1657). Although awake during most of the
night on 4 December 1601, Vere leaps from his nap in early morning when he
hears that the "English trenches [at Ostend] were assaulted." "Pulling on his
stockins, with his sword in his hand, he ran in all haste unbraced with some
souldiers. . . . The Enemy being retreated into his works, Sir Francis Vere called
me to him, and said, boy, come now pull up my stockins, and tie my points"
(pp. 141-42).

"into frequent Swoonings." But within fifteen minutes the enemy approached, forcing him to continue the retreat. Whether faced with insubordinate troops or "a Body so full of pain, and a Mind yet fuller of anxiety and trouble," Fairfax never fails. His every action seems dictated by the lessons in other men's books. He provides a model for men in the New Model Army by being both martial and moral: "I must acknowledge it as the infinite goodness of God, that my Spirit was nothing at all discouraged from doing still that which I thought to be my Duty" (pp. 54-56).

All this close observation of war's minutiae satisfied a warning articulated by Vegetius: the man "that desyreth peace, let him prepare for warre: he [that] coueteth the victorye, let him diligentlye trayne and enstructe his souldiours: he that wysheth for prosperous successe, let him fight with art and pollicye, not at all aduenture and by chaunce" (Sig. D$_1$^{v}). Even after the defeat of the Armada, a fear of invasion or foreign-inspired sedition stalked most Englishmen. They may or may not have had reason to worry. Undeniably, though, they were targets for certain English patriots who fired off inflammatory pamphlets that reduced history to a sequence of treachery, deliverance, and new treachery. These alarming works claimed that foreigners were gliding throughout the land, plotting destruction. William Leigh, who was chaplain to Prince Henry, fosters both zeal and suspicion with tracts like *Great Britaines, Great Deliverance, from the Great Danger of the Popish Powder*. With reckless simplicity, Leigh "proves" that treason at court during the previous half century is only part of a nationwide plot: "euer since the first yeare of *Elizabeth*, our late Queene of famous memory, euen to this day . . . factious Priests & Iesuites, . . . vermine of the Church, and bane of Christendome" have raised "Rebellions." Infamous traitors like "*Saunders, Morton, Felton, Edmond Campion*, and *Robert Parsons*" still live in the person of other agents, as yet undetected.[41] Trueborn Britons must guard against such villains

---

[41] *Great Britaines, Great Deliverance, from the Great Danger of Popish Powder* (London, 1606), Sig. B$_1$^{r}.

since, as Leigh explains in *Queene Elizabeth*, Catholics "*hold it not onely lawfull and meritorions [sic] to kill Kings*" of other faiths, "*but with all an* heroicall *acte.*"[42] Although God has preserved England's monarchs, danger still threatens. Leigh betrays a certain anxiety even when he boasts

> it is not in you, or your *Romane* God (ô yee popish repin-
> ers) its not your boysterous bull can pull downe a Prince,
> its not the croaking of your frogges, and Locusts, your
> Iesuited crew and Seminarie broode, can blast our doctrine,
> blemish our state, or bereaue vs of our Soueraigne, dis-
> quiet you may, destroy you may not. (p. 10)

Leigh's opinion that England would triumph against its foes must have struck some readers as questionable. There was a glum tradition in philosophy that said everything decays. The noblest families decline, brave peoples become servile, liberty is bartered for ease. Even Robert Ward, who usually emanates reasoned optimism, explains why he devotes such care to his military book:

> our people are so metamorphiz'd from that true worth
> which in former ages was inherent to our English, but now
> so effeminiz'd by their voluptuous living, that they are not
> fit to undertake the paines and care of a Souldier; their
> hearts melting like butter, upon the supposition of meeting
> death in the face. (*Anima'dversions*, p. 167)

Wherever Englishmen turned, outward toward enemies or inward toward their melting hearts, they saw a need to study soldiering. No doubt the martial details of *Paradise Lost* seemed welcome to most casual readers.

Milton had two final public reasons for keeping Satan under arms after the war in Heaven, artistic and propagandistic. On a level of esthetics, the numerous allusions to military costume and behavior provide a solidity to characters who otherwise might fade into abstractions. "He saw," as Dr. Johnson did,

---

[42] *Queene Elizabeth, Paraleld in her Princely Vertues, with David, Josua, and Hezekia* (London, 1612), Sig. A4ᵛ.

"that immateriality supplied no images."[43] Satan and his de-
mons may be described as envious, proud, wrathful, deceitful,
cunning—assertions that are theologically correct but visually
barren. When pictured as a commander with his legions, how-
ever, the adversaries borrow something from portraits by
Greek, Roman, and Renaissance war theorists. Theology said
that fiends from some nonhuman world oppose us in a baffling
war whose weapons "are not carnal" (2 Cor. 10:4). Thus our
darkened understanding may have difficulty comprehending
the concreteness of evil. But minds that have mastered military
books can (to use an artillery term) bracket soldierlike devils be-
tween doctrine's cloudy horizon and the familiar field of human
squabbles. Satan and his crew lose the camouflage of their
abstract attributes when they surge toward us equipped like sol-
diers we have seen already and, because of our pugnacious
urges, will see again.

Let me give one preliminary example of how military de-
scriptions help to illustrate *Paradise Lost*. Azazel carries Satan's
flag, but Milton says little to particularize this "Cherub tall."
Azazel seems merely to act: during the demons' dress review,
he "forthwith from the glittering Staff unfurl'd / Th' Imperial
Ensign" (1. 534-36). We moderns may not respond to Milton's
short references. However, generations of army writers before
him had specified so many qualities for a standard bearer that a
late Renaissance man probably would feel Azazel leap fully
armed from his memory. Each of Milton's few words pertaining
to the guidon has authority from *artes militares*. The demon
claims a "proud honor" (1. 533) since, as Thomas Trussell
explains,

> The Ensigne is the foundation of the Company, . . . there-
> fore the Ensigne-bearer ought to bee not onely a good
> Souldier, bold, and valiant, but as neere as may be, the
> Captaines equall in valour, discretion, and counsell. (*The
> Souldier*, pp. 48-49)

[43] Selections from Lives of the Poets, ed. Edmund Fuller (New York, 1965),
p. 92.

Other writers agree that the soldier who carries a flag must have outstanding moral and physical traits. Gerat Barry knows from his life as an Irish mercenary that the "Alferis or Ansign bearer" should be

> a brave Souldier. . . . He oughte to goe galante and well armed. . . . he is to sheow himselfe dreadfull and terrible, with his sowrde in the righte hande, and his culores in the lefte, bravely displaying the same, sheowinge him selfe valiante, and givenge goode examples to the Souldieres, and animatinge them. (A Discourse, pp. 16-17)

Both Trussell and Barry give an added depth to Azazel. The fiend is more than a disembodied name. Rather, he represents functional courage and marches with a traditional posture. John Smithe's Instructions, Observations, and Orders Mylitarie furnishes the most complete physical picture of this functionary in Satan's militia:

> I would wish that all Ensignebearers should bee armed in this sort following (viz) a light vpright & sharp crowned Spanish burgonet, a Coller, a Cuyrasse with short tasses, or without tasses, and a backe with a paire of sleeues and gloues of fine maile, . . . to the intent that they may carry their Ensignes with the more ease; and his said armour I would wish to bee of a good and a hard temper to resist the point of a pique.

Not only may we now see what Azazel wears, but we also can visualize where he marches ("in the midst of the piques accompanied with halbarders") and how he holds the flag: he

> ought to carry his Ensigne open and vpright, and not wound vp about his Ensigne staffe, nor yet the lowest part of the Taffata of his ensigne gathered into his hand, and leaned vppon his shoulder, but vpright as aforesaid.[44]

---

[44] Instructions, Observations, and Orders Mylitarie (London, 1595). The first quotation ("I would wish") is from page 19; the second ("ought to carry") is from pages 18 and 19.

Both readers and viewers know that Azazel typifies a very special kind of soldier. Thomas Styward reminds us in *The Pathwaie to Martiall Discipline* that a standard bearer has vowed to make the ensign "his winding sheete" rather than lose it.[45] Thus, we properly see Satan's Ensignbearer "marching in battalia," as The Lord of Praissac describes him in *The Art of Warre, or Militarie Discourses*: "he is to march courageously without bowing himself to any."[46]

In addition to recalling current events and picturing angels, martial parlance aimed at a third target, this one moral. Although Milton's military allusions represent a minority view, they try to convince readers that armed assault, except in certain cases, is futile. Until Book 6, the fallen angels seem to be perfect soldiers. The similarity between damned angels and ideal human warriors itself rebukes armies. Milton does indicate before the Son's victory that Satan's mutineers should not be praised without reservation. But such caveats, couched as many are in technical language, work most effectively when the rebels lose the war in Heaven. The power that defeats them is clearly spiritual and superior to any work-a-day efficiency to which mortals may rise if they follow the maxims of war books. In short, Milton gives some credit to military endeavor but reserves his highest praise for better fortitudes. Like a philosopher-king who sagely employs one mercenary army to destroy another, Milton drafts the soldiers' lexicon into a crusade against war itself. By militarizing the fallen, he renders them palpable, thus satisfying literary requirements for visual *energeia*, and reprehensible, thereby fulfilling his ethical belief: war is the utmost that vice promises to her followers.

Milton's Disapproval of War

Milton's private feelings about war lend special urgency to his widespread use of technical expressions. We should not be sur-

[45] *The Pathwaie to Martiall Discipline* (London, 1581), p. 37.
[46] *The Art of Warre, or Militarie Discourses* (Cambridge, 1639), p. 128.

prised, given his temper, that ethics rather than relevance or picturability superintends his utterances. There are relatively few military references in Milton's early work, although bloody Mars imposed upon him several times. Having returned from Italy sooner than desired because an English war was brewing, he later laments to Carlo Dati, "What safe retirement for literary leisure could you suppose given one among so many battles of a civil war, slaughters, flights, seizures of goods?" (*Fam Let* No. 10. C.E. 12. 51). His cherished plan to write of King Arthur "waging his wars beneath the earth" (*Manso* 81, Hughes' tr.) is forcibly postponed during the terrible period when actual English leaders clash at places like Marston Moor. Even when he seems to confront war, Milton displays a certain aloofness. Sometimes he alludes to war in passages making no judgment. *L'Allegro*, for example, humorously describes a rural morning when "the Cock with lively din, / Scatters the rear of darkness thin" (49-50). Elsewhere his references are more satirical, but their victim is not conflict itself. Here he mocks the behavior of clergymen by linking them to captains:

> For Divines, if ye observe them, have thir postures, and thir motions no less expertly, and with no less variety then they that practice feats in the Artillery-ground. Sometimes they seem furiously to march on, and presently march counter; by and by they stand, and then retreat; or if need be can face about, or wheele in a whole body, with that cunning and dexterity as is almost unperceavable; to winde themselves by shifting ground into places of more advantage. And Providence only must be the drumm, Providence the word of command, that calls them from above, but always to som larger Benefice, or acts them into such or such figures, and promotions. At thir turnes and doublings no men readier; to the right, or to the left; for it is thir turnes which they serve cheifly. (*TKM*. C.E. 5. 56)

Whatever Milton's purposes in these works, metaphorical or polemical, he expresses himself with the same precision that will characterize his later uses of war terms. Observant but not involved, Milton almost resembles the Satan of *Paradise Regained* who proudly displays his Parthians to tempt Christ: "See how in warlike muster they appear, / In Rhombs and wedges, and half-moons, and wings" (3. 308-309). I often suspect that Milton uses these highly controlled early utterances to seal off his imaginative world from the rowdy dither of combat. "On the Morning of Christ's Nativity," for example, commemorates two unique incidents, the birth of Jesus and Milton's own coming of age. Yet the speaker, who invokes a "Heav'nly Muse" "to welcome" "the Infant God" (15-18), uses stereotyped language. An honor guard of predawn stars is described quite conventionally: "all the spangled host keep watch in squadrons bright" (21). Their silence in the sky parallels the tranquility of earth, where war ceases: "The Trumpet spake not to the armed throng" so that "spear and shield" as well as "hooked Chariot" lie unused (53-58). Even when divine music begins, Milton speaks competently but unadventurously:

> At last surrounds their sight
> A Globe of circular light,
>   That with long beams the shame-fac't night array'd,
> The helmed Cherubim
> And sworded Seraphim
>   Are seen in glittering ranks with wings display'd,
> Harping in loud and solemn choir,
> With unexpressive notes to Heav'n's new-born Heir.
>   (109-116)

This smooth stanza expresses an idea that other writers had often thought: God's angels sometimes appear as soldiers. Milton had earlier assigned a troop of winged soldier-angels (*Volatiles . . . milites*) to escort the Bishop of Ely to heaven (*Ely* 47); later his *Christian Doctrine* (1. 9) will limit the guise to occasions when good angels execute God's vengeance. Similarly, "the damned crew" (228) who flee at the Lord's coming are predictably nonmartial, "brutish gods" (211) following "Th' old Dragon" with his familiar "folded tail" (168, 172). Both good and evil angels appear as background characters and do not disturb the nativity's solemn pageant by exhibiting novel attributes.

A few years later, Milton calls upon the same good angels who heralded Jesus' birth. These "flaming Powers, and winged Warriors bright" are invited to "mourn" the first shedding of Jesus' blood. "Upon the Circumcision" also expects soldier-angels to be members of a static chorus, not a functioning military unit. Milton returns to singing angels in "At a Solemn Music," once more unmoved to assign them martial duties.

War seized his imagination after the grand tour of 1638-1639. Asking why leads to a simple answer (England's Civil War had begun) and a more complex answer (Italian academicians may have convinced him that combat was a valid topic for serious poetry). Milton's first extended meditation on war deals with the old *paragone* between Mars and the Muses. Sonnet 8 opposes "Captain or Colonel, or Knight in Arms" to the poet. (The antagonist's rank is unknown but unimportant: he is the enemy.) Properly classical in expression, intended (perhaps humorously) to be placed "On his door when the City expected an assault" (probably during November 1642), the poem nevertheless communicates a certain home truth. Alexander and Pindar reappear in every age, but the former is always a "Conqueror" and the poet "defenseless." Only the magical songs ("charms") of a consummate artist may protect him from war's spoliation. Yet even with the precedent of salvation through artistry in mind, a dweller in "the Muses' Bow'r" who plies his pen will forever depend upon the whim of any soldier who wields a "spear." Their encounter takes place in an ambiguous arena that is equally past and yet-to-come.

Milton's reluctance to be mastered by war helps organize *Of Education*. He suggests the establishment of a Renaissance Sandhurst, but his major interest is in a thoroughly rounded course of study. Ignoring the frantic calls for military preparedness that issued from many of his contemporaries, Milton dreams that pupils at this academy will polish the dark glass of their fallen intellects in order "to repair the ruins of our first parents" (C.E. 4. 277). The curriculum, however, is only partly theological and includes grammar, mathematics, agriculture, geography, biology, wrestling, and "military motions." Such training, claims Milton, "fits a man to perform justly, skilfully, and magnanimously all the offices, both private and public, of peace and war" (C.E. 4. 280). Other writers since the time of Plato agreed, using almost identical phrases. For example, Ceriol's *Very Briefe and Profitable Treatise* reminds any citizen who wishes to aid his king that "the counseler had neede to be skilfull as vvell in martiall affayres, as in cyuill gouernement" since all nations face problems whether at war or peace.[47] Although the goals of education were expressed in clichés, the intent of much early seventeenth-century training was to habilitate soldiers. Milton provides a careful balance in his essay so that warlike activities do not dominate his pupils' lives. The ideal is harmony, symbolized by music and army maneuvers. The first trains an individual's soul to integrate all his talents into a coherent pattern, while "battling, marching, encamping, fortifying, besieging, and battering" provide discipline on the social level. Adam and Hercules stand for those admirable men who repay their debts by committing themselves to a complete program of self-improvement.

Milton himself abides by his own advice when he writes the two sonnets of 1652. Each has a similar structure and both urge their addressees to balance past accomplishments in conflict by social achievements in peace time. Cromwell is first praised in the octave of Sonnet 16 for being a warrior who triumphed because he was "Guided by faith and matchless Fortitude." The sestet looks to Cromwell's future, reminding him that "peace hath her victories / No less renown'd than war." Likewise, Sonnet 17 to Henry Vane the Younger piles up opposites such as "young in years, but in sage counsel old," "gowns not arms," "settle peace, or . . . advise . . . war," "Iron and Gold," and "spiritual power and civil." Vane heroically reconciles antitheses. The octave and sestet, while less distinct than in the previ-

[47] Federico Furio Ceriol, *A Very Briefe and Profitable Treatise* (London, 1570), Sig. F4^{r,v}.

ous poem, trust that the political wisdom Vane displayed in the past will control England's debate on liberty of belief. Both men are urged to transfer soldierly virtues and political astuteness into civilian channels to meet the less dramatic but still important religious problems that battle had not solved.

Perhaps Milton's logical training superintended the artful balance in *Of Education* and Sonnets 15, 16, and 17. Such equipoise is found in war books, too. They regularly divide time and space into two contiguous arenas. Past and present cease to exist because military manuals import ideas from Greece, Rome, and the Bible to enrich modern operations. Francesco Patrizi's literate works, for instance, continually compare ancient and current practices in order to correct recent imperfections. His titles indicate how war writers insisted upon the relevance of the past: *La militia romana . . . Ma ancora, in paragone, farà chiaro, quanto la moderna sia difettosa & imperfetta* (Ferrara, 1583); *Paralleli Militari . . . Ne'quali si fa paragone delle milizie antiche . . . con le moderne* (Rome, 1594). In the same manner, martial authors juxtapose discrete regions of the physical world. The needs of England's armies are provisioned by practices from Spain, Turkey, Switzerland, Italy, and Sweden. Binary thought is so basic to martial works that it appears in countless forms: win/lose, Christians/infidels, English/foreign. No matter how zealous a war writer may be, he usually expresses his message in terms of an opposition that balances at some point. The most simple form, that of two armies, appears in a translation of "Signior Valesco's" *Newes from Rome* (London, 1606?). This odd work (which mentions a Jew named "Shilocke") describes *"two Mightie Armies . . . : The First of the Great Sophy, the other of an Hebrew People"* (Title Page). More sophisticated examples of military balance appear in illustrations. To the left on the engraved title page of "Philanactophil's" *Nero Caesar* (London, 1624) stands "Roma." Treading on a globe, armed with spear and shield ("SPQR"), this allegorical figure matches a female to the right labeled "Londinium." Although London's left hand touches a sword, she holds a cornucopia and displays the anchor of hope.

Her relations to the world, while equal in magnitude to Rome's, differ in quality. The same "blessings of war and peace" motif introduces Ed[ward] Grimeston's *Generall Historie of the Netherlands*. With relentless symmetry, Pallas on the left confronts Pax on the right. The former's spear, helmet, and aegis lie across from an olive branch and book in the two hands of peace. Below Pallas is a battle scene; beneath Pax, ships trade, men make music, couples dance. Belgia in the middle is prepared for either alternative—"*In Vtramq[ue] Parata*." Like the ideal soldier who opened Kellie's *Pallas Armata*, Belgia holds a sword in her right hand and olive wreath in the left, undaunted by the choices, equal to both.[48] Those who read war books or tracts on education or sonnets about conduct had the same lesson drummed into them: recognize life's antagonistic circumstances and prepare to deal with the extremes of battle or peace.

Obviously Milton pondered his own role as writer in a country boiling with conflict that seemed to require flesh-and-bone brawlers on real battlefields. He participated in battle, vicariously but willingly, by mastering treatises like Machiavelli's *Art of War*, Frontinus' *Strategems*, and Ward's *Anima'dversions*.[49] Also, he required Edward Phillips to read Frontinus, Aelian's *Tactics*, Polyaenus' *Strategems of War* and works of Xenophon often cited by theorists, *Cyropaedia* and the *Anabasis*.[50] He gives the impression that he has courageously undertaken to familiarize himself as completely as possible with what he detests. Perhaps his motive for reading so many martial texts in the late thirties and early forties was to use their lucid pronouncements as mental stepping stones into the Lernian swamp of actual fighting. He probably did not consider becoming a soldier, but his study for once aligned him with a

[48] *A Generall Historie of the Netherlands . . . 1608 . . . till . . . 1627* (London, 1627), title page.
[49] William Riley Parker, *Milton: A Biography* (Oxford, 1968), 2: 893. Parker mentions here that "perhaps the study of them had something to do with the abortive notion of making Milton an Adjutant-General in Waller's army about this time."
[50] Phillips, "Life of Milton." In Hughes, p. 1029.

majority of his contemporaries. They saw great merit in such reading. Seasoned veterans like Robert Monro, recently returned from seven years' campaigning in Germany, says approvingly,

> I dare be bold to affirme, that reading and discourse doth as much or rather more, to the furtherance of a perfect Souldier, than a few yeares practise without reading.[51]

'Even Milton's father could not have supported his son's course of study with more encouraging words.

The enormous amount of information Milton gleaned from war books did not shake his faith in the high worth of his own vocation. Against the author of the vindictive *Regii Sanguinis Clamor* (*Cry of the Royal Blood* by Peter du Moulin, 1652), he asserts,

> it is not true, that I am thus lean beyond example; on the contrary, I possess that spirit and strength, that, when my age and manner of life so inclined me, I was neither unskilled in handling my sword, nor unpractised in its daily use. Armed with this weapon, as I commonly was, I thought myself a match for any man, though superior in strength, and secure from any insult which one man could offer to another. (*Def.2. C.E.* 8. 61)

Milton's personal memory cooperates with a belief articulated earlier in the *Second Defence*, a trust that

> courage shines out not exclusively in war and arms, but displays its intrepid power equally against every species of

---

[51] *Expedition*, Sig.)(4ʳ. War writers resemble teachers in their praise of reading. Sutcliffe cajoles his audience: "Admit a mans experience bee neuer so great, yet shall hee learne much by reading of Military discourses, more then euer his owne experience could teach him" (*Practice*, Sig. A4ʳ). Leighton bullies: "The greatest schollers haue been the greatest souldiers" (*Speculum*, p. 33). Ward repeats: "by the reading of History a man may learne, and conceive more in a yeere then he possibly can see practised in his lifetime; by reason whereof the worthies of ancient times, were portraited with a Booke in one hand, and a Sword in the other." *Anima'dversions of Warre. The Second Booke* (London, 1639), p. 3. Subsequently cited as *Anima'dversions II*.

fear. . . . For, if I avoided the toils and the perils of war, it was only that I might earnestly toil for my fellow-citizens in another way, with much greater utility, and with no less peril. In doubtful postures of our affairs, my mind never betrayed any symptom of despondence, nor was I more afraid than became me of malice, or even of death. Devoted even from a child to the more humanizing studies, and always stronger in mind than in body, I set an inferior value upon the service of the camp, in which I might have been easily surpassed by any ordinary man of a more robust make, and betook myself to those occupations, where my services could be of more avail; that, if I were wise, I might contribute my utmost power, from the higher and more excellent, not from the lower parts of my nature, to the designs of my country, and to this transcendent cause. I thought, therefore, that if it were the will of God those men should perform such gallant exploits, it must be likewise his will, that when performed, there should be others to set them forth with becoming dignity and ornament; and that the truth, after being defended by arms, should be alike defended by reason—the only defence which is truly and properly human. (*Def.2. C.E. 8. 7, 9, 11*)

This credo brilliantly creates a public image. Its expression honors his favorite historian, the respected Sallust, and its logic parallels that of Vegetius. The latter already had furnished a noble example of literate patriotism to the Renaissance in his account of Cato the Elder, who,

often Consul, and always victorious at the head of armies, believed he should do his country more essential service by writing on military affairs, than by all his exploits in the field. For the consequences of brave emotions are only temporary, while whatever is committed to writing for the public good is of lasting utility.[52]

[52] *Military Institutions of Vegetius, in Five Books*, tr. John Clarke (London, 1767), p. 39. I use this version in subsequent references since Sadler's quaintness sometimes gives a false impression of Vegetius' straightforward Latin.

With a coincidence rare in polemical statements, Milton's passage both preserves him from obloquy because of the prestige attached to writers who immortalize fighters and defines a theory of accomplishment to which he was genuinely attached. His *History of Britain* (written in the half decade before the *Second Defence* appears in 1654) repeats the concept of creative symbiosis in which doer and teller exist in a close but hierarchical relationship, the first subordinate to the second. Yet each contributes his effort to advance an ideal. For "worthy deeds," Milton says,

> are not often destitute of worthy relaters: as by a certain Fate great Acts and great Eloquence have most commonly gon hand in hand, equalling and honouring each other in the same Ages. . . . [H]e whose just and true valour uses the necessity of Warr and Dominion, not to destroy but to prevent destruction, to bring in liberty against Tyrants, Law and Civility among barbarous Nations . . . hath recourse to the aid of Eloquence. (*Britain* 2. C.E. 10. 32-33)

If we inquire no more deeply into Milton's early views of war, we would conclude that by about 1642 he loyally responds to a subject that gripped his countryman but held little attraction for him. Milton evaluates his talents as a writer and offers them to a troubled nation. His objective statements satisfy a call from military authors such as Thomas Stafford, who sounds much like Milton when he says in *Pacata Hibernia*:

> The great Actions of Worthie and eminent Persons, haue ever been esteemed so powerfull for the instruction of succeeding times, that all Ciuill States haue made it their principall care, to preserue and transmit them to Posteritie, for their Example and Imitation. . . . The omission of this hath been a great defect of some ages foregoing ours, being the Middle times betweene learned Antiquitie and this latter age, wherein Language, Arts and Elegancie have revived and flourished . . . A want of which many haue complained, but few haue laboured to supply.[53]

[53] *Pacata Hibernia* (London, 1633), Sig. A₂ᴿ.

On paper, Milton's chosen role of polemicist fulfills his personal desire and his country's need.

Milton the Civilian

Milton's statements are quite logical. But whenever he justifies his own activities during the Civil War, he exhibits a curious intensity. Milton considered himself both patriotic and useful. Yet he dwells upon the specific fact that he served his cause although not as a soldier. Other writers who were his near contemporaries do not feel obliged to vindicate their actions at such length and do not return to the question of whether they enlisted in the army. The Royalists counted many educated soldiers among their supporters. However, those without the poetic and martial talents of a Lovelace do not offer extenuating biographies. Cowley is not dismayed that he labored for the exiled court doing work roughly like Milton's. Henry Vaughan, who probably was present at Rowton Heath during the king's Welsh campaign of 1645, does not brag of his service. Isaac Walton, connected by his second marriage to the Royalists, does not exculpate his lack of service. Those religious supporters of the king like Herrick, Crashaw, Thomas Fuller, and Jeremy Taylor do not apologize for their spiritual callings during wartime. Even Royalists who disgraced themselves do not pen lengthy defenses. Denham was high sheriff for Surrey but does not worry that he speedily surrendered Farnham Castle to Parliament. His friend George Wither shared in the debacle but does not relive the experience even in later life when he becomes a Puritan. Waller's confession to Parliament in 1643 that he was involved in a plot, an apparently cowardly act that betrayed others, does not torment him to a reasoned excuse. And Suckling does not feel compelled to explain his retreat from Duns with the Earl of Holland. Nor does he rebut the sarcastic ballad by Sir John Mennes, "On Sir John Suckling's Most Warlike Preparations for the Scottish War." Despite the length and acrimony of the civil war, no one heaped opprobrium upon Thomas Browne when he preserved a mystic's aloofness from the commotion. Even those who bent with the wind such as

Marvell or Peter Lely, painter of both Charles and Cromwell, do not review their past errors to win forgiveness from succeeding administrations. Among notable artists, only Milton doggedly returns to his contributions as a civilian to the Good Old Cause.

Perhaps Milton's reluctance toward direct involvement was conditioned by his close Royalist connections among relatives (such as Thomas Agar) and friends (such as the Rugeleys). Still, I suggest that Milton's most personal concern with the military began when he returned from Italy. There was another John Milton in London at this time, a soldier. He probably was about the poet's age. A portrait of him, showing a serious man in sober uniform, was painted to commemorate his induction into the Honourable Artillery Company on 2 June 1635. His participation in military matters may be documented further if all the following data refer to the same man. In 1642 he was quartermaster to Colonel Isaac Penington in the White Regiment of the London trained bands. On 23 July 1647 he had advanced to the rank of sergeant major in the London militia. The House of Lords appointed him on 24 April 1648 to bring "in the Arrears of the Assessments for the Army" from Tower Ward. (Our poet at this time lived rather far from the Tower.) The wife of a John Milton was buried at St. Dunstan in the East in 1658, a resting place to which he followed her on 7 June 1661.[54] So far, the facts exist in various accounts without making special appeal to a student of the poet.

The major document I have found concerning this warrior Milton, however, contains numerous assertions that would have been of importance to the returning poet. Published on 28 August 1639, approximately a month after the tour ended, Wil-

[54] These facts have been assembled by J. Milton French in *The Life Records of John Milton* (New Brunswick, N.J.): vol. 1 (1949), p. 294; vol. 2 (1950), pp. 86, 200, 218; vol. 4 (1956), pp. 383, 398-99. See also Parker, *Milton*, vol. 2, p. 894n, and Robert T. Fallon, "John Milton and the Honorable Artillery Company," *MQ*, 9 (1975), 49-51. The latter rightly (I think) concludes, "the poet was never a member of the Honorable Artillery Company." David Masson has a readable if inconclusive summary of facts available to him in *The Life of John Milton*, vol. 2 (London, 1871), Chapter 2.

liam Barriff's book *Mars, His Triumph* is a detailed "Description of an Exercise performed the xviii. of October, 1638. in Merchant-Taylors Hall by Certain Gentlemen of the Artillery Garden *London*." An epistle dedicatory to the forty-eight page program appeals to the scholarly reader with examples from Greece and Rome to prove "that the wel *disciplin'd* have alwayes been the very *Bulwarks and impalements* of their Countreys. Whereto the contrary, neglect of *discipline*, and the *Art Military* have been always the forerunners of destruction both to the *Province and people*." If the young poet, near thirty and relatively unknown, read more of Barriff, he found stings to his character other than this standard call for drilling. To cite only one possible goad: a doggerel poem urges the audience to

> Behold how *Londons armed Infantry*,
> Through *practise* in true *Rules of Souldery*,
> By the *Drums martiall Musick* often led
> The *Pyrrhic* dance do now *distinctly tread*:
> Which if *industriously* they do pursue,
> And use that timely custome that is due
> To *warlike practice*, in despight of hate,
> Which evermore upon *desert* doth wait;
> Times *Finger* may *engrave* their *Industry*,
> Vpon *Fames Pillars* to *posterity*.
>
> (Sigs. ★3^{v,r})

Its casual references to practice and true worth rewarded by fame had already become part of Milton's ongoing inner monologue. Sonnet 7 ("How soon hath Time") and *Lycidas* show that he yearned for the "happy-making sight" ("On Time") of proper recognition. No matter what Milton desired, advisors like Barriff urged him to become a soldier. If he was patriotic and if he paid attention to political news, then, concludes George Marcelline in *Vox Militis*,

> *Will not the Schollar to himselfe take heede,*
> *When as the rod doth make the others bleede.*[55]

[55] *Vox Militis* (London, 1625), Sig. B1^{v}.

Marcelline as well as Barriff sponsors a simplistic dualism: either a man enlists or he hinders his nation. Only cowards, misers, and lechers will not step forward. All right-thinking men realize that an army career can save England and win praise:

> *Then on my Lads, doe not lie slugging heere,*
> *To smoake tobacco pipes, and sucke the beere;*
> *But rather arme, and for your Countrey stand,*
> *Remember Honours haruest is at hand,*
> *In which you reape renowne, if vile digrace,*
> *And cowardize produce not shame of face*
> (Vox, Sig. B2^r)

Barriff's exercise was carried out by 80 men uniformed as soldiers from various times and places: 18 with *"Morions[,] swords* and *Targets,"* "22. *Sarracens,"* and "40. *of the moderne Armes"* (p. 1). The second act consisted of "Captain *Mulli-Aben-Achmat* with his *Saracens* in great state" (Figure 4). Among the troopers, "all of them habited after the *Persian* and *Turconian* maner," was "Iohn Melton" carrying a *"steel"* target (p. 2). The infidels followed a banner (illustrated in the text) on which appeared the *"halfe moon"* of Islam plus Arabic letters proclaiming *"Alli and Mahomet"* (p. 3). Obviously well practiced, the pagans drew themselves up into various formation *"without any present directions"* from their commander who supervised them silently "with a stately survay" (p. 4). After they withdraw, the modern Christian troops appear and one of their number addresses the assembled dignitaries. Here, too, are harsh words for the young poet:

> *Behold the* Souldier *and the* Citizen
> *Make but* one man: *these to* Mars *encline,*
> *And though like* fiery Comets *now they shine*
> *Threatning prodigious ruine to their foes,*
> *Each man can gain a* Conquest *without blows.*
> . . . .

Not one of these but can instruct a Band,
But each Commander, *discipline a* Land.
(pp. 7-8)

The performers appear as ideals who win in war and provide exemplars of disciplined utility during peace. Noble soldiers such as these were stock characters in English drama during the seventeenth-century's second quarter, repeatedly urging their audiences to respect martial virtues.[56] On stage as well as in books, men who are "skilfull as vvell in martiall affayres, as in cyuill gouernement" aid their nation (Ceriol, *Treatise*, Sigs. F4^{r,v}).

There follows a long exhibition of the manual of arms that need not detain us. The postures for musket drill and facing movements, with doublings, marches, countermarches, wheelings and "figures of battell," can be duplicated in the pages of innumerable *artes militares* familiar to Milton and his contemporaries.

The climax of this evening's entertainment is the mock combat between "The Christians and Sarracens." At first, leaders and troops on both sides of the dubious battle "shewed themselves to be no younglings in the *Art Millitary*" (p. 39). Although the Christians force Mulli Achmat to retire, he draws up his men in the garden and, canny general that he is, "sends a spie to see what the Christians are doing." Learning the floor is vacant, he "returns with great *Triumph*, and with much vaunting insolence" (p. 40). Not realizing that the Christians have been keeping "good *espiall* upon him," he chortles about their "*Temeritie*" (p. 42). Soon they return and join in battle. There is a duel between the rival lieutenants and finally an even more epic encounter between the Christian commander and "*Inraged* Achmat *even foming with anger* that he could not work his designe" (p. 45). The Turkish soldiers are beaten but so well

---

[56] Marilynn Strasser Olson studies the convention in *Nil Medium: Noble Soldiers in the Drama in English, 1625-1660* (Duke Dissertation, 1975). She also shows how playwrights used topics like court versus camp, the blunt-spoken soldier, and duelling.

treated they convert to Christianity. As for their military profession, they leave "that course of life, and are now either *Merchants* or *Shopkeepers* for the most part" (p. 48).

In reports of this exercise, Milton would have found enacted, neatly but unacceptably to him, the common way for Englishmen to meet danger. It is no exaggeration to say that a worthy man both in the books and the opinion of war-jittery Londoners was like that "forward youth" in Marvell's "Horatian Ode" who knew when it was time to "forsake his muses dear." The conversion of Saracens to businessmen, however bathetic it may seem to us, apparently justified any loss of life that even a staged conflict entailed. After all, Francis Markham's *Five Decades of Epistles of Warre* had explained that only during peacetime, when "*Minerua* hath cast away her lance, & the Booke of the seuen Arts is become both her playmate and pillow," could the nation "let Souldiers now turne Tradesmen."[57] In *Mars, His Triumph*, Milton the soldier, with full community support, thus offered Milton the poet a role to emulate with automatic honor and clear distinction.

If we combine the generally positive attitude toward war, which Milton's contemporaries shared but he rejected, with the presence in London of a martial shadow, then we have a more complex explanation for his antipathy to militarism. A Jungian critic might well emphasize two meanings of shadow—a soldier enrolled but not physically present, and the opposite of the persona, an unsuspected dimension of everyday personality that contradicts its usual manifestations. Whether Milton actually met his martial double is unprovable, of course, but I suspect that the returning poet carefully noted accomplishments of his fellow citizens. Certainly the nervous atmosphere of London did not facilitate his willed development, and beleagured people tend to be highly sensitive to alternative careers pursued by those within observing distance.

The doppelganger might have had any number of effects upon him. A rising trooper with his name could have func-

---

[57] *Five Decades of Epistles of Warre* (London, 1622), p. 3.

tioned as a constant reproach in the years after the poet learned of his namesake, spurring him to find a socially acceptable vent for his talents. One might argue that Milton's untiring combat in the pamphlet wars of the next decade or so represents his incorporation of the shadow's apparent pugnacity into his own personality. By absorbing the energy imputed to soldiers, he enlarges himself and can proceed to further stages of mature individuation. Conversely, the poet could have vicariously lived his double's active life since inclination and ability (his eyesight was soon to diminish) forbade him "the labors of a camp." In any case, knowing about a soldier named Milton might have actualized traits in the poet that otherwise would have remained dormant.

Did Milton ever long for a life of sensation rather than thought? If so, the paradigm of a soldier provides the perfect form. We might remind ourselves of the anguish he may have experienced by learning that there was a soldier with his name. It is interesting to wonder why, near the end of his life (c. 1669), hedged in by blindness, gout, and an uncongenial government, he moves to a modest home in Artillery Walk, close by the drill field of the London Artillery Company. The other John Milton, legally dead for nearly a decade, should no longer have been able to affect him. Still, were we able now to ask Milton the mournful question of Shallow in 2 *Henry IV*, "Is old Double of your town living yet?" (3. ?. 45-46), I think he would pause significantly before replying.

Summary

This congeries of public traditions and private ideals suggests why Milton devotes so much space to martial matters in his epic. Western civilization and seventeenth-century Englishmen approved of war and understood its parlance. War was both easy to visualize and thrilling to contemplate. While Milton himself habitually mistrusted war, the widespread belief in its efficacy prompted him to study it closely and evolve a subtle, learned, and progressive argument against it. His biography, provable and circumstantial, shows how often he encountered a soldierly ideal. As with other painful topics like death or divorce or temptation, he faces that which disturbs him. Reason carefully modulates his expression so that frequent military references make *Paradise Lost* not a pedantic hypomnema but rather a skillful indictment of mankind's most vulgar error. Coming as it does toward the end of a tradition that appreciated aristocratic war—the new fashion was bourgeoise and biblical—Milton's janus-faced epic looks backward to innumerable poems after Homer that elevate conflict between families, cities, nations, or faiths to an awesome height. *Paradise Lost* also looks forward to the poetry that it helps to create. This new verse ridicules established custom, emphasizes motive rather than means, and concerns an entire society rather than some few champions. The didactic poems of the next century that attack misconceptions about poetry, nature, and society evolve directly, I think, from Milton's way of reexamining such major questions as this one of war.

II

The fallen angels give us the first hint that Milton will simultaneously use and criticize the venerable machinery of war. They regularly appear as military creatures throughout *Paradise Lost*. In obvious and subtle ways, they conform to precepts about soldiering, a conformity that is boldly original. Before Milton's innovation, bad angels almost always appeared in mufti, while good angels (as his early poems show) went about in arms. He insists, however, that the evil are weapon-wielding campaigners and thereby effects a genuine revolution in angelology. Even a brief review of Jewish, Christian, and Islamic angel lore demonstrates that no significant precursor of Milton viewed angels as he did. Milton claims the fallen express their ingratitude to God, loyalty to Satan, and hostility to man in a martial manner. Surprisingly, perhaps, but uniformly, the demons act like trained professionals. Before considering the many specific ways by which angelic activity in the epic imitates soldiering on earth, let us recall how novel Milton's view is.

Background

The Old Testament mentions in passing some defeated monsters like Rahab and Leviathan. But whatever cosmic battles Yahweh fought against them or what weapons he employed or what strategies he devised have all slipped from Scripture. Unlike the authors who gave such a graphic account of the duel between Marduk and Tiamat in Babylon's creation hymn, the Hebrews rigorously expunged almost every detail of the Most High's contentions. One obscure passage may preserve a mythological episode concerning collision between two groups: some mysterious "sons of God" (Gen. 6:2) mate with the daughters of men and sire a race of giants. But Jewish authors neither claim that the sons were angels nor imply that the miscegenation was sinful—Noah's flood (which follows this account) specifically punishes not these couplings but rather the evil each man has in his own heart. Most important, sexual appetite and not aggressive militarism is the only accusation that may be leveled at the unknown sons of God.

Other spirits in other passages are as visually empty. Even if wicked angels do the same things as the good ones—and Milton knew that their primary identity was as messengers (ἄγγελοι, מַלְאָכִים)—even so, bare assertions that these supernatural beings eat, drink, walk, speak, and think roughly like men give little reason to assign soldierly roles. Angelic powers of flight and sudden appearance, while impossible to humans, would be useful for war; yet they are not emphasized in military contexts. That some angels make wrong choices does not even remotely force one to conclude they are warriors. Far superior to men yet infinitely below Yahweh, Old Testament angels live a relatively complete life without much army activity.

Almost the only Hebrew authority Milton can enlist for his own conception of angelic fighters is the divine being who defeats enemies of the Lord (Ps. 35:5-6) and camps around the faithful (Ps. 34:7). Other than this guardian, there are few canonical Hebrew angels from which to fashion epic legionnaires, good or bad. Names and titles sprinkled in such books as Daniel and Zechariah suggest a hierarchy that can, by extension, be martial. Yet the social organization is equally comprehensible as a heavenly analogue to earthly courts.

Even extratestamental writings, some of which Milton might have known, contain almost nothing to inspire the fiction of fallen angels whom humans can comprehend most directly as warriors. Those strange tales recorded in Tobit or 1 Enoch or 2 Esdras beguile us with the activities of unwelcome beings like Asmodeus, Samael, Matatron, and Matanbuchus. But none is a soldier. And assertions that angels guard nations and armies (2 Macc. 3:25 ff) receive little military elaboration.

To be sure, Paul's famous exhortation to the Ephesians postulates a universe seething with evil hosts:

Put on the whole armor of God, that ye may be able to stand against the wiles of the devil. For we wrestle not against the flesh and blood, but against principalities, against powers, against the rulers of the darkness of this world, against spiritual wickedness in high places. (6: 11-12)

But Paul inherits his notion of demonic attack from his age; it is superfluous to his theology. The Fall of Man sufficiently explains human ill in terms of an original crime whose punishment justly afflicts all Adam's descendants. Also, Paul's references usually come from athletic contests, not battlefields. The Gospels barely hint at some evil army arrayed against us. Jesus expels bad spirits without military paraphernalia. His words alone conquer Satan in the wilderness and various demons during his ministry. Only a supremely imaginative synthesis of the scattered New Testament allusions to angelic hostility, numbers, organization, and leadership would label them "military."

If Milton's fully armed rebels spring from any one Colchian field, it is from the short passage in Revelation that mentions some war in Heaven:

Michael and his angels fought against the dragon; and the dragon fought and his angels, and prevailed not; neither was their place found any more in heaven. (12:7-8)

John emphasizes that the bad are limited; he does not suggest they are armored. The mutineers in Revelation fulfill a capacity for bringing evil that earlier writers had darkly described.[1] No matter what cryptic significance originally lay beneath this passage, its surface pictures an insurrection by creatures who serve

---

[1] There are many Old Testament passages in which angels bring woe to men: 2 Sam. 24:16-17; 2 Kings 19:35; Ps. 78:49; Job 33:22; Prov. 16:14. Also see I Macc. 7:41-42.

their own ends and not those of deity. The author obviously emphasizes the negative side of rebellion by having his dragon parody other, more excusable defiances of authority such as exhibited by the Maccabees, Spartacus, and the zealots of Masada. That ethical dualism which made a belated entry in Jewish writing here erupts with a mixture of terror and trust characterizing later Christian apocalypses. Evil changes: the perverse inclination emanating from deep within an individual's heart becomes a cosmic power largely external to humans. Governed by Satan and aimed against both God and hapless man, this energy cannot be a mere platonic privation of goodness. Rather, it is tangible and imaged by many-headed beasts or scarlet women. However, it lacks the automatic linking of sin and soldier that Milton perceives and whose origin we seek.

For the sake of completeness, I should also note that Talmudic and Midrashic statements about fallen angels may be spellbinding yet are not part of the legitimate genealogy of Satan's troopers.[2] Wicked spirits (*mazzikin*, "injurers") abound, but they exhibit no connection to *Paradise Lost*. They are less organized than a pack of wolves and may be warded off by various acts, some pious and others superstitious. Their leader is often a buffoon and the Talmud even implies that these demons are not completely depraved. Similarly, the henchmen of Iblis (from *diabolos*) in Islamic lore are neither martial nor particularly organized.

Although these and many other speculations about reprobate angels were largely available to Milton, his own discussion in *De Doctrina Christiana* comes from the Bible and the interpretation of a few commentators like Calvin, Ames, and Wolleb. Unlike several of his contemporaries, Milton does not spend much time on angels. His single terse chapter refreshes any reader who has perused tomes like *The Hierarchie of the Blessed Angells*, Thomas Heywood's more than six hundred

---

[2] For this paragraph I rely upon Bernard J. Bamberger, *Fallen Angels* (Philadelphia, 1952) and the collection of odd tales in Leo Jung, *Fallen Angels in Jewish, Christian and Mohammedan Literature* (1926, rpt. New York, 1974).

pages of meditation, assertion, and translation.[3] The chief points in Milton are simply that

> There are . . . both good and evil angels. . . . It is well known that a great many of them revolted from God of their own free will before the fall of man. . . . Sometimes they [the good angels] are the ministers of divine vengeance. . . . As a result they often appear looking like soldiers. . . . Bad angels are kept for punishment. . . . But sometimes they are able to wander all over the earth, the air, and even heaven, to carry out God's judgments. . . . But their proper place is hell. . . . Their knowledge is great, but it is a torment to them rather than a consolation. . . . The devils have their prince too. . . . They also keep their ranks. . . . Their chief is the author of all wickedness and hinders all good.[4]

One would hardly think that this slender scaffold could support the numerous and complicated angels in *Paradise Lost*. The basic theological facts Milton allows himself admit only one visual detail: "looking like soldiers." The other details granted by Scripture are of low descriptive density: "punishment . . . wander . . . knowledge . . . prince . . . ranks." Yet poetry luckily snaps up unconsidered trifles.

We must then assign the noticeable soldierliness of Milton's bad angels to his own conclusions rather than to some tradition. It might seem that the many discussions about a war in Heaven which filled volumes before his day should have given him some aid. But the commentaries I have read share a grim resolve to clip the wings of imagination. Fra[ncis] Du Jon, for example, spends more time in *The Apocalyps* on the good angels' song of triumph than on "the combat begunne by the Deuill and his souldiers against Christ and his elect Angels."[5]

[3] *The Hierarchie of the Blessed Angells* (London, 1635).

[4] 1. 9. Tr. John Carey in *Complete Prose Works of John Milton*, ed. Maurice Kelley (New Haven, 1973), 6:343-50, *passim*.

[5] *The Apocalyps, or Revelation of S. John the Apostle* (Cambridge, 1596), pp. 147-48.

John Salkeld's *Treatise of Angels* gathers learned opinions about Satan's revolt only to squelch further elaboration by creative humans:

> these two, as it were, armies of Angels, being contrary in manifested affections the one to the other, resisted mutually, and as it is expressed in the *Apoccalipse* Chap. 12. spiritually fought together. This is that which *Aquinas, Alensis, Albertus Magnus, Durand,* and other Schoole-Diuines hold, but whether it was so, or by some other expression of their particular affect, it is as *Durand* well noteth, a thing (or rather the manner of it) vncertaine.[6]

From Salkeld's barren tentativeness, from "as it were," "spiritually," "whether it was so," and "vncertaine," Milton conceives the glittering legions of Heaven and Hell. Undeniably, personal concerns about the innate evil of war overrode any lack of cultural support when he turned to the description of angels.

The most coherent tradition of soldierly angels from which Milton might have borrowed is in the plastic arts.[7] Illuminated manuscripts, frescoes, carvings, paintings, and statues had pictured supernatural beings in combat long before the composition of *Paradise Lost*. Generally, however, visual artists chose separate, dramatic incidents such as the expulsion from Heaven or Michael's subduing a dragon. Graphic art is not durational, but artists gave viewers little encouragement to suppose damned angels remain under arms after the battle. The devil in Pisa's Camposanto, though dressed as a warrior, presides over a conventionally nonmilitary Hell (Figure 5). Indeed, the collective impression an observer has from these scenes is that suits of armor, swords, shields, spears, penants—all the trappings of chivalric war—symbolize goodness. Contrary to Milton, plastic artists see loyal angels as armed and demons as monsters or naked men (Figure 6). If Milton noticed Guido Reni's *St.*

---

[6] *Treatise of Angels* (London, 1613), p. 347.

[7] Roland Mushat Frye's sumptuous volume on *Milton's Imagery and the Visual Arts: Iconographic Tradition in the Epic Poems* (Princeton, 1978) agrees that showing "demonic forces in armor . . . was not common" (p. 46, fn. 15).

Michael Binding the Devil in Rome's Santa Maria Della Concezione, he would have found an up-to-date summary of angel iconography that conflicts with his later poetic renderings (Figure 7). Completed in the decade before the Englishman's visit, Reni's canvas allots a sword and armor to the blond Michael while it hypostatizes Satan as a partially-bearded, partially-bald man, naked, and prostrate. Although the epitome of evil, this latter figure is merely dark and resentful, recognizable for no attribute except his confining chains and an unobtrusive tail (Figures 8, 9, and 10).

Milton, however, repeatedly directs our attention to the martial attributes of his fallen spirits. Sometimes the referents are clear. The damned "Legions" (1. 301) have an identity that depends upon our ability to recognize a Roman military word. Other times, the references are clear but unexpected. Satan addresses his battalions as "Princes, Potentates, / Warriors" (1. 315-16). The first two epithets, common in angelology, designate two Dionysian orders; the last title of "Warriors," which Zanchy alone uses,[8] is both innovative and significant. It neatly reminds us that we are dealing with rebels who regularly exhibit positive traits extrolled in manuals of military deportment. Only the catalogue that identifies these soldiers with pagan gods interrupts the consistent connection between Satan's infernal followers and earthly armies. And the catalogue, we should remind ourselves, arises from the common military practice of holding a command review.[9]

Organization

The warriors whom Satan addresses seem to be a perfect fighting unit when judged by conventional criteria. The soldierly

---

[8] Jerome Zanchy, "De Operibus Dei" 2. 14. 95. In *Operum Theologicorum* (Geneva, 1613). Robert H. West also mentions "Warriors" in *Milton and the Angels* (Athens, Ga., 1955), p. 202, fn. 28.

[9] The epic practice of cataloguing is certainly involved here, perhaps for ironic effect. Other ways in which Milton comments upon epic conventions are mentioned when I turn to the characterization of Satan in the first part of Chapter III.

skill of these former inhabitants of "The Quarters of the North" (5. 689) in Heaven would not surprise any Renaissance geopolitician since it was a byword "that Northren people are commonly more valiant and venturous, then those of Asia & Afrike" (Sutcliff, *Practice*, p. 64). Unlike the headstrong heroes in sagas, however, they willingly submit to a strict chain of command that reflects the dreams of human theorists concerning a favorite topic: what is the best organization for an army? Satan is clearly the *imperator* and Beelzebub his chief *legatus*, "*next in Order and Dignity*" (Argument to Book 1). There is also a general staff attending the Great Consult and troopers with specific military operating specialities.

The most obvious indicator of this superb organization is that Satan's legions, which comprise vast numbers, arrange themselves in orderly "Files" (1. 567) and "Ranks" (1. 616). Asclepiodotus speaks for the innumerable analysts coming after him when he emphasizes the need for clear subdivisions in formation and illustrates his text with many diagrams. "It is necessary," he says,

> first of all, to divide the phalanx, that is, to break it up into files. Now a file is a number of men dividing the phalanx into symmetical units. . . . And those who stand behind one another in this formation are said to form a file, . . . but those who stand side by side are said to form a rank. (*Tactics* 2. 1; 6)

The devils' formal arrangement is more than an artistic device by which Milton helps us visualize them as easily as we see pictures in manuals; it also underscores his moral point that assaults on men are not random expressions of hostility. An assertion that demons as dissimilar as Moloch and Belial can stand correctly in a "Battalion, . . . thir order due" (1. 569) reminds us how professionally the powers of darkness organize themselves. United, ironically, for the purpose of disrupting unity in Heaven and later sowing discord on Earth, they embarrass humans who seldom confederate even to accomplish good ends. "The weakenesse of the armies of our time," scolds one vet-

eran, "proceed[s] of contempt of military arayes, and orders.
. . . [I]f the army be a body, then euery souldier ought to be
taught, that he may knowe to stand in his place, as euery mem-
ber is placed in the body" (Sutcliffe, *Practice*, p. 114).

Other references to Hell's militia mix unit designations from
many periods in history. They are a "Host" (1. 37), "Legions"
(1. 301), "powers" (2. 522) and a "Brigad" (1. 675). Satan is
surrounded by a loyal "Globe of fiery Seraphim" (2. 512) who
are distinguished not so much for their circularity as for their
relation to the *globus*, or tightknit platoon of legionnaires who
march resolutely across the pages of Livy, Virgil, Tacitus, and
Vegetius. Viewed from afar, the rebels exhibit a well-practiced,
mutually agreed-upon order that must impress all readers—
those who resemble Pistol's recruits as well as those who dili-
gently march and countermarch on St. Martin's Fields. The
"perfect *Phalanx*" (1. 550), at once the ancestor and the de-
scendant of Alexander's indominable φάλαγξ, bespeaks cun-
ning arrangement for maximum impact. Visually and morally
such a prospect should stun individual readers. By mingling
terms associated with classical and modern armies, Milton con-
vinces us that we are witnessing the ultimate military machine.
Like Vegetius, Milton drafts terms from many eras when he
pictures how "every Band and squared Regiment / By place or
choice the worthiest . . . / With hunderds and with thousands
trooping came / Attended" (1. 758-61). There, parading before
us, are units called by contemporary names like "Band" and
"Squared Regiment" that drill in close order with units called
"hunderds" and "thousands," names used by biblical and clas-
sical armies.

Obedience

The devils do much more than arrange themselves in impres-
sive formations. They act in a proper military manner and
exemplify "that absolute discipline which the Romans ob-
serued, and by which they conquered so many nations." A
fallen human reader, knowing how "The vvant of this discipline

hath dishonoured the martiall gouernment of this age" (Edmunds, *Observations 1604*, pp. 52, 67), might assume that Satan's followers are permanently out of action. The Argument to Book 1, after all, emphasizes their double affliction—"thunderstruck and astonished" are cognate terms hinting that God, like Zeus, confounds his antagonists with spears of lightning. Yet no sooner do the rebels hear a command to "Awake, arise" than they

> were abasht, and up they sprung
> Upon the wing; as when men wont to watch
> On duty, sleeping found by whom they dread,
> Rouse and bestir themselves ere well awake.
>   (1. 330-34)

While still in shock, the demons instantly obey an order from their superior. Because Satan mobilizes his army to continue hostilities, I suggest Milton uses the standard formula of Roman generals addressing Mars in his shrine: "*Mars, vigila!*"[10]

The martial simile following Satan's call shows how obedient his troops are. It gains force when juxtaposed to passages found in many texts about punishments for negligent sentries. If Roman guards were discovered by officers of the watch ("whom they dread") to be asleep, they were reported and often courtmartialled. Any sentinal unlucky enough to be convicted was liable to suffer the infamous *fustuarium*:

> The tribune [explains Polybius] takes a cudgel and just touches the condemned man with it, after which all in the camp beat or stone him, in most cases dispatching him in the camp itself. But even those who manage to escape are not saved thereby: impossible! for they are not allowed to return to their homes, and none of the family would dare

---

[10] For "*Mars, vigila!*" see Servius on *Aeneid* 8. 3 and fn. 45 below. Servius explains that a general about to declare war would enter Mars' temple at Rome and clatter the sacred shields and the god's own spear. Servius, *Commentarii*, ed. Georgius Thelo (Leipzig, 1883), 2:200.

to receive such a man in his house. So that those who have once fallen into this misfortune are utterly ruined.[11]

Notorious throughout antiquity, the *fustuarium* could be (and was) imposed on derelict groups as well as individuals. Sometimes unwary companies were decimated as an example to survivors. In any case, this Roman penalty for failure on guard duty epitomizes the extraordinary means that commanders had to adopt in order to maintain constant vigilance. Renaissance writers differ from classical theorists only in denying the culprit any chance to run the gantlet. Henry Hexham speaks for all who offer rules to govern a camp when he flatly states, "If any souldiour shalbe found sleeping on his centinel, he shal without any mercy be punished with death."[12] Callot's eighteen engravings show that some of the war's "great miseries" for careless soldiers included execution by firing squad or on the wheel.

Milton's simile does more than remind us of the difficulties that attend guard duty for humans; it defines several new facts about the demons. They carry out their assignment instinctively and despite momentous distraction. Men, on the contrary, have shirked their most critical missions throughout recorded history. Adam's "First Disobedience" (1. 1) and that of Eve are failures to keep proper watch against an enemy whose

---

[11] *The Histories* 6. 37. 1-4. Loeb ed., 3:353. See also Polybius 6. 38 and Frontinus 3. 12 and 4. 1 for other harsh ways (including decimation) to stimulate vigilance. The Duke of Rohan, *The Complete Captain, or, An Abbridgement of Cesars Warres, with Observations upon Them,* tr. J[ohn] C[ruso] (Cambridge, 1640), p. 90 sums up the *fustuarium*. Roman discipline had a lasting appeal to Englishmen. See the fourteen illustrations for John Beaver's *The Roman Military Punishments* (London, 1725) engraved by William Hogarth in *Hogarth's Graphic Works,* rev. ed., ed. Ronald Paulson (New Haven, 1970), plates 60-74.

[12] *The Principles of the Art Militarie; Practised in the Warres of the United Netherlands* (London, 1637), Appendix, p. 11. The death penalty is routinely recommended: William Garrard and Captain [Robert] Hichcock, *The Arte of Warre* (London, 1591), p. 39; Sutcliffe, *Practice,* p. "323," misnumbered for p. 331; Ward, *Anima'dversions,* p. 196; also, Ward, *Anima'dversions II,* p. 45. Styward's *Pathwaie,* pp. 52, 61 recommends death for even straying off one's post.

attack they expected. But Milton seldom allows one action to remain unqualified. Sin and Uriel also fail as sentinels and perhaps mitigate our Parents' neglect. It is thoroughly in line with the author's subtle treatment of military references that he allows the fallen angels to be more successful sentries than any other characters. Yet, simultaneously, he undercuts their Prussian alacrity by comparing them to frightened watchmen who experience present fear about future punishment. As even the most impercipient reader knows, they already have been exiled from Heaven and already are undergoing punishment. No action on their part, not even Pavlovian obedience in a martial situation, can ever mitigate their pain. The demons' obtuseness should moderate our surprise that they function at all.

Organization and obedience, admirable as they are by themselves, have political implications that would not be lost on Milton's readers. Historians routinely said that nations with triumphant armies abroad have united forces at home. An army's behavior is the sure index of a nation's health. For example, Polybius marvels how well all branches of civil government cooperate at Rome. When danger threatens, consuls, Senate, and populace "act in concord and support each other. . . . All are zealously competing in devising means of meeting the need of the hour" (*Histories* 6. 18. 1-4). Polybius turns immediately to his description of Rome's carefully articulated army, the most obvious sign of constitutional harmony. Similarly, the faultless military posture of Satan's devils indicates a strength for more than mere display. Milton's picture of trim soldiers is a common shorthand device to suggest their complete accord in all enterprises. Until the Great Consult, we usually assume that they are as united as an army of warrior ants.

The narrator furthers this conclusion about the devils' unity which their martial bearing encourages us to make: he comments emotionally, "O shame to men! Devil with Devil damn'd / Firm concord holds, men only disagree" (2. 496-97). His outburst is traditional in the pages of militarists. With masochistic fervor they recount "to the great shame of the confusion of Christians" (Garrard, *Arte*, p. 30) and stress "to the shame of the *Christian*"[13] the unity of heathen armies. They imply that success in the field naturally results from homogeneity of purpose at home. While English soldiers are said to be "rogues, loyterers, pikars, & drunkards, and such as no other way can liue" (Sutcliffe, *Practice*, p. 63), infidel soldiers have learned in their own society that war should be more like a crusade than a robbery. Spaniards were highly professional in their camps and, as Robert Ward notices, "we may learne even of the brutish Turke" (*Anima'dversions*, p. 151). The English expected many of their own soldiers to be "insolent, seditious, and impatient" (Garrard, *Arte*, p. 33) or "lewd and wicked men" (Achesone, *Garden*, p. 27) who spend their time in "whoorehunting, dronkennesse, common swearing, quarrelling, fighting, defrauding" (Styward, *Pathwaie*, p. 35). Their miscreant opponents, however, behaved themselves so well that military writers were almost required to praise "the marvellous obedience [of] . . . those enumerable Armies."

> this mighty Army of the Turkes [continues Ward] were so
> well governed, that no quarrells, mutinies, nor distractions
> was ever seene, nor heard through the whole Army, but
> low and soft speeches; Alwayes both evening and morning
> recommending themselves, their safeties and prosperous
> successe of their actions to their God; The consideration of
> this should make us that are Christians, if not surpasse,

[13] The Duke of Rohan, *A Treatise of Modern War*, tr. J[ohn] C[ruso] (Cambridge, 1640), p. 106. Rohan later calls most Christian soldiers "vagabonds and evil livers, and such as cannot live but by robbing" (p. 113). Many of the following observations are based upon Ovid's maxim in *Metamorphoses* 4. 428: *fas est et ab hoste doceri*. As far back as Xenophon's *Cyropaedia*, writers from one country claimed that soldiers from another were ideals to emulate. Coleman O. Parsons collects many quotations, some antiwar, in "The Classical and Humanist Context of *Paradise Lost*, II, 496-505," *JHI*, 29 (1968), 33-52. He offers these words from Thomas Paynell's *The Complaint of Peace* (London, 1559), a translation of Erasmus' *Querela Pacis*, as parallel to Milton's: "O Shame, they [Christians] fyghte more cruellye than Jewes, than Ethnyckis [heathens], than wyld beastes." An informative study is C. A. Patrides, " 'The Bloody and Cruell Turke': The Background of a Renaissance Commonplace," *Studies in the Renaissance*, 10 (1963), 126-35.

yet equall them in such laudable actions. (*Anima'dver-
sions*, p. 151)

Theorists develop ingenious variations for this embarrassing
question: "if the infidels obserue such strict discipline, why
should not we that be Christians indeuour our selues to sur-
passe them" (Garrard, *Arte*, p. 30). Military writers belabor
their readers by recalling "the Turke; whose observancie of
Discipline to his advantage, & our losse, may make us blush"
(Leighton, *Speculum*, pp. 34-35). Thus when Milton pictures
the infernal cadres "Breathing united force with fixed thought"
(1. 560), he communicates more than Nurnberglike army preci-
sion. He connotes selfless devotion to a common psychological,
political, and religious ideal.

Milton also abides by the same tradition that locates such
military and social solidarity in the East when he stresses the
devils' orientality. Their crusade is led, significantly, by a
"great Sultan" (1. 348) or "great Emperor" (1. 378), titles redo-
lent of Asiatic regimentation. Even as late as the middle fifties,
when Milton was still composing *Paradise Lost*, Francis Os-
borne's *Politicall Reflections upon the Government of the Turks*
speaks ruefully about "the Shame and Terror they have
brought upon *Christondome* (through the division of whole
Princes they have attained this grandure)."[14] Osborne sums up
a century of tradition when he blames Western social disorgani-
zation: Turkish soldiers aim "to the propagation of honour and
dominion" while their counterparts "in such narrow yet fruit-
full Cockpits as *England*, breed nothing but *Sedition*." Like Sa-
tan's troops, these idolators follow their *"Grand Segnior"* (p.
65) and fight well.

Equipment

The demons' equipment complements their organization and
obedience. Their weapons are so splendid that the most accu-
rately a poet can describe them is to say,

---

[14] *Politicall Reflections upon the Government of the Turks*. (Oxford, 1656),
p. 2.

> they stand, a horrid Front
> Of dreadful length and dazzling Arms, in guise
> Of Warriors old with order'd Spear and Shield,
> Awaiting what command thir mighty Chief
> Had to impose.
> (1. 563-67)

The rebels give no indication that the rout in Heaven and head-long fall have lowered their morale or impaired their competence. Milton's reference to the "dazzling Arms" is yet another symbol by which he can paint a picture and point a moral. Like the disciplined armies that exist by themselves as artistic objects and simultaneously imply a harmonious nation, well-maintained weapons appear in many military texts as evidence of first strike capacity. Onasander recommends that

> the general should make it a point to draw up his line of battle resplendent in armour—an easy matter, requiring only a command to sharpen swords and to clean helmets and breastplates. For the advancing companies appear more dangerous by the gleam of weapons, and the terrible sight brings fear and confusion to the hearts of the enemy.[15]

Since we are the enemy and since an expert soldier is one with his weapon, it is natural that we transfer our awe at the demons' arms from the inanimate objects to their wielders. Thus Milton does not need to particularize individual warriors. Their effect is meant to be cumulative and impersonal.

Readers of war books were familiar with a second point about "dazzling Arms." "Nothing does so much honor," says Vegetius, "to the abilities and application of the Tribune, as the appearance and discipline of the soldiers, when their apparel is neat and clean, their arms bright and in good order" (2. 12). Unlike human Tribunes, Satan does not bully his followers about equipment. Renaissance writers, fully expecting conscripts to neglect or even sell their armament, usually insist that "all souldiers must keepe their armor and weapons faire,

---

[15] *The General* 28. Loeb ed., *Aeneas Tacticus*, etc., pp. 469-71. See also Suetonius, *Julius*, 67 and Polyaenus *Stratagems of War*, 8. 23. 20.

cleane and seruiceable" (Garrard, *Arte*, p. 42). Styward repeats
these same words and unconditionally demands the "paine" of
death for any trooper luckless enough to lose his equipment
through negligence or gambling (*Pathwaie*, pp. 56, "59," the
first of two pages numbered 59). Unlike human troops, the
devils exhibit well-tended weapons proving their owners' de-
pendability. The arms cast picturesque gleams of light in Hell,
thereby reemphasizing the self-generated pride that seldom
animates earthly forces.

Other Traits

Other physical descriptions reverberate with significance when
we comprehend their full military meaning. Sometimes a word
taken in its martial sense unexpectedly amplifies the ordinary
meaning of a statement. For instance, the rebels assemble and
then Satan

> through the armed Files
> Darts his experienc't eye, and soon traverse
> The whole Battalion views, thir order due,
> Thir visages and stature as of Gods;
> Thir number last he sums.
>
> (1. 567-71)

The last line may mean, "Finally he counts how many are
present." But Milton uses many technical terms ("Files . . .
traverse . . . Battalion") and "Darts" cleverly denotes the re-
viewer's act as it connotes the weapons he sees. Thus "number"
may signify not only a general mathematical total but also
numerus. Tacitus, Pliny, Suetonius, Ammianus, and others
employ this specialized word to designate "troop, band, cohort,
division." Such a unit was "often drawn from a markedly less
civilised stratum of the frontier population and probably neither
so highly trained nor so highly paid"[16] as regular Roman
legionnaires. With one word Milton may be preparing us to live
with these infernal hosts since he hints that, for all their admi-

---

[16] Graham Webster, *The Roman Army* (Chester, England, 1973), p. 6.

rable traits, they are inferior to some (as yet unmet) other army. We shall return to "number" when Satan's behavior as a general is discussed; here let us remember that "number" may have two meanings.

Other words communicate an obvious civilian meaning and a concomitant martial significance that expands our awareness. When the fallen stand "in guise / Of Warriors old with order'd Spear and Shield" (1. 564-65), a noncombatant comprehends that their spears are "neatly arranged" while a soldier understands that the spears are ordered, that is, "upright but at rest" in response to an unspoken yet obeyed command such as "Order your picke."[17] The civilian connotation of "order'd" should upset our expectations concerning a realm that borders geographically and morally on Chaos and whose activities are usually described as "wand'ring" (e.g. 2. 561). The soldier's meaning reintroduces a painful awareness that demons perform admirably so far as the manual of arms is involved. We are given, in short, two views of the fallen, esthetic and efficient, both of which should unnerve us by their superhuman perfection.

Milton uses a similar two-level description to remind readers that, unlike many English shire levies, the damned crew cares for its commander as well as its weapons. While Satan prepares to speak,

> thir doubl'd Ranks they bend
> From wing to wing, and half enclose him round
> With all his Peers: attention held them mute
> (1. 616-18)

Here again common assertions coexist with the vocabulary of war books. One may paraphrase the action in ordinary terms: standing in double rows, the winged spirits form a semicircle

---

[17] Kellie, *Pallas*, p. 23, quoting "*The Exercise Military of Ye English* by ye Order of That Great Generall Maurice of Nassau." See also Ward, *Anima'dversions*, p. 222 and *The Tactiks of Aelian, or Art of Embattailing an Army after ye Grecian Manner*, tr. J[ohn] B[ingham] (London, 1616), p. 155; "Lords of his Maiesties . . . Privy Counsayle," *Instructions for Musters and Armes* (London, 1623), Sig. A4ᵛ; and many other drill books (Davies', Trussell's etc.).

about Satan and, eager to hear him, remain silent. Yet an ear attuned to the phraseology of drill masters can hear the more accurate implications of "doubl'd Ranks . . . wing . . . mute." One message communicated by this tableau is the devils' familiar forgetting of self. They place their general in the midst of their *alae* and form a "lunula" or "cyrte"—a half-moon formation "wherein the Turk especially delights" (Figures 11 and 12).[18] Garrard and Hichcock picture this "Battell in Forme of a Moone" commenting that it is "of great force for the night" (*Arte*, bound at end). They also place Satan in the center of their concern. Obliterating the recalcitrant desire shown by human troops to move or talk, they instinctively conform to Aelian's maxim that "aboue all things silence is to bee commanded, and that heed be giuen to directions."[19] And on his part Satan apparently has fulfilled the Lord of Praissac's advice (a commander "ought to acquire the love of all men") as well as Gerat Barry's dictum: "prudent cariadge and amiable behaveure [of a leader] are muche esteemed, obeyed, honored, and respected, by the Souldieres, and doe binde them in obligatione and repose of minde" (*The Art of Warre*, p. 150; *A Discourse*, p. 36).

Communication

The fact that Satan's army obeys his wishes redounds to his credit, to the shame of men, and to the advice of theorists about the need for communication. As Machiavelli ruefully warns, "Many armies have been thrown into great confusion when the

[18] Quotation from Thomas Digges' *Stratioticos* (London, 1590). In Henry J. Webb, *Elizabethan Military Science: The Books and the Practice* (Madison, Wis., 1965), p. 21. For a diagram of this lunate formation see picture facing p. 148 in *The Tactiks of Aelian*.

[19] *Tactiks*, p. 150. Repeated in *The Second Part of Aelians Tactiks* (London, 1629), p. 83. Compare Xenophon's *Cyropaedia* 5. 3. 43: "Take care to march in silence, both officers and all who are wise." Loeb ed., 2:61. With Elizabethan severity, Styward also calls for silence "in all places of service." Anyone who makes inappropriate noise "shall die." *Pathwaie*, pp. 46, 60.

general's orders have been either not heard or mistaken."[20] In Hell Satan's commands are transmitted so quickly and accurately that no reader would ever suppose some light cavalry might go astray. The precision with which the infernal legions respond to signals of brass and banner links them to idealized armies in text books. Satan

> Then straight commands that at the warlike sound
> Of Trumpets loud and Clarions be uprear'd
> His mighty Standard; that proud honor claim'd
> Azazel as his right, a Cherub tall:
> Who forthwith from the glittering Staff unfurl'd
> Th'Imperial Ensign, which full high advanc't
> Shone like a Meteor streaming to the Wind
> With Gems and Golden lustre rich imblaz'd
> Seraphic arms and Trophies: all the while
> Sonorous metal blowing Martial sounds:
> At which the universal Host upsent
> A shout that tore Hell's Concave, and beyond
> Frighted the Reign of Chaos and old Night.
> All in a moment in the gloom were seen
> Ten thousand Banners rise into the Air
> With Orient Colors waving: with them rose
> A Forest huge of Spears: and thronging Helms
> Appear'd, and serried Shields in thick array
> Of depth immeasurable: Anon they move
> In perfect Phalanx to the Dorian mood
> Of Flutes and soft Recorders; such as rais'd
> To highth of noblest temper Heroes old.
>
> (1. 531-52)

Theorists would be amazed how rapidly Satan's entire army receives and executes the order to march. Vegetius rightly says,

> The particulars [of military service] necessary to be observed are many and various; but none more essential to

[20] Niccolò Machiavelli, The Art of War, tr. Ellis Farneworth and rev. Neal Wood (Indianapolis, Ind., 1965), p. 138.

success than entire obedience to signals: on this depend
both the victory and safety of the troops. (3. 5)

Despite Machiavelli's grim reminder of the potential for failure
in all human attempts to communicate, the "Trumpets loud and
Clarions" galvanize every soldier in Satan's troop. Perhaps Mil-
ton thinks of Roman *tubicines* and *cornicines* whose functions
are described by Vegetius:

> The music of the legions consists of trumpets [and] cor-
> nets. . . . The trumpet sounds the charge and the retreat
> [hence Milton's "warlike"]. The cornets are used only to
> regulate the motions of the colors ["be uprear'd / His
> mighty Standard"]. . . . In time of action, the trumpets
> and cornets are found together. (2. 22)

Satan's "Imperial Ensign" is probably the *signum imperatoris*[21]
carried, as was the Roman custom, by one whose merit had
earned him the proud honor of *signifer* (Figure 14). And the
banners anticipate as well as reproduce what Romans call
vexilla.[22] Judged by the standard of any military text, evil
manners do not corrupt good communications in Hell.

Milton helps his audience perceive Satan's army both vis-
ually and morally when he mentions the "Ensign" and the
"Banners" (Figure 15). War books assumed they were indis-
pensable items of martial equipment since they symbolized each

[21] Vegetius 2. 7 and 2. 13 say that the ensign of a cohort pictured a dragon.
Perhaps readers are expected to remember this information when imagining the
army of "th' infernal Serpent." In heraldic language, a snake symbolized reli-
gious heresy. Also, cannon of different calibers were called dragons, serpen-
tines, and basilisks. Even pictures of armies on the march often curled across
war books' pages: one fine example appears in Samuel Pitisk's edition of Quin-
tus Curtius Rufus, *De Rebus Alexandri Magni* (Utrecht, 1685), between pp.
26-27 (Figure 13).

[22] More information on Roman standards is contained in G. R. Watson, *The
Roman Soldier* (Ithaca, N.Y., 1969), *passim,* and Graham Webster, *The
Roman Imperial Army of the First and Second Centuries A.D.* (London, 1969),
pp. 134-41. Milton may remember Dante's ironic introduction to Dis at *Inferno*
34. 1: "*Vexilla regis prodeunt inferni,*" a parody of the hymn by Venantius
Fortunatus (who, of course, does not use "*inferni*").

unit's identity. "[T]*here is nothing more venerable,"* says Leighton, *". . . in the eyes of souldiers then the Majesty of the colours"* (*Speculum*, p. 56). By specifying "Orient Colors," Milton directs his readers' eyes to the warmest hues of the spectrum. Thanks to a common heraldic belief, these colors could readily be translated into ethical qualities:

> *Yellow* betokeneth *Honour,* or height of Spirit, which being neuer separate from vertue in all things is most iealous of disgrace, and may not indure the least shadow of imputation. . . . *Red* signifieth *Iustice,* or noble and worthy Anger in defence of Religion or the oppressed.[23]

If we were encouraged to look no deeper into the significance of the standards, then we would have to praise the infernal host as an assemblage of right-minded crusaders.

But Milton almost always allocates ambiguous traits to the fallen. "Orient Colors," for example, may signify *"Honour"* and *"Iustice"*; just as easily, however, they may refer to those garish hues military writers condemned. Markham continues his explanation of primary color symbolism by warning,

> Now from these Colours and their mixtures, are deriued many Bastard and dishonourable colours, as *Carnation, Orangetawnie, Popeniay,* and the like, all which haue Bastardly significations, as Craft, Pride, Wantonnesse, and such like. (*Epistles of Warre,* p. 75)

Although "Orient" is broad enough to mean either desirable or undesirable hues, it suggests Eastern devices like those of janissary or Mameluke units and at least impedes unqualified approval.

Moreover, Milton exaggerates so much that he brings our response to that ambivalent point between awe and absurdity. No army that readers could picture would need "Ten thousand Banners." And the historic *vexillum* measured only fifty cen-

---

[23] Francis Markham, *Epistles of Warre,* p. 75. Three years after Francis, G[ervase] M[arkham] repeats the same words in *The Souldiers Accidence* (London, 1625), pp. 31-32.

timeters square.[24] In fact, Satan's "streaming" ensign resembles the unwieldy seventeenth-century flags that Bingham scornfully describes as *"made of many ells of Taffaty"* and as hindering communication between human soldiers (*Tactiks*, p. 68). Certainly the signalling devices stun us with their richness ("Gems and Golden"), number, size, exoticism ("Orient Colors") and sinister implications ("Meteor"). Yet overstatement only partly explains how Milton arranges his data. He gives more than baroque amplification to a common military practice; he records a magical process. Everything happens quickly ("straight . . . forthwith . . . All in a moment . . . Anon"). The movement, sound, and glitter are part of an infernal act of creation: "Banners *rise. . . . / . . .* with them *rose /* A Forest huge of Spears. . . . / . . .* Anon they *move / . . .* to the *Dorian* mood / . . . such as *rais'd /* To *highth* of noblest temper Heroes old." All this upward movement of an *"uprear'd"* standard, of the "Ensign, which full *high* advanc't," of a shout *"upsent,"*[25] anticipates the surging vitality of God's creation in Book 7. Reinforcing the martial atmosphere in Book 1, however, the infernal forest contains deadly spears, not fecund trees. But this passage and the account of divine creation have a common bond: both show how an awesome force banishes inertia and transforms mere being into being-in-motion. Certainly the Hell passage contains more innuendo of sexuality, of prodigious but blind erections; so it reinforces the tie between sex and aggression that our Parents discover immediately after their Fall, and it explains the presence of phallic deities in Satan's army.

[24] There are, so far as I can discover, few factual bases for Milton's battle banners. *Vexilla* are pictured on many Roman coins, especially from the war-torn later Empire, but they are reasonably well proportioned. Perhaps Milton combines functional standards like these with gaudy banners from masques, civic pageants, and military reviews such as detailed in Barriff's *Mars*. The only similar pictures I can call to mind are Albrecht Altdorfer's swirling *Battle of Issus* (1529, now at Munich's Alte Pinakothek) and Piero della Francesca's Arezzo frescoes (Figure 15).

[25] My italics. Don Cameron Allen, *The Harmonious Vision: Studies in Milton's Poetry* (Baltimore, 1954), p. 108 and Jackson I. Cope, *The Metaphoric Structure of Paradise Lost* (Baltimore, 1962), pp. 97-99 mention the verticality in this passage. "Orient" may be a pun in keeping with the rising motions.

By showing how martial activities can briefly raise the fallen both literally and metaphorically, Milton makes credible their otherwise absurd wish to recapture Heaven. And, perhaps most devastatingly, this impressive display of demonic magic develops quite naturally from the common military *topos*, "how may a commander quickly mobilize his men."

Talents

Effective communication down the chain of command in Satan's army indicates that still another dream of theorists has been fulfilled: individual talents are efficiently used. One demon serves as "Standard" bearer (1. 533), others as "Heralds" (1. 752) and others, the "numerous Brigad" (1. 675) of Mammon, as engineers. Ever since Plato's *Republic*, theorists have wondered how best to apportion work. But among well-trained human soldiers, there probably always will be those who lament the waste of their skill. Yet Hell's recruits never complain that they are "the unwilling led by the unfit doing the unnecessary." Efficiently and with no hint of recalcitrance, they perform their tasks. For example, specialists construct Pandaemonium. First miners hurry to a volcanic hill:

> As when bands
> Of Pioners with Spade and Pickax arm'd
> Forerun the Royal Camp, to trench a Field
> Or cast a Rampart. *Mammon* led them on.
> (1. 675-78)

Milton's simile identifies the demons as pioneers, soldiers who (in the phrase of William Bourne) are skilled at "the intrenching either of an armie, or the inclosing of a Towne."[26] Milton curiously neglects a common and perhaps anticipated Renaissance connection between miners and underground demons. He passes over those strange tales found in Georg Agricola's *De Animantibus Subterraneis* (1548), Burton's *Anatomy of Melancholy* (1628. 1. 2. 1. 2) and Thomas Heywood's *Hierar-*

26 *Inventions* (London, 1578), p. 56.

chie of the Blessed Angells about *cobali* or (as the latter author-
ity explains) "Mountaine-Dwarfes": "because not full three
hand-fulls hye" (p. 568). Instead Milton stresses the pioneers'
methodical division of labor: "a second multitude . . . / A third"
(1. 702, 705).

Their skillful teamwork erects Pandaemonium. Milton uses
the same complex of magical ideas that characterized the
response to "Trumpets loud and Clarions": Speed / Organiza-
tion / Creation. Here, too, everything happens quickly ("has-
ten'd . . . Forerun") with machinelike orderliness. Most impor-
tant, Milton again speaks of the result in terms of creative
elevation ("*Rose* like an Exhalation." 711, my italics). By
attributing these acts to division of labor in a military setting,
he implies that talents found in Hell may be immoral, but are
perfectly acceptable by mechanical or martial standards.

Furthermore, Milton implies Satan has solved a question that
exercised human theorists: should a general use pioneers and, if
he does, how many? The Duke of Rohan pleads that "pioners
. . . are necessary to make the inclosures of the camp, the
trenches in a siege, the accomodation of the wayes" (*Treatise*,
p. 158). But he would limit their number to five hundred, ap-
parently forestalling criticism such as that articulated by Gen-
eral Monk who flatly states, "Pioners shall [not] be entertained
to make the Souldiers lazy: For each Souldier ought to know
what belongeth to his duty" (*Observations*, p. 22). (John Smith
dreams of four thousand "pioners" in his ideal army of
twenty-eight thousand men. *Instructions*, p. 81.) Theorists
usually sneer that "expert Enginers and men of exquisite
knowledge" (as Ward calls them in *Anima'dversions II*, p. 4)
are Johnny-come-latelies to war. According to Sutcliffe, they
are "but of a late inuention, since ye use of artillerie came in,
and souldiers through slouth began to refuse the labours of
warre" (*Practice*, p. 62). Although the fiends invented cannon
and although Mammon worships "peaceful sloth" (2. 227), the
construction of Pandaemonium is still "wondrous art" because
not one angel tries to duck his duty.

Given the low view of human pioneers—Markham refuses to

call them soldiers: "a raskally, rude, ragged, and vnciuill regi-
ment of barbarous and ill-taught people . . . [A] confused masse
. . . without any ciuill nourture" (*Epistles of Warre*, p. 129)—
we again must pay respect to Hell's unprecedented efficiency.
Mammon and his crew may be judged by two different
yardsticks when they accomplish a mission without evaluating
its morality. As creatures in God's universe, they are reprehen-
sible since their building contributes to a corrupt war effort. But
as soldiers they are superb exemplars of *immunes* or troops
with specific skills released from ordinary fatigue duties (*vaca-
tio munerum*) in order to practice their crafts. Milton treats
them as a separate unit, as do military writers like Paternus
who lists some of the professions that merit special notice:
"surveyors, . . . ditchers, farriers, the architects, smiths, . . .
coppersmiths, blacksmiths, stonecutters, limeburners, wood-
cutters, and charcoal-burners."[27] In Hell, as in ideal armies,
these talents are identified, used, and rewarded. The chief tech-
nician, Mammon, epitomizes his subordinates. He has won
fame in Heaven for building "many a Tow'red structure high"
(1. 733), constructs Pandaemonium, an unparalleled temple,
and later will be regarded as the patron god of blacksmiths,
Mulciber (1. 740).

In addition to having engineering ability that wins respect in
all times, Mammon embodies among Satan's army one trait
eliciting the most praise from military theorists. They insist it
is not so much a man's talent to construct "all . . . Engines" (1.
750) that qualifies him for induction. Rather, a good recruiting
officer will seek some internal quality of stabilizing pride.
"Smiths, carpenters, butchers, and huntsmen," says Vegetius,

are the most proper to be taken into [the army]. On the
careful choice of the levies depends the welfare of the
republic. . . . The soldiery, to whom the defence of the

[27] *Digest* 50. 6. 7. Quoted in Watson, *Roman Soldier*, p. 76. Note that even
in this practical survey, miners are not mentioned. For an interesting summary
of attitudes toward the profession, see George Coffin Taylor, "Milton on Min-
ing," *MLN*, 45 (1930), 24-27.

empire is consigned, and in whose hands is the fortune of war, should, if possible, be of reputable families, and unexceptionable in their manners. Such sentiments as may be expected in these men will make good soldiers: a sense of honor, by preventing them from behaving ill, will make them victorious. . . . A trust of such importance should be committed to none but men of merit and integrity. (1. 7)

In his discussion of the ideal recruit, Machiavelli repeats much of Vegetius and emphasizes, "I should not so much consider the nature of their profession as the moral virtue of the men, and which of them could perform the most services" (*Art*, p. 33). Mammon's versatility is mechanical—in both senses of the word. An adept at machines and techniques, Mammon blindly obeys his master. Like the broom in "The Sorcerer's Apprentice," Mammon does not care why he acts. He is the perfect technician for an army that serves without protest in a thoroughly insane war. Milton carefully chooses his epithet to reflect both military efficiency and moral failure. "Architect" (1. 732) is the correct army term (*architectus*) attested to by Roman inscriptions; but the related word *architecton*, as used by Plautus and others, connotes trickery, deceit, or false appearance.

Both meanings of architect cooperate to characterize this craftsman who can build Pandaemonium. At first, the structure argues for his competence; finally, it must be understood as insubstantial, the bees' "Straw-built Citadel" (1. 773). Whatever power this ornate pentagon may have to stun the viewer, it clearly disqualifies Mammon for any lasting praise since, after describing its lavish decorations, the narrator pointedly adds, "The Roof was fretted Gold" (1. 717). Used only here in all of Milton's work, the word "fretted" simply means coffered. Like the Pantheon or the Vatican Library, Pandaemonium's ceiling consists of recessed panels. But simplicity, as Jebb reminds us, does not characterize a literary epic. Used in conjunction with gold, Milton's phrase accurately translates the Latin *aureum lacunar* or *aurea laquearia*. An entire subgenre of classical diatribe uses this architectural feature to condemn the buildings that have it and the persons who reverence it. Gold-fret-ceiling is a shorthand sign warning readers that such buildings are loci of impiety, depravity, tyranny, and demons. The chorus of pagans who denounce temples like Pandaemonium—authors as varied as Lucretius, Livy, Statius, Virgil, Horace, Apuleius, and Lucan—is swelled by Christian voices from Cyprian, Arnobius, Jerome, and Ambrose to Richard Crashaw. All agree that fretted gilt ceilings symbolize immorality. During his trip to Catholic Italy, Milton would have had many chances to see golden ceilings and to reinforce the literary prejudice against them (Figures 16 and 17). Once again, symbol and *significatio* present themselves to us with apparent clarity; then, with a phrase that jogs our memory, Milton sunders the original connection and replaces the first lesson by a second. Thus the plain fact Pandaemonium demonstrates—Mammon is loyal and capable—fades, soon to be replaced by a new and more potent truth—Mammon is loyal to an unworthy master and capable only of creating an evil structure.[28]

The phrase "wondrous Art" (10. 312. Compare 1. 703) connects Pandaemonium to a second building project of Satan's followers. The bridge from Hell to Earth, "this new wondrous Pontifice" (10. 348), has already suggested to previous readers Rome's Pontiff, Dubartas' "Stygian Bridge," God's benign creation, the frozen north, Gorgon, "asphaltic slime," and the broad way leading to destruction. Now we should focus on new connections to magic, militarism, and politics. Despite the commercial utility, architectural beauty and military innocuousness of some bridges, the Ponte Vecchio, perhaps, or London Bridge, a preponderance of literary allusions to them is negative and paves the way for the invention of Sin and Death.

To construct a bridge over troubled water has inevitable associations with magic. Tales of the other world commonly include a bridge upon which the pilgrim must travel if he wishes to

---

[28] There is full documentation for this topic of moral diatribe in my article, "The Roof Was Fretted Gold," *Comparative Literature*, 27 (1975), 254-66.

reach Heaven or Hell. Present in many folklores from India to Scandinavia, the bridge often arches over some water barrier. Hel, the Germanic underworld, is surrounded by a roaring river that can be crossed only on Gjallabrú, the high span with red and gold pinnacles. Sometimes the mythological bridge is constructed of exotic material: in the *Voyage of Maeldúin*, a Celtic tale from about the tenth century, it is of glass. Other times it is endowed with a life of its own: the "Bridge of the Cliff" over which Cú Chulainn must pass routinely bucks off travellers. Also, there are judicial bridges to the lower world: two described in the mid-twelfth-century *Vision of Tundale* allow only the elect to pass, pitching sinners into either a bottomless valley or a stormy lake filled with monsters. Bridges like these are so conventional in accounts of visits to supernatural realms that they may be said to form the archetypal pilings upon which Sin and Death erect their bridge.[29]

Another point about magic and bridges: the demons' span defies destructive elements beneath it. Their skill obviates any need to sacrifice some "fair lady" to insure that resentful forces below will not make the bridge come "falling down." Thus it demands our admiration. Sin and Death successfully defy an ancient taboo against erecting permanent bridges and do so without propitiating the governing deity. (Even Satan had mollified Chaos before crossing the latter's territory.) They control the "raging Sea" (10. 286) and "vext Abyss" (10. 314), thereby reminding us of humans such as Odysseus and Philip II who were defeated by a "boiling Gulf" (2. 1027). Like Mammon's temple, the bridge of Sin and Death chastens us with its triumphant sorcery.

But they base their structure less upon thaumaturgy than upon solid soldierly practice. As the simile reminds us, Xerxes tried to link his despotic realm with that of liberty-loving Greeks by a bridge over the Hellespont. Quite probably

[29] I owe these examples to Howard Rollin Patch, *The Other World* (Cambridge, Mass., 1950). Gregory tells of a slippery bridge in *The Golden Legend*, tr. Granger Ryan and Helmut Ripperger (New York, 1941), p. 653.

Herodotus' account is uppermost in Milton's mind since he specifies that when Sin and Death first use their bridge,

> the blasted Stars lookt wan,
> And Planets, Planet-strook, real Eclipse
> Then suffer'd.

(10. 412-14)

Likewise an eclipse accompanied Xerxes' first crossing (*Histories* 7. 36). However, Milton's generation had many bridges recommended to its attention in military works. Almost every schoolboy recognized Caesar's over the Rhine, pictured by (among others) Fra Giocondo of Verona in his edition of the *Gallic War* (Verona, 1510), Andrea Palladio in his *Archittetura* (Venice, 1570), and an anonymous edition of *C. Iulii Caesaris Commentarii* (London, 1585). Milton himself could easily have seen that the lower bands of Trajan's column in Rome depict two bridges, one on boats and the other, designed by Apollodorus of Damascus, a permanent one over the Danube that elicited mention by Dio Cassius (*Roman History* 68) and Pliny (*Letters* 8. 4). Certainly the causeway by which Alexander the Great captured Tyre, hitherto impregnable, remained in people's memories. Throughout all time, one requirement of an army engineer is the ability to construct bridges for invasion (Figures 18 and 19). Yet once more, magic and military necessity lie behind an infernal triumph.

I think it fair to add bridges have political associations that, given the symbolism of *Paradise Lost*, are largely pejorative. The first bridge was constructed, according to Herodotus, by Nictocris, Queen of Babylon.[30] She united the two halves of her

---

[30] *Histories* 1. 185. E.M.W. Tillyard has a note on "Milton and Philostratus" in *Studies in Milton* (London, 1951), pp. 171-72. He postulates that the tunnel which Medea, a queen of Babylon, built under the Euphrates may have inspired some of the wording in Book 10. I suggest, first, that Philostratus may himself be indebted to this passage in Herodotus and further that the *Histories* give a recognizable enough "source." Nictocris' bridge is stone, fastened (it is true) not "with Pins of Adamant / And Chains" (*PL* 10. 318-19) but with metal.

city by a bridge whose lower part was stone, secured with iron and lead, but whose superstructure was of planks that were taken up at night to interdict the free movement of robbers. If Babylon stimulates technical innovation, then Babylon, in the sinister vision inherited from Revelation, inspires the mechanical skill of Sin and Death. Also, Darius the Persian despot marched over the Bosporus because he had the services of an extraordinary engineer, Mandrocles the Samian (*Histories* 4. 85). Sin echoes the praise that Darius heaped upon his technician when he greets Satan as "prime Architect" (10. 356) of the new bridge to Earth. This bond between bridges and dictatorships is more than literary, of course. It may be recalled that Michelangelo, galled by the demands of Julius II, considered an offer from the Sultan to take refuge in Constantinople and there superintend construction of a bridge from the city across the Golden Horn to Pera.[31] Routinely, then, bridges have a political dimension that makes them more than objects of magical fascination or military utility. They assist untoward happenings like sudden assault by remote foes. All these social disruptions result directly from the "portentous" (10. 371) project completed by Satan's master builders.

When estimating the value of these constructions that Mammon, Sin, and Death complete for their liege, we may wish to sidestep our responsibility. Both *praetorium* and *pons* are "wondrous": large, quickly built, efficiently used and exactly what the war effort requires. Indeed, the narrator insists we admit that these products of Satan's combat engineers outdo the most elaborate enterprises of Babylonian, Egyptian (1. 694), and Persian (10. 307) builders. But we also know that each project is evil and should be condemned. An unwilling reader can minimize headquarters and bridge by summoning up moral clichés (those three countries were idolatrous and tyran-

---

However, just before Herodotus' account of this bridge he talks of the region from which Babylon got its bitumen, a possible clue in Milton's adhesive mind for his phrase, "*Asphaltic* slime" (*PL* 10. 298).

[31] So says Ascanio Condivi in his life of Michelangelo. See Robert Coughlan, *The World of Michelangelo, 1475-1564* (New York, 1966), pp. 109-10.

nic) or ethical analogies (like bees, Satan's workers demonstrate only mindless instinct). Although these disclaimers may be true, we are once again forced to admire successful military fabrications even while we admit they do not automatically merit unqualified praise. Milton carries on his campaign for a permanent divorce between the results of military effort and the acceptance which a Christian audience usually accords such results.

Rewards

The high morale in Satan's army may seem implausible—they have been roundly defeated and chased from their home—but it is credible when one analyzes the conditions of military service. First of all, the soldiers know that their talent will not only be used properly but even rewarded. Azazel is granted the position of *signifer* because of his stature ("a Cherub tall") as well as "his right" (1. 534).[32] Mammon is respected and the peers are asked for their advice during the Great Consult. This consistent recognition of merit fosters high spirit in an ideal army. Polybius gives examples of just recompense and concludes:

Considering all this attention given to the matter of punishments and rewards in the army and the importance attached to both, no wonder that the wars in which the

[32] Robert H. West comments that Milton may here be using cabalistic material garnered from Robert Fludd: "As there are four commanders in the Army of God, . . . so in the Army of Satan are four standard-bearers ("signiferi"), Samael, Azazel, Azael, and Mahazael." *Milton and the Angels*, p. 155. Contrast the professional way by which Azazel wins his position to this disgracefully human episode from the battle of Naseby (1645), "where *Fairfax* killed the [King's] Ensign, and one of *D'Oyley's* [Puritan] Troupers took the Colours, bragging of the service he had done in killing the Ensign and taking the chief of Colours.

"*D'Oyley* chid the Trouper for his boasting and lying, telling him how many witnesses there were who saw the General doe it with his own hand, but the General himself bad *D'Oyley* to let the Trouper alone, and said to him, I have honour enough, *let him take that honour to himself*." See Bulstrode Whitelock, *Memorials* (London, 1682), p. 146.

Romans engage end so successfully and brilliantly. (*The Histories* 6. 39. 11)

Promotions in the devil's army have been earned and not, as in the case of human armies, "solde at the pleasure of barbers, & scriuenoes, and . . . giuen for ye loue of ladies" (Sutcliffe, *Practice*, p. "62," misnumbered for p. 61). Bacon paints a gloomy picture of honors that, in his debased modern times, "are conferred promiscuously, upon Soldiers, & no Soldiers" (*Essays*, p. 129). Apparently the facts of seventeenth-century army procedure justify these jeers. When Francis Markham reviews traditional ways to earn rank, he turns venomously upon modern "*Dunghill*, or *Carpet-Knights*" who attain their offices because they intrigue at court rather than perform on the battlefield.[33] Milton's contemporaries must have envied the professional way that the fiends merit advancement. Competent soldiers such as Sir Charles Morgan often had to report how they found "most of our best men run away, through the ill usage of their officers." Writing in 1627, Morgan excoriates his officers' lack of experience: they come from "Gray's Inn, Lincoln's Inn, or Middle Temple, where they have learned to play mauvais garcon that they can hardly be made fit to know what belongs to command."[34] Little wonder that our first estimate of Hell's evaluation process must be positive. Satan's army seems above reproach in the vital area of promotion. No investigator could charge the Fiend with falling to human levels. Barry sums up a professional's despair: "In thies oure later warres for the moste parte all electiones goes by favor[,] frindshipp or affection to the greate discomoditie of his majesties service." Inevitably, "the prudente and brave Souldier remaineth almoste oute of all hope, . . . seeinge that *Bisones* and men of litl skill are prefered before them" (*A Discourse*, pp. 170, 20).

To be sure, Satan's system of reward also contains much

[33] *The Booke of Honour. Or, Five Decads of Epistles of Honour* (London, 1625), p. 69.

[34] Quoted by E. A. Beller, "The Military Expedition of Sir Charles Morgan to Germany, 1627-9," *The English Historical Review*, 43 (1928), 530.

irony. Although he seems to correct one failure of human generals by awarding distinction in Hell only to those troops who merit it, his own incredible urge to receive promotion far above his own deserts in Heaven precipitated the disastrous war. Similarly, none of the honors that Satan distributes gives any of his subordinates the slightest hope of succeeding him as commander. Although the demons are immortal and thus not concerned with orderly transfer of power from aging leaders to deserving junior officers, it is interesting that Satan forestalls any possible competition for leadership by volunteering to scout Earth alone:

> this enterprise
> None shall partake with me. Thus saying rose
> The Monarch, and prevented all reply,
> Prudent, lest from his resolution rais'd
> Others . . .
> . . . [who] might in opinion stand
> His Rivals.
>
> (2.466-72)

Yet no one of his subordinates whines as Iago does (and as Satan probably did in Heaven):

> 'Tis the curse of service,
> Preferment goes by letter and affection,
> And not by old gradation, where each second
> Stood heir to the first.
>
> (Othello 1. 1. 35-38)

Despite the triviality of its recompense, Hell's army appears to be satisfied with the recognition that Satan grants.

Drill

Inconsequential but public rewards help to prevent the dissatisfaction that threatened even Roman armies under competent generals like Sulla, Pompey, and Caesar. So does a busy schedule of activities. When asked how to deal with an idle army, theorists unanimously agreed with Xenophon "that an army must never be left idle" (*Cyropaedia* 1. 6. 17). Appian, for example, tells how between battles Scipio Africanus the Younger

> daily fortified new camps one after another, and then demolished them, dug deep trenches and filled them up again, constructed high walls and overthrew them. (*Roman History* 6. 14. 86)

Admirable armies trained so constantly that Tertullian uses the idea to encourage those who are about to be martyred:

> Even in peace soldiers inure themselves to war by toils and inconveniences—marching in arms, running over the plain, working at the ditch, making the *testudo*, engaging in many ardous labors. . . . In like manner, O blessed, count whatever is hard in this lot of yours as a discipline of your powers of mind and body. You are about to pass through a noble struggle. ("To the Martyrs," in *Writings* 1. 3-4)

Later military theorists like Jacopo di Porcia,[35] the Duke of Rohan (*Treatise*, p. 116) and General Monk (*Observations*, p. 17, a paraphrase of Rohan) also applaud exercise that increases the stamina or skill men need in war. James I, who disliked conflict, defends playing games on Sunday since the "common and meaner sort of people . . . make their bodies more able for war."[36] Milton himself echoes these sentiments in several passages.[37] Perhaps nearest to Milton's mind when he turns to the brisk drill of Satan's followers is the praise elicited from Augustan historians for emperors like Hadrian and Probus: they considered it wrong for troopers (as the latter says) "to eat lazy-man's food" (*annonam gratuitam milites comedere non*

---

[35] *The Preceptes of Warre*, tr. Peter Betham (London, 1544), Sec. 99.

[36] *The Book of Sports* (London, 1618). Quoted in Henry Bettenson, *Documents of the Christian Church* (New York, 1947), p. 390. Although James' clergy refused to read it from the pulpit, Charles I ordered it recited in 1633.

[37] See, for example, *RCG* (C.E. 3. 239-40) and *Of Ed* (C.E. 4. 289). Also, Mohl, *Milton's Commonplace Book*, p. 311.

debere).[38] The consensus implies that uninterrupted training benefits the physical soldier—he hardens his body and perfects his skills—as well as the moral soldier—he justifies his expense to the state.

When applied to Satan's troops, these physical and financial rationales for exercise seem illogical. A Dr. Johnson could say that angels are mainly immaterial and completely free from economic considerations. However, we leap over such anti-metaphorical quibbles since training underscores what we already know to be demons' most important qualities. Tirelessly hostile to men, they pursue means to overthrow us. They drill ceaselessly because their enemies, "Th' unarmed Youth of Heav'n," also "exercis'd Heroic Games" within reach of their "Celestial Armory, Shields, Helms, and Spears" (4. 551-53). Since the host of Hell is *semper paratus* and Heaven's guards are ever vigilant, those humans who do not prepare for assaults from unfriendly powers should feel chagrined.

Another reason for exercise among Satan's crew is to dissipate any thoughts of mutiny. As one who apparently had leisure to hatch rebellion, Satan would be the first to agree with "a maxime which must be exactly observed, never to suffer your souldiers in any place to be idle, especially when the army is brought together in a body; for if you imploy them not in that which is good, they will busie themselves in that which is naught" (Rohan, *Treatise*, p. 116). When Satan leaves on his scouting expedition, his well-trained troops engage in *ambulatura*, those drills recommended by experts for filling time. To practice, some engage in *decursio*, whereby the participants divide in half, wheel about to face each other and form fronted brigades,

> As when to warn proud Cities war appears
> Wag'd in the troubl'd Sky, and Armies rush
> To Battle in the Clouds, before each Van

---

[38] *Probus* 29 by Falvius Vopiscus. Also *Hadrian* 10. 3 by Aelius Spartianus. Milton mentions both of these disciplinarian emperors in *B* 2 (C.E. 10. 81-89, *passim*). He may have read the *Scriptores Historiae Augustae* in any one of three editions: Erasmus' (1518), Casaubon's (1603) or Salmasius' (1620).

Prick forth the Aery Knights, and couch thir spears
Till thickest Legions close; with feats of Arms
From either end of Heav'n the welkin burns.

(2. 533-38)

Like a merchant who baits our attention with one kind of mer-
chandise and later switches to a less desirable kind, Milton
offers a plain description of war games. Then his sky simile
merges so closely with the demons' activities that for an imagi-
native moment their games and men's hallucinations are one.
He replaces our admiration for an army that trains continually
with the apprehension felt by Jews who witnessed before
Jerusalem's fall "chariots and troops of soldiers in their armour
running about among the clouds."[39]

The simile that grows from the devils' drill and qualifies it
may also expand an association between Satan's troops and in-
fidels. During their parade in Book 1, they appeared as pagan
gods. Now they behave as the worshippers of similar gods.
Turkish sultans, says a translation of Lazaro Soranzo's *The Ot-
toman* "take the onely ende of warre to bee warre." Accord-
ingly, they keep "their subiects occupied and busied" with
army matters, "and so haue diuerted them from ciuill seditions
and insurrections, which for the most part are bred & nourished
by ease and idlenesse."[40] The well-practiced pagan soldier often
appears in illustrations. For example, the title page to Richard
Knolles' *Generall Historie of The Turkes* shows a wary Chris-
tian gazing at a turbaned Turk who holds his war hammer with
insolent ease. Below them, Christian cavalrymen rout the mis-
creants in a panel that may ease a viewer's anxiety.[41] Yet men
of Milton's generation connected soldierly exercise with non-
Christians. The title page of Th[omas] Herbert's *Description of
the Persian Monarchy* sums up this cliché: "A Coozel-bash,"
or turbaned warrior, stands defiantly with his scimiter, glaring

---

[39] Note in Hughes to Josephus, *Wars* 6. 5. 3. Both *ambulatura* (mounted
drill) and *decursio* (dismounted) appear on Roman coins of the Empire.

[40] *The Ottoman* (London, 1603), Fol. 41r.

[41] *The Generall Historie of the Turkes* (London, 1603), title page.

into space. Below him, three Persians pray to a statue of their deity which has wings, horns and a bestial face.[42] Whatever theological contempt such prayer may arouse, the pagan's military prowess, like that of Satan's army, deserves attention.

The Great Consult

In addition to rewards and drill, the Great Consult is a third device by which Satan maintains stability. Generations of military writers agreed that a prudent commander must have a competent general staff whose advice could be sought in times of crisis: "there was neuer man of so great prudence, and of such singuler experience, that hee was able to discide and discypher all things of himselfe" (Garrard, *Arte*, p. 337). No matter how much of the debate has been engineered by Satan, he still gives the outward impression that he listens to his *evocati*, the advisors "called out [from muster], being all men of speciall note and seruice, and such as were able to giue sound aduice for matter of warre" (Edmunds, *Observations 1600*, p. 89). They possess "Many eyes" (Sutcliffe, *Practice*, p. 47) or are pilot fish to "the great Whale" (Leighton, *Speculum*, p. 91). Although Satan ("that Sea-beast / Leviathan." *Paradise Lost* 1. 200-201) has comparatively few advisors—L. Furius had five, Julius Caesar ten, and Pompey fifteen (Sutcliffe, *Practice*, p. 47)—they vary in manner and message. Their debate occupies nearly half of Book 2 and shows their awareness of a truism in war books:

> There is nothing in this sublunary World, which requires more mature Consultations, Deliberations, and grave advise then the Subject of Warre; in regard the welfare of Citties, Countries, and Kingdomes, wholy depends upon it. (Ward, *Anima'dversions*, p. 209)

Milton may give such prominence to the staff discussion for an historical reason.[43] During the spring term of 1647, the

[42] *A Description of the Persian Monarchy* (London, 1634), title page.
[43] Milton's attitude toward Leveller agitation may best be judged after read-

Long Parliament allowed an innovation: two representatives elected from each squared regiment were allowed to appear on behalf of the army. No doubt competent spokesmen, these "Agitators" brought into Parliament the acrid smell of powder and disturbed those who did not wish to extend any more privileges to the restive veterans. In their writings, too, the Leveller agents were unwearied: they assailed the public with pamphlets, manifestoes, and proclamations demanding certain benefits. *"These things we declare to be our* native Rights," says one pronouncement, *"and therefore are agreed and resolved to maintain them with our utmost possibilities, against all opposition whatsoever."*[44] Articulate, truculent, determined, the speaking soldier was familiar to Englishmen before they read *Paradise Lost*.

Among Satan's counsellors, Moloch is the only professional soldier. As such, he disclaims any skill in casuistry: "Of Wiles / . . . I boast not" (2. 51-52). When we first hear Moloch's words, they merely seem to distill the sentiments usually expressed by other professional fighters. James Achesone modestly acknowledges that his essay on "Martiall affairs" will "be roughlie drawne, as it were with the Picke and Musquet of a Souldier, and not trimmed with the delicate pen of an orator, for I haue ever judged it more becomming a Souldier to vtter himselfe by workes than by wordes (*Garden*, p. 36). Yet Moloch delivers a polished oration that first suggests a policy and then defends the proposal against imagined objections. Also, bluff man of practical action though he claims to be, Moloch "reveals a vast capacity for self-delusion, for inhabiting an unreal world where facts no longer matter."[45] He believes

ing Joseph Frank's standard book on *The Levellers* (Cambridge, Mass., 1955) and Christopher Hill's *Milton and the English Revolution* (New York, 1977), Chap. 11.

[44] Edmond Bear plus "Agents coming from other Regiments," "An Agreement of the People for a Firme and Present Peace, upon Grounds of Common-Right and Freedome" (London, 1647). In A. L. Morton, ed., *Freedom in Arms: A Selection of Leveller Writings* (New York, 1975), p. 141.

[45] John Peter, *A Critique of Paradise Lost* (New York, 1960), p. 43.

that the devil's army actually can reconquer Heaven, revenge itself on God and easily ascend. (Any schoolboy knows that only the *de*scent to Avernus is easy.) The more he speaks, the more he deflates himself. Where tradition has taught us to expect an agitator whose words, though rough, respond accurately to actual events, we instead meet another smooth-tongued swindler, soul mate of Beelzebub and Satan, who oozes sophistry. Of all the demons he comes nearest to John Earle's character, "A Blunt Man": "He is not easily bad in whom this quality is nature, but the counterfeit is most dangerous since he is disguised in a humour that professes not to disguise."[46] Like his leader in Hell, who rewards although he has no idea of true merit, Moloch falls between two stools: he fails as a soldier since he has no steady vision of actuality and he fails as an orator since those who speak later easily outpoint him. His speech impresses us more for its snideness than its reasoned military utility. He is as sorry a verbal tactician as he is a poor counsellor.

Limitations

Milton does not make his careful disproof of martial commonplaces depend upon one speech. Certainly Moloch's tirade most concisely epitomizes Hell's deceptive militarism. He demotes himself from a model of the *via activa* to a beef-witted hypocrite. But Milton constantly qualifies language when dealing with war topics so that the other demons, perfect troopers though they are, cannot satisfy an audience, even one predisposed to admire good soldiering. To further our newly-perceived suspicion of armies and to reassure us that God alone is invincible, Milton employs three significant reservations in his account of Hell's host. The first restraint depends upon a knowledge of Christianity. Although the narrator tells us the fallen "Legions" (1. 301) are "Innumerable" (1. 338), "numberless" (1. 344), and "without number" (1. 791), and al-

---

[46] *Microcosmography*, ed. Harold Osborne (London, n.d.), p. 97.

though they are drawn up as if on the pages of a war manual, we can mitigate their awesomeness. All we need to do is recall how Jesus cast out "Legion" from the Gadarene demoniac (Mark 5:9; Luke 8:30) and how he also assured his followers that he personally could summon "more than twelve legions of angels" (Matt. 26:53). The rebels only temporarily represent omnipotence. Until we meet in Book 3 the power which Revelation hints has defeated them, the renegades are like primates in one category on the scale of nature. Milton makes us realize that they win their high status in Books 1 and 2 by default and prompts us to remember the infinitely more potent forces existing above them. Our noble surrogate Abdiel senses the gap between mere numbers and meaningful power when he addresses Satan (and us, if we have praised Hell's multitudes):

> fool, not to think how vain
> Against th' Omnipotent to rise in Arms;
> Who out of smallest things could without end
> Have rais'd incessant Armies to defeat
> Thy folly; or with solitary hand
> Reaching beyond all limit, at one blow
> Unaided could have finisht thee, and whelm'd
> Thy Legions under darkness.
>
> (6. 135-42)

Jesus' example and data assumed from Revelation cooperate with Abdiel's words so that both Bible and Bible-inspired epic show us how premature was our fear of Satan's "Innumerable force of Spirits arm'd" (1. 101).

The poem also reverses a New Testament distinction between quality and quantity. Where early Christians felt that a valiant few were obliged to combat wicked multitudes, *Paradise Lost* inverts the proportion of good to evil. Only a minority of angels choose to fall, but Milton temporarily conceals this fact so its eventual discovery particularly heartens us. Satan claims his cause was so just that the exile of his "puissant Legions" has "emptied Heav'n" (1. 632-33). We initially expect to witness a celestial archetype for our outnumbered state here below, yet we later grasp the truth: Satan only "Drew after him the third part of Heav'n's Host" (5. 710), a much more agreeable proportion. While victory on Earth is not always gained as it is in Heaven, the same moral force superintends both realms. Somehow, whether by numbers or by faith, goodness triumphs. The different percentages of loyal and lapsed reminds us that angels can perceive rectitude more directly than humans. We require time to see how satanic catchwords like "numberless" and "innumerable" may properly be used to describe Heaven and even Earth, not just Hell. By progressively revealing truth, the epic allows our souls to move upward from fear in the presence of evil to a high point where we feel that, "as a good soldier of Jesus Christ" (2 Tim. 2:3), we are lent strength from many sources to "war a good warfare" (1 Tim. 1:18).

Sometimes the epic alone constricts our first impression that the fallen are invincible. Even without recalling the Bible, we can learn that there are alternatives to the devils' behavior. For instance, we may be impressed that "thir General's Voice they soon obey'd" (1. 337), but ignoble fear motivates their promptness. Once we see that the loyal angels act as impressively "With solemn adoration" (3. 351), we can discard much of our praise for Hell's training. Its result is cacophonous and hostile, far less attractive than the product of Heaven, where warriors "thir gold'n Harps . . . took, / Harps ever tun'd, that glittering by thir side / Like Quivers hung" (3. 365-67).

Milton uses a third group of qualifications that functions independently from our memories of Scripture or of the epic. Frequently he calls upon our knowledge of military custom to dampen admiration for the fiends. The way in which the demons respond to Satan's words may impress a reader who does not know certain martial customs. After Satan speaks,

> to confirm his words, out-flew
> Millions of flaming swords, drawn from the thighs
> Of mighty Cherubim; the sudden blaze
> Far round illumin'd hell; highly they rag'd

Against the Highest, and fierce with grasped Arms
Clash'd on thir sounding shields the din of war.

(1. 663-68)

Bentley, for one, is taken in by this scene: "The known Custom
of *Roman* Souldiers, when they applauded a Speech of their
General, was to smite their Shields with their *Swords*."[47] Cer-
tainly the superficial setting might lead us to see this as Mil-
ton's verbal equivalent of the numerous *adlocutiones* pictured
on Roman coins and Renaissance walls: an emperor harangues
his adoring troops as they crowd around him in full battle dress
(Figures 20 and 21).[48] Yet the plain fact is that only barbarians
acclaim their chieftain by "the din of war." With the clinical
awe of an anthropologist who has discovered a bizarre custom,
Tacitus tells how Germans clash their spears if the advice of
their overlord pleases them (*Germania* 11). To show their ap-
proval of a speech urging battle against Rome, some Germans
"applauded these words by clashing their arms and by wild
leaps, as is their custom" (*Historia* 5. 17). Caesar, too, remarks
on the uncouth applause that rebellious Gauls accord to Ver-
cingetorix in a statement which I suspect is less ethnological
than derogatory: Caesar fought no more noble foe (*Gallic War*
7. 20-21).

The normal method of Roman approbation was a joyous

---

[47] *Paradise Lost. A New Edition, ad loc.* Two editions of *Paradise Lost,
Books I and II* repeat the error: that of F. T. Prince (Oxford, 1962) and that of
B. Rajan (New York, 1964).

[48] Handsome *adlocutio* coins or medallions were issued by Caligula,
Claudius, Nero, Galba, Marcus Aurelius, and Lucius Verus, Caracalla, Gor-
dianus III, and Diocletian. During his Italian journey, Milton may have seen
Luca Signorelli's tondo in the San Brizio Chapel of Orvieto Cathedral (painted
after 1499) that illustrates "Greek" soldiers listening to their commander. With
somewhat more fidelity to classical antiquity, Domenico Ghirlandaio decorated
the Sassetti Chapel of Florence's Santa Trinità with a grisaille *adlocutio* in the
1480s. Perhaps most stunning is Giulio Romano's *Constantine Addressing his
Troops* in the Vatican. These familiar scenes of martial harangue not only
clarify Satan's action but Milton's observation, "What you call the right of the
Roman emperors was no right, however, but downright force, a power gained
through no law but that of arms" (*Def 1*. 5. C.E. 7. 317).

shout and occurs in *Paradise Lost* when the good angels hear of Christ's exaltation:

> all
> The multitude of Angels with a shout
> Loud as from numbers without number, sweet
> As from blest voices, uttering joy, Heav'n rung
> With Jubilee, and loud Hosannahs fill'd
> Th' eternal Regions.
>
> (3. 344-49)

Having heard this sacred *clamor*, we can understand how repugnant was the devils' noisy *vápna-tak*, or "weapon-grasping." Associated with Germans and Gauls, the gesture characterizes creatures who once inhabited "The Quarters of the North" (5. 689) in Heaven and now resemble "barbarous Sons" of "the populous North" (1. 351 ff), a region where soldiers are "hardy and brave, but dull and slow to understand" (Machiavelli, *Art*, p. 25). Thus "the din of war" should quash our initial verdict of admirable fidelity. Hell contains no rational crusaders but rather a *comitatus* of uncivil brawlers who embolden their war lord.[49]

---

[49] Fuller documentation of *vápna-tak* may be found in my article, "Satan, Bentley, and 'The Din of War,' " *MQ*, 7 (1973), 1-4. I have discovered only three instances of Romans responding to a *contio* by clanging shield and weapon, each of which is clearly repugnant. In one, troops approve Scipio's harsh and unprecedented death sentence for mutineers in New Carthage, Spain, during 206 B.C. (Livy 28. 29). In the other two, Ammianus Marcellinus says such a gesture represents "angry indignation" or a suicidal resolve to die for Julian the Apostate (*Roman History* 15. 8. 15; 25. 3. 10). Other weapon-clashing references are plainly negative (e.g. Turnus *concussit arma* in *Aeneid* 8. 3, probably, as Servius explains, to wake up Mars). I think the clanging together of arms at Opheltes' funeral is meant to frighten away evil spirits and is thus another matter (Statius, *Thebaid* 6. 218). Similarly, when Aeetes prays that Gravidus keep watch over the Golden Fleece in Valerius Flaccus, *Argonautica* 5. 251-52, the request to "let weapons and trumpets ring" (*arma tubaeque sonent*) is a precaution against theft, not assent to a harangue. The Curetes likewise protected baby Zeus from Cronus with clashing (Apollodorus, *Library* 1. 1. 7). The one positive allusion to shield-and-weapon clanking I have found is the sonic defence made by Xenophon's exhausted troops in *Anabasis* 4.

Milton's long passage recounting the exploration of Hell likewise uses traditional military ideas to trap the unwary.

> Another part in Squadrons and gross Bands,
> On bold adventure to discover wide
> That dismal World, if any Clime perhaps
> Might yield them easier habitation, bend
> Four ways thir flying March. . . .
> . . . through many a dark and dreary Vale
> They pass'd, and many a Region dolorous,
> O'er many a Frozen, many a Fiery Alp,
> Rocks, Caves, Lakes, Fens, Bogs, Dens, and
>   shades of death,
> A Universe of death.
>   (2. 570-74, 618-22)

We might admire the perseverance of these "discoverers" (as they are technically known) if we read their exploit as a martial one, performed in a Poe-like landscape. Indeed, the list of "Alp, / Rocks, Caves, Lakes, Fens, Bogs, Dens, and shades of death," while remarkable in English poetry for having eight accents in one pentameter line, sounds exactly like the phrasing of English military writers. Sutcliffe urges that the wise commander have "espials secretly sent" to reconnoiter plains, woods, mountains, straights, and rivers that may harbour the enemy (*Practice*, p. 116). Similarly, Ward says the general "must be truly informed by Intelligencers, and Guides . . .; he must not be ignorant of the Hills, Vallyes, Wayes, Straights, Passages, Lakes, Rivers, and Bridges" |(*Anima'dversions II*, p. 5). Also, Edward Cooke cautions that the enemy may try an ambush: "You must therefore appoint some to march before to discouer suspected places; as Woodes, Mountaines, Forests,

---

5. 18 and this desperate gesture was to scare pursuers, not agree with a leader. In *Paradise Lost*, undisciplined noise is regularly pejorative. Milton probably associates it, as does Virgil, with "bloody Mavors" who clangs his shield (*clipeo intonat*) to start war (*Aeneid* 12. 332). Classical authors regularly connect the clatter of weapons with war. Hannibal tries to encourage his downhearted troops by banging his shield loudly (*clipeoque tremendum/ increpat. Punica* 12. 684-85); Ovid points to noisy iron-age warriors in *Metamorphoses* 1. 143.

1. Peter Paul Rubens: *The Consequences of War* (Florence)

2. (*top*) Illuminated capital: Pygmy Strangling Crane (From Flavius Vegetius Renatus, *The Foure Bookes*); 3. (*bottom*) Title page: The Ideal Soldier Holding Sword and Book (From Thomas Kellie, *Pallas Armata*)

PALLAS ARMATA,
O R,
Militarie Inſtructions for the Learned:
And all Generous Spirits,who affect the Profeſſion of Armes.

THE FIRST PART,
Containing the Exerciſe of Infanterie, as well
Ancient,as Moderne: Wherein are Clearely ſet downe all the
Poſtures and Motions,belonging to Battallions of Foote.

PRO PRINCIPE ET PATRIA   IN VTRVMQVE PARAT

MARTE MVSISQVE

C. dickesonn Sc.   Exc.ſfinLason.

Printed at *Edinburgh*,by the Heires of *Andro Hart.* 1627.

4. Peter Paul Rubens: *Portrait of Mulli Achmat* (Boston)

5. (*top*) Nardo di Cione: *The King of Hell* (Pisa);   6. (*bottom*) Luca
Signorelli: *Hell* (Orvieto)

7. (left) Guido Reni: *St. Michael Binding the Devil* (Rome); 8. (right) Illuminated page: St. Michael Defeating the Dragon (From the *Sforza Book of Hours*)

9. (*left*) Spinello Aretino: *St. Michael Defeating the Dragon* (Arezzo); 10. (*right*) Andrea Bregnò: *St. Michael Overcoming Satan* (Rome)

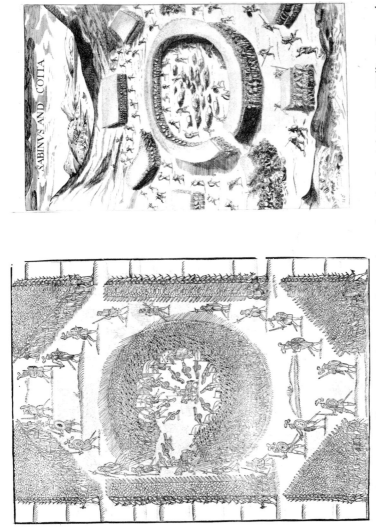

11. (*left*) "The Battell in Forme of a Moone, being of great force for the night" (From William Garrard and [Robert] Hichcock, *The Arte of Warre*); 12. (*right*) "Sabinus and Cotta" (From Clement Edmunds, *The Commentaries of C. Julius Caesar*). The author explains on page 116 that "an Orbe . . . is the best manner of imbattelling for a defensive strength, and therefore never used but in extremitie." Note that the Father's loyal troops "stood/ Orb within Orb" (*PL* 5. 595–96).

13. *(top)* The Persian Army on a March (From Quintus Curtius Rufus, *De Rebus Gestis Alexandri Magni*); 14. *(bottom)* Commander and Standard Bearer (From [John ?] Norris, *A True Discourse*)

15. Piero della Francesca: *The Defeat of Chosroes* (**Arezzo**)

16. (*left*) Melozzo da Forli: *Pope Sixtus IV Appointing Platina as Prefect of the Vatican* (Vatican); 17. (*right*) Pinturicchio: *Aeneas Silvius Piccolomini before Pope Eugene III* (Siena)

18. (*top*) "The Bridge made over Danubius" (From Richard Knolles, *The Generall Historie of the Turkes*); 19. (*bottom*) Three military bridges (From Robert Norton, *The Gunner*)

20. (*top*) *Adlocutio* (On reverse of sestertius of Galba, minted c. 69 A.D.);
21. (*bottom*) Domenico Ghirlandaio: *Adlocutio* (Florence)

22. (*top*) Simone Martini: *Guidoriccio da Fogliano with a Bastone* (Siena);
23. (*bottom*) Robert Walker: *Oliver Cromwell with a Baton* (London)

24. Portrait of George Carew (From Thomas Stafford, *Pacata Hibernia*)

25. (*top*) Unknown: *Charles I with a Baton* (London);   26. (*bottom*) Diego
Velásquez: *Philip IV of Spain with a Bastón* (Florence)

27. "The Action neer Turnhoult" (From Francis Vere, *The Commentaries*)

Rockes, Bankes of Riuers, Caues, Hills, hollow and deepe wayes. The most of which are rough and intricate, and scarce passable for the heauy Armed and horse."[50] Later, Cooke varies his brachylogia slightly when he says, "If your Enemy be in a Wood, Fenne, Hill, Fort, Towne, or other place of strength, that admitteth no accesse, send your Musketteers to . . . bring him into the field" (*Glasse*, p. 11). Markham too urges "Vant-currers" to "obserue all *Hils, Valleys, Straits, Woods, Bogs*" (*Epistles of Warre*, pp. 113-14). Since Milton's phrase sounds so tritely martial, we may automatically conclude that the infernal reconnaissance is an unexceptional example of intelligence gathering.

Yet, in harmony with the epic's critique of war, Milton bends the tradition so that it works against itself. Satan's "Squadrons" are not exploring the territory of an enemy but their own land, duly claimed for them by Satan, its "new Possessor" (1. 252). Also counter to the usual situation in books of strategy, Hell has no external enemy who lurks in ambush. The true foe of the demons is their own perverse will. What they survey symbolizes their inner condition: "perpetual unfulfilled search, unending grief, eternal deprivation of light and grace and satisfying rational meaning."[51] Milton gives a final twist to tradition: the scouts of this landscape, besides not realizing it is wholly theirs and really internal, are characterized as "gross" (570) and "bold" (571), "roving on / In confus'd march forlorn" (614-15). The last phrase reminds us of the military *enfants perdus*: "Wee call them," explains Sutcliffe, "the forlorne

[50] *The Prospective Glasse of Warre* (London, 1639), p 8.

[51] David Daiches, *Milton* (New York, 1966), p. 174. Note how the epic repeats different lists of geographic features with similar military words. The following passages point out, subtly but evocatively, deficiencies in Hell's landscape: 2. 948; 6. 475, 645; 8. 262-63, 275; 9. 116-18; 10. 860. Early in his life, Milton had associated vain activities with wasteland terrain. Compare his dismissal of scholasticism in the Third Prolusion, a rejection written before his close study of army phrasing: "[W]hen I go through these empty quibbles . . . it seems to me as if I were forcing my way through rough and rocky wastes, desolate wildernesses, and precipitous mountain gorges." Tr. Phyllis B. Tillyard, *Milton: Private Correspondence and Academic Exercises* (Cambridge, 1932), p. 69.

hope" (*Practice*, p. 174). Left behind by their commandant, they lose their drill team precision. Their disarray reassures any reader who had been overwhelmed by their earlier May Day parades. Without God or with a false god, these troops are incapable of independent action. All their splendid adherence to copybook precepts has failed, finally, to produce anything more impressive than puppets who collapse when the puppet master leaves. We should be chastened as readers if we ever thought that standard operating procedures could secure for the damned any but a temporary illusion of order.

The demons' last corporate act perhaps best symbolizes their specious perfection. After hearing of Satan's raid in Paradise, they are turned to serpents and tormented by hunger. "There stood / A Grove hard by, sprung up with this thir change" (10. 547-48), the narrator explains, "laden with fair Fruit, like that / Which grew in Paradise, the bait of *Eve*." The ex-soldiers "could not abstain": "greedily they pluck'd." But for their trespass, "instead of Fruit / Chew'd bitter Ashes" (10. 550-66). Milton neatly combines data from the three kinds of limit on Hell's glory. He copies biblical mythology about the "Apples of Sodom" that Tertullian describes: "They still smell of burning, but attract the eye. Once touched, however, they turn to ashes" (*Apology* 40. 7). Milton also equates the fallen angels' fruits with that which tricked Eve in *Paradise Lost*. Finally, Milton may allude to one of the most common stories used by military writers to illustrate the behavior of a faultless army. Under the discipline of "Great *Tamberlan*," the Scythians conquered all their enemies. Barry admiringly recalls that the Tartar chief

> did soe corecte and feare his vvhole army, that vvhere his campe did continue three dayes togither, a tree full loaded vvhith fruite at there departeture remayned vvhole and untuoched [*sic*] (a mervayllouse example to all Souldiores to imitate this vertue) and abstaine from all disordered apetites. (*A Discourse*, p. 4)

Even with Satan present, Hell's host breaks ranks—"they roll'd in heaps" (10. 558)—to satisfy private cravings. Their panic destroys any assumptions we might have formed earlier concerning their automatic professionalism. All their rectilinear files and ranks, as well as all the stable qualities which correct military array connotes, here collapse. Milton leaves us with a knot of vipers that obeys nothing except the basest of personal hungers. No Philip Sidney offers to share with his comrades and no Agamemnon stems the grotesque stampede. By seizing fruit that Tartar soldiers scrupulously avoided, Hell's army reveals its nature. Each trooper mutinies against the purposeful unity that the narrator had commended by imitating Eve during her solitary sin: "Greedily she [and now they!] ingorg'd without restraint" (9. 791). The spectacle of these "disordered appetites" should convince every witness that the martial excellence of Satan's army is as thin as whitewash over a sepulcher. Their wholesale disobedience also mocks standard advice such as that given by "Leo the Emperor": when friends or relatives are assigned to the same unit, they will naturally care for each other (*De Bellico Apparatu*, Sig. D2ʳ).

Failure

The soldiers of Hell fail to sustain our unqualified acceptance for one basic reason: they worship a false god. Satan's troops obviously embody many dreams of military theorists by having a firm chain of command, precise formations, unquestioning obedience, fine equipment, swift communications, sensible operating specialties, high performance, and buoyant morale. Yet their numbers, ferocity, and expertise recall Pharaoh's "*Memphian* Chivalry" (1. 307), another sophisticated but doomed unit. Theorists dependably say that a successful army must display religious orthodoxy. Their suggested laws for camps usually include strictures against crimes like blasphemy as well as provisions for morning and evening worship. Ministers, they say, should be present and protected since victory comes from piety.[52]

---

[52] War writers assure their pupils that one vital part of a functioning army is

The connection between faith and fighting, held to be self-evident, was rationalized in several ways. Xenophon stands first in a long line of advisors who equate waging war with gambling on the future, that mysterious realm only deities can enter. He closes his first book concerning Cyrus's education as a leader by making Cambyses emphasize how important it is to ask the gods whether or not one should take up arms:

> mere human wisdom does not know how to choose what is best any more than if any one were to cast lots and do as the lot fell. But the gods, my son, the eternal gods, know all things, both what has been and what is and what shall come to pass as a result of each present or past event; and if men consult them, they reveal to those to whom they are propitious what they ought to do and what they ought not to do. (*Cyropaedia* 1. 6. 46)

Centuries later Sutcliffe voices a Christianized version of this lesson. A just deity governs our universe and apportions triumph only to believers:

> no good successe can be expected at Gods handes, where hee is not serued; and . . . such wicked men as they shew themselues to be, are rather to feare the wrath of God, then to hope for victory or other fauour; let them if they be but mother-wise, desist from scoffing at Religion, & if they be Christian-wise, let them learne to serue him, that is Lord of armies, and giuer of victory. (*Practice*, p. 306)

Achesone's opinion contains irony when applied to Satan's crew:

> First the Souldier, of all men ought to set the feare of God before his eyes, to haue a cleare conscience, & to be of

---

an effective minister. "[H]ave a goode Chapleyn," says Barry (*A Discourse*, p. 26), just before urging the commander to provide a good barber. Leighton perhaps remembers some time in his own career when his vocation was ignored by superiors: *Speculum* devotes several pages to prove that everyone in an army has "neede to be hedged in by the Lords husbandmen, with the pale of the word" (p. 105).

honest conversation, least in runing vpon the Pickes hee fall into the hell-fire. (*Garden*, p. 26)

Perhaps Richard Bernard offers the most comprehensive explanation of a perfect soldier. He envisions an extremely talented recruit, one moderate in passion and aware of his place in a system of mutually dependent responsibilities:

That Calling must needs be honourable which requireth so many honourable parts and praise-worthie endowments requisite to make a man deserving to be admitted into militarie profession, as to be a man of vnderstanding, of sharpe and quick apprehension, of a stout and vndaunted courage, and yet not foolehardy but prudent and patient; of an able body, yet no lubber of a luskish and sluggish Disposition, but nimble and liuely, to execute designments, and crowning all this with true religion and zeale towards God, with a loyall and faithful heart to his King and Country. (*Bible-Battells*, p. "24," misnumbered for p. 36)

The criteria from martial books by which we had judged at least some of the devils' behavior to be temporarily acceptable cannot finally exculpate Satan's soldiers. Those precepts assume a god-serving human. Milton leaves us, however, with "that Godless crew" (6. 49) or that "Atheist crew" (6. 370), a conglomeration of angels whose outward signs of military virtue can never repair the lack of energizing piety. Since the bad angels accept their identity as soldiers, they must also accept the European rule for proper spiritual behavior. According to *The Swedish Discipline*, Gustavus Adolphus' second general order to all his troops says,

If any shall blaspheme the name of God, either drunke or sober; . . . he shall be put to death without all mercy.[53]

Almost every code of military justice forbids impiety and allows no extenuation for irreligious conduct. Satan's army exists for the sole purpose of attacking God.

[53] [William Watts ?,] *The Swedish Discipline* (London, 1632), pp. 40-41.

We should also deplore the emblems of their actions. However much we respect the two symbols of their soldierly capability, Pandaemonium and the great bridge collapse when we pierce through their showy exteriors to examine the blasphemies they connote. Unless we operate exclusively on a low level of sensitivity that assumes surface and reality are always congruent, we shall be disturbed by the results of blind skill rising before us. If humans have dreamed of technicians who are both loyal and competent, if armies need command posts and bridges, if, in short, our accumulated experience has made us long for the objects that Mammon, Sin, and Death can construct, then we must decide whether we can afford the terrible moral price that their completion demands. The elegant *praetorium* and solid bridge insinuate such unsavory wizardry that the normally perceptive reader must reject them despite (and because of) the pride which Satan takes in their existence. They may stand for all the other indications we have been offered that Satan's soldiers fail. If Milton's careful manipulation of military references has succeeded in educating us about apparent and absolute valor, we realize that what once appeared to be the "perfect militia" is only a "rebellious rout" (1. 747), fit subordinates to no leader except Satan himself.

III

SATAN THE GENERAL

To appreciate most fully the pervasive use of military topics in *Paradise Lost*, we can outline Satan's career. He is a general who has lost the opening battle of a war. Reacting to his defeat in the manner recommended by martial manuals, he composes himself, musters his despondent legions, harangues them optimistically, consults with his staff, announces new strategy to the assembled troops, and sets off on a scouting expedition. His manuevers in the no man's territory around Chaos and on the disputed fields of earth, like his reported behavior during the battle for Heaven, keep close dress and cover with tactics discussed in innumerable treatises. We err, though, if we accept this character of a demon soldier as inevitable. Never before in literature had Satan been assigned a military part with such scope, accuracy, and duration. In this our "westward and setting" age of criticism (as Thomas Browne would call it), we should first understand the public and private reasons that prompt Milton to select *dux belli* as the devil's primary role. Then we may turn to the particular ways in which *Paradise Lost* deals with a fiend who vows "To wage by force or guile eternal War" (1. 121).

Reasons for Satan's Military Role

Although Milton's characterization is original, his audience[1] was conditioned by sermons, war books, and epics to accept

---

[1] There has been debate about the notion of a poet's audience. While not taking sides here, I simply assume that often-repeated ideas indicate an interested public. See Walter J. Ong, "The Writer's Audience is Always a Fiction," *PMLA*, 90 (1975), 9-21 and Robert Crosman, "Some Doubts About 'The Reader of *Paradise Lost*.' " *CE*, 37 (1975), 372-82.

Satan as leader of belligerent spirits. Other accounts of the devil
do not make him so exclusively martial, but the biblical empha-
sis on a cosmic battle between good and evil cooperates with a
secular awareness that, as "Plato in his booke of lawes" says,
"*all cities haue by nature unproclaimed warre one against
another.*"[2] Preachers regularly remind their flocks that they are
soldiers engaged in a lifelong crusade against Satan. A few ser-
mons indicate the religious basis of Milton's decision to prolong
his Adversary's time on active duty: John Downame, *The
Christian Warfare* (1609); William Gouge, Πανοπλια του
Θεου: *The Whole-Armor of God . . . provided to keepe safe
every Christian souldier from all the assaults of Satan* (1616);
Thomas Taylor, *Christs Combate and Conquest* (1618) and
Christs Victorie over the Dragon (1633); John Preston, *The
Breastplate of Faith and Love* (1630); Richard Sibbes, *The
Soules Conflict with it selfe* (1635); John Goodwin,
ΘΕΟΜΑΧΙΑ; *or the grand imprudence of men running the
hazard of fighting against God* (1644); and an anonymous
translation of Jacob Acontius' famous work *Satans Stratagems*.
Although a prefatory letter by J[ohn] Goodwin casts doubt on
the efficacy of temporal warfare ("whilest men arm themselves
against Satan, with the material sword, they do but insure his
victory and triumph"), the Englishman still maintains that
Acontius' century-old treatise is valuable: "They that desire to
serve as *good souldiers of Jesus Christ*, against Errors and
Heresies, must first conscienciously study the Christian Art,
and Method of this Warfare."[3] Like many religious tracts
printed during the first half of Milton's life, sermons routinely
characterize Satan as a military antagonist.[4]

[2] Aelian, *Tactiks*, p. 7. The quoted words appear in the opening section of
Plato's *Laws*.

[3] *Satan's Stratagems* (London, 1648), Sig. a4ᵛ.

[4] William Haller discusses many of these in *The Rise of Puritanism* (New
York, 1938). He reproduces John Downame's title page, a fine picture of the
armored believer vigilant against a grotesque devil who wields dagger-like ar-
rows. Everett H. Emerson has a more current bibliography of secondary sources
in *English Puritanism from John Hooper to John Milton* (Durham, N.C.,
1968). J. R. Hale lists and discusses a large number of sermons that prove how

Despite occasional stylistic felicities, these pious works blur into a single fervent warning. The majority of religious tracts vary the theme spelled out in John Gough's *A Godly Boke wherein is Contayned Certayne Fruitefull, Godlye, and Necessarye Rules, to bee Exercised & Put in Practise by all Christes Souldiers Lyuyne in the Campe of This Worlde* (1561). Gough's message and the messages of those who follow in this homogeneous tradition spring from the meaning of Job 7, a chapter which, he says, "mouethe and prouoketh euery good man, dylygently to remember that the lyfe of man in this worlde is nothing but continuall battell & conflyct."[5] Like other divines, Gough employs concrete martial parlance to clarify spiritual conditions. He and his brothers in the pulpit deny any gap between "reality" and metaphor. The sermons move easily from physical activities such as baking bread, building houses, or waging war to activities of souls. *Paradise Lost* likewise mingles concrete and imaginative references. Alexander Leighton explains why Milton is not atypical when he ranges from material to intangible topics: "As the spirituall warfare of a Christian is the matter of greatest moment under the heaven; so next unto it, in my judgement, is the bodily warre" (*Speculum*, p. 77). Regardless of how sermons are partitioned, they nearly all praise conflict. Ministers urge Englishmen to crush continental degenerates or domestic traitors or private vices, all the while playing "the fife to the recruiting officer's drum" (Hale, "Incitement," p. 374).

Sermonizing literature also uses military metaphors, but often with a more generous dash of wit. Consider the conclusion to Thomas Dekker's *The Seven Deadlie Sinns of London*:

---

united the clergy was in favor of war. Hale's masterful essay should be read for its comprehensive and intelligent scholarship: "Incitement to Violence? English Divines on the Theme of War, 1578-1631." In *Florilegium Historiale: Essays Presented to Wallace K. Ferguson*, ed. J. G. Rowe and W. H. Stockdale (Toronto, 1971), pp. 368-99. Michael Walzer, *The Revolution of the Saints* (Cambridge, Mass., 1965) also shows that Puritan sermons contained military images and supported soldiering.

[5] *A Godly Boke* (London, 1561), Sig. A1[R].

"Is it not now hye time to sound a *Retreate*, after so terrible a battaile fought betweene the seuen *Electors* of the *Low Infernall Countryes*, and one little *Citty*? What armyes come marching along with them? What bloudy cullors do they spread? What Artillery do they mount to batter the walls? How valiant are their seuen *Generalls*?"[6]

Whether moral tracts originated from the pulpit or from popular writers, they sponsored a siege ethic and tried to keep their auditors combat ready. So common is this trope of investment that Ben Jonson uses it, cleverly but urgently, to request money from the government after his paralyzing stroke in 1628:

> *Disease*, the Enemie, and his Ingineeres,
> *Want*, with the rest of his conceal'd compeeres,
> Have cast a trench about mee, now five yeares.
> And made those strong approaches, by *False braies*,
> *Reduicts, Halfe-moones, Horne-workes*, and such close
>   wayes,
> The *Muse* not peepes out, one of hundred dayes.
> . . . .
> Unlesse some saving-*Honour* of the *Crowne*,
>   Dare thinke it, to relieve, no lesse renowne,
> A *Bed-rid* Wit, then a *besieged* Towne.[7]

Jonson dramatizes his plight without self-pity or obscurity. His pun on "*Crowne*" ("government"; "coin") lightens the familiar body-as-city metaphor. Unlike most valetudinarians, he does not force private symptoms upon his listener. Rather, Jonson draws from a widespread admiration for cities that stand firm against attack. Memories of Ostend (1602), La Rochelle (1628), and Straslund (1628) make the trope particularly effective. Underlying Jonson's brave words is the common knowl-

---

[6] *The Seven Deadlie Sinns of London* (London, 1606), p. 57.

[7] "To the Right Honourable, the Lord High Treasurer of England. An Epistle Mendicant, 1631." In *The Complete Poetry of Ben Jonson*, ed. William B. Hunter, Jr. (Garden City, N.Y., 1963), p. 228. Jonson, a veteran, also contributed two dedicatory poems to the 1609 edition of Edmund's *Observations*.

edge that unscrupulous enemies may strike at any moment. Everyone knew how the villainous Spaniard had starved Breda into submission. Gerat Barry's translation of *The Seige of Breda* by Herman Hugo has pictures that both illustrate the poem and prod viewers to arm themselves. The title page shows a dejected female with a mural crown—the city of Breda—being choked by a gaunt female representing hunger. In addition, there are engravings of fortifications and of emergency money, proof that war requires special efforts in architecture, economics and will.[8]

Any researcher can multiply examples. The point is, in case modern wishful thought has obscured it, that pacifism and sentimental benevolence had almost no part in mainstream Christianity until very recent days. With remarkable unanimity, Milton's audience and that of, say, Cyprian of Carthage felt in their hearts that Satan "goeth about each of us; and as an enemy that makes siege upon men who are shut within, he spies the walls, tries whether there may be some part of our members less stedfast and less sure" (*Treatise* 12. 1). Time collapsed for the seventeenth-century believer. Satan had been his first adversary, was now plotting against him and surely hoped to trap him in the future.

Since sermons so often belabor their audience with language from the camp, there is a certain propriety in those war books that appropriate phrases from the pulpit. Preachers understand Plato's maxim in terms of New Jerusalem fighting against Satan's City of Destruction; military theorists easily substitute London, Madrid, Rome, Paris, Constantinople—always as sure as their religious comrades that good must fight error. Aelian sounds like a chaplain in the field: "what discipline is more to bee esteemed, or more avaylable to mans life, then this of warre" (*Tactiks*, p. 7). Another theorist hopes his war treatise ("the *Breuarie* of soldiers") might be "a spur to glory" by helping us gain "the knowledge of our owne fortune" and "foresee the ende of that race which we haue taken" (Edmunds,

[8] *The Siege of Breda* (Louvain, 1627), title page; fortifications, *passim*; money, between pp. 84-85.

Observations 1600, Sig. ★ ij; *1604*, p. 6). This ethical tone, reminiscent of innumerable pathways to heaven and ladders to God, often appears in war texts. Still a third military expert shows how closely religion leagued with war in commentaries. "[E]very man," claims Robert Ward,

> of what degree and quality soever, must and ought to be diligent, and carefull to learne the art of Warre; Whereby we may not only be equall in skill and judgement to our Adversaries, but also to exceed and transcend them, so that our Valour, Obedience, and Policy, may bee antidotes, sufficient to qualifie, and reprocusse the venomous treacherie, and subtill actions of the Enemie. (*Anima'-dversions*, p. 150)

Caught in this crossfire from saints and soldiers, Milton's contemporaries certainly recognized the propriety of his choosing a military role for Satan. Clergymen and campaigners assured them that Satan constantly menaced both the little world of man and the great world. Almost everyone must have felt "the devil striving against him with all the myghte and slyghte that could be invented."[9] Besieged by powers of darkness, human beings had an urgent prior interest in the demons' leader: he was key to their sinister maneuvers. By carefully observing his looks and actions, mortals might guard themselves against his hostile onslaughts.

There are other public reasons for Milton to keep Satan under arms after the war in Heaven. The same audience that wanted to learn about the devil from *Paradise Lost* in order to perfect its theological defense also expected an epic would record the deeds of a warrior. Milton appreciated those other fighters who survived their own time in echoing song—figures like Achilles, Aeneas and Turnus, Caesar and Pompey, Roland, Arthur, Godfrey, Rinaldo and Red Crosse. Milton knew that Tasso, Vondel, and Phineas Fletcher had presented soldier-devils. He deals with

[9] Samuel Clarke, *The Marrow of Ecclesiastical History* (London, 1650). Cited in *OED*, *s.v.* Sleight, 1 B.

this convention as with many others. On the one hand, he immediately presents us with the expected warrior; on the other hand, his exemplary soldier debases everything he touches.

We should note in passing that another victim of *Paradise Lost* is the Renaissance paradigm of epic.[10] Milton proves he knows epic customs, although he comments adversely upon many features of the "full" heroic poem. Without analyzing all the ways in which he remolds our expectations, we can point to some places where Satan-as-warrior parodies epic conventions. Milton introduces the fiend at a low point in his career, thus reminding us of archetypes like Odysseus and Aeneas. (Satan's very first words echo the distraught Trojan's.) The battle Satan has lost forces him to leave his former home and dwell in the underworld, a traditional place for a hero to receive guidance that will help him repair his loss. Yet Hell is clearly not a region of foresight: Satan's subsequent bustlings do not return him to a lost Ithaca or to a future homeland like Latium. Nor do they even disrupt an enemy's realm like the deeds of Eteocles and Polynices in the *Thebaid* or of Hannibal in the *Punica*. He returns, ironically, to the place where he began, the physical reminder of his abject spiritual state. (Perhaps his humiliating *nostos* implies that he accomplishes less than Odysseus or Aeneas, who go on from their unhappy returns to Aeolus' island and Helenus' false Troy.) Satan's great construction projects, Pandaemonium and the bridge, are evil, and the long voyage away from Hell is illusory: "myself am Hell" (4. 75). In addition to his unheroic movements—like Pope's contemptible "dab-chick," Satan, "swims or sinks, or wades, or creeps, or flies" (2. 950. Compare *Dunciad* 2. 59-66)—his martial deeds are perverse or shabby. Insidious confrontations such as those with Sin, Chaos and Uriel, while allowed in war books that

---

[10] There are several passages that support my contention about epic in John M. Steadman, *Milton and the Renaissance Hero* (Oxford, 1967). As most histories of literature affirm, the military poem was going out of fashion by mid-century, losing its heretofore hynoptic appeal because of triteness. The new mode was Biblical and "middle class." Neither subgenre of epic attacked war so relentlessly as does *Paradise Lost*, however.

admit the utility of deception, contravene the face-to-face combats sponsored by epics. Satan's voyage, like that of Mulli Achmat, is humiliatingly observed by those he thinks to surprise. More embarrassingly, he cannot sustain an assumed identity like Odysseus or Jason: his cover as a toad is blown. Even his campaign on Earth degrades the memory of epic. He attacks Eve since he fears Adam. (Satan himself seems ashamed of his role as seducer rather than duelist. While reporting to his troops he brags ambiguously, "Man I deceiv'd," 10. 496.) Like other epic captains, he appears to his followers mysteriously. But instead of communal exaltation, they experience a grotesque theriomorphosis. Instead of a victory feast, they gnaw illusory apples like those of Sodom (10. 547-70). Instead of hearing they have regained a kingdom or golden fleece, they lose the only tools that had hinted there was some possibility of earning autonomy: "down thir arms, / Down fell both Spear and Shield, down they as fast" (10. 541-42). In short, Milton manipulates epic commonplaces by conforming to them in a thorough but independent way, at once fulfilling expectations and provoking surprise.

These precedents for a warrior figure found in sermons, soldiers' books, and epics are, of course, after the fact. Just as knowing a statue may be sculpted from a lump of metal does not explain the final form Verrocchio gives to his statue of Colleoni the Mercenary, so knowing prototypes does not determine why Milton insists upon Satan's thorough-going soldierliness. I suggest he again faces the public need for pictorialism. Although underrated in Milton, it is one of his goals. He and his readers knew the truth of Quintilian's famous rationale:

> Oratory fails of its full effect, and does not assert itself as it should, if its appeal is merely to the hearing, and if the judge merely feels that the facts on which he has to give his decision are being narrated to him, and not displayed in their living truth to the eyes of the mind.[11]

[11] *Institutio Oratoria* 8. 3. 62. Loeb *Quintilian*, 3: 245.

Yet Satan was notoriously difficult to describe. The Bible furnishes our enemy with some titles that Milton expands as well as he can. However, assertions that the devil is a "spirit" (Eph. 2:2), "liar" (John 8:44), "tempter" (Matt. 4:3), "wicked one" (1 John 2:13-14), "seducer" (2 Cor. 11:2-3), "accuser" (Rev. 12:10), or being which can take on the guise of "an angel of light" (2 Cor. 11:14) are more useful for narrative than for description. Even definite images such as serpent (Rom. 16:20. Alludes to Gen. 3:15) or "dragon" (Rev. 12:7-9) chained in a pit (2 Peter 2:4) and "prince of this world" (John 12:31) have only a temporary utility.

Christians often seem eager to deny the devil any significant identity. John Ball, for one, tantalizes the literary detective who searches for an ancestor to Milton's Satan. Ball couches his *Treatise of Faith* in metaphoric language and even uses many military allusions. Yet, when he turns to the Adversary, Ball rejects our basic human need to see: "Sathan was the strong man armed, who possessed all in peace: but our Saviour hath overcome him, taken from him all his armour, and divided his spoiles" (p. 291). Ball leaves us with no visual stimuli; he neglects any mention of, say, chains such as confined Guido Reni's nude devil at St. Michael's feet.

Other Christian literature shortly before Milton's time displayed a similar lack of iconic imagination. Sometimes it resorted to animal images, but these were either lifted from the Bible or based upon stale comparisons. John Bradford, for example, draws upon 1 Peter 5:8 when he prays, "O good Christ, open our eyes to see and shun Satan his subtlety against us and never to forget that 'as a roaring lion' he seeketh to destroy us."[12] Thomas Becon, compelling speaker though he was reputed to be, is not particularly original when he says,

---

[12] *The Writings of John Bradford*, ed. Aubrey Townsend, Parker Society Reprint (Cambridge, 1848), 5: 256. Similarly Robert Burton says in *The Anatomy of Melancholy* 1. 2. 1. 2, ed. Floyd Dell and Paul Jordan-Smith (New York, 1927), p. 171: "Thus the Devil reigns, and in a thousand several shapes, as a roaring lion still seeks whom he may devour."

> There is no ravening wolf that so earnestly seeketh greed-
> ily to devour his prey, as this enemy of mankind: That old
> serpent hunteth and studieth every moment of an hour,
> how he may destroy and bring to everlasting damnation
> mortal man.[13]

Milton pays homage to this tradition of devil-as-animal by hav-
ing Satan disguise himself as an animal in Paradise and, more
subtly, by comparing Satan to animals in several similes.

Although religious imagery is usually stereotyped, Milton
probably felt that a conventional beast was not sinister enough.
While animals embody a certain "living truth" about Satan,
they might affect Milton's audience as the devils of Italian art
had affected him. Lewd and memorable as are the horned, leer-
ing demons of Florence, they do not emanate the intellectual
menace that evil must possess. The three-headed brute in the
Baptistry and in Fra Angelico's Last Judgement, Andrea di
Bonaiuto's technicolor ghouls in Santa Maria Novella, Vasari's
and Zuccari's lop-eared persecutor in the Duomo, Spinello
Aretino's winged dark things in San Miniato—all exist in an
outer darkness of mental incapacity. So do the king of Hell pic-
tured by Giovanni da Modena in San Petronio at Bologna and
the frenetic demons of a Last Judgement mosaic in the Basilica
on Torcello, near Venice. Likewise, Pisa's Camposanto im-
pounds a mindless, three-faced beast who chews sinners, defe-
cates fire, and nauseates viewers (Figure 5). In fact, almost
every Italian church that Milton could conceivably have visited
pictures the enemy as a shaggy horror who differs from its Eng-
lish cousins only in greater sophistication of artistic technique.
Examples of these ignorant beasts are (to use the devil's own
word) legion. Taddeo di Bartolo offers viewers a pornographic
swarm, goggle-eyed and vindictive, in his fresco of the Last
Judgement at the Cathedral of San Gimignano. His marmot-
like torturers erupt from men's nightmares as do the emotion-
less devils who punish the unjust in the Maestro delle Vele's

---

[13] *The Catechism of Thomas Becon*, ed. John Ayre, Parker Society Reprint
(Cambridge, 1844), 3: 149.

fresco in the Lower Church of Assisi. They are degenerate country cousins to Michelangelo's donkey-eared devil in his Sistine Last Judgement or Rubens' hydraheaded catcher of the damned (now in Munich's Alte Pinakothek). Even those demons pictured as advisors are carnal, not reasoning creatures. Signorelli's Master of Deceit in the Anti-Christ section of his Orvieto Cathedral frescoes shares the fluorescent animality of those phallic devils that face it on the opposite wall. For all Giotto's skill, his devil coaxing Judas in the Arena Chapel at Padua resembles a sooty poodle standing awkwardly on hind legs. And Ghiberti's devil, who fails to tempt Christ, differs from other figures on the North Door of Florence's Baptistry: robed and bearded, he repels because of his prominent reptilian foot and bat wing. Pulpit carvings of Last Judgements, such as those by Giovanni Pisano in the Cathedral and Baptistry at Pisa and by Nicola Pisano in the Cathedral at Siena, also impress more for the number of figures squeezed into a modest space than for the intellectual quality of their fiends.

Milton was not completely alone in his dissatisfaction with previous portraits of the Prince of Darkness. His friend Henry Lawrence wondered how to assign a role to Satan that would be theologically correct as well as visually effective. "[W]ee are apt," says Lawrence,

> to feare onely, what wee see, but invisible things are the best and worst, they are the greatest, as our originall sin which wee see not but by its effects; and this great invisible prince that casts so many darts at us, the blowes of which wee feele, but consider not the hand that gives them, whence comes all our mischeife: I would set out this enemy a litle in his owne coulours, that wee may knowe him, and knowe how to deale with him.[14]

Interestingly enough, Lawrence himself experiments with similes in order to discover Satan's "owne coulours": "the

---

[14] *An History of Angells*, p. 6. Paul Carus conveniently gathers together pictures of demons from many cultures in *The History of the Devil* (1900, rpt. New York, 1969).

divell like a cunning fencer hath his faints, knowes how to take his advantages, and like a great commaunder hath his stratageꭤes, by which hee doth as much as by fine force" (p. 3). Although Lawrence does not develop these characterizations, they indicate the artistic problem that Milton masters when he gives Satan a consistently martial part to play. Clearly, any writer who wishes to picture a devil operating on several plateaus of iniquity has to go beyond animals and abstract villains to discover a role that automatically connotes capacity for violence controlled by intelligence, a part, finally, filled by the character labeled "Commandant of hostile armies."

To sum up these public goals that Milton accomplishes when he portrays Satan as a military officer is a short matter whose brevity should not bely the importance of such imaginative innovation in demonology. First, Milton intensifies the preachers' warnings about universal conflict by showing, over and over, how wily and desperate the opponent is. Possibly the specter of an implacable foe will accomplish the clergy's goal by making us gird up our spiritual loins to fight a better fight. Furthermore, Milton reinforces the admonition of war books to prepare always for combat. By seeing how Satan employs his strength during *Paradise Lost*, we may learn to thwart later assaults by his earthly myrmidons. Third, a war lord satisfies readers of epic since they may compare him to predecessors like Turnus or Caesar or Hannibal. Classical references encourage them to weigh Satan in the balance of heroic poem as well as holy Bible. And, perhaps most important, Satan-as-General expands without breaking his biblical form of militant rebel against God, campaigner against men and "prince of the devils" (Matt. 12:24). Satan can arrogate to himself the physical trappings of other commanders, thus satisfying "the eyes of the mind." His high rank suggests an efficiency more terrible to contemplate than bogey-man horns or tail. Identified as a general, Satan satisfies requirements from each category of public expectation, religious, martial, epic, and pictorial.

Milton also had personal reasons to portray Satan as the very model of a modern major general. If the fiend meets so many requirements of the complete commander and still fails, then with him falls the whole warlike mystique. Whether we replace the popular notion of heroism with his more mature one lies, of course, beyond the scope of the epic, but Milton offers us manifold proof that war cripples men physically and spiritually. When Milton debases Satan, he may be exorcising the shade of that other John Milton who made his way upward in the profession of arms. Satan resembles the defeated villain of the Artillery Exercise. Like Mulli Achmat, the Devil in *Paradise Lost* is an oriental war lord, transported by rage, scornful of his opponents, yet observed by those whom he hopes to harm.[15] Because many of our most urgent reasons to act are undocumentable, let us conclude that the verifiable public motives for militarizing Satan reinforce the possible individual motives. Both combine to demonstrate the validity of Milton's conviction that one who wishes to "put on the whole armor of God" need not be an army officer.

The Role of General in War Books

Military books of Milton's time say, oddly, little and much about the character of a successful general. They devote most of their space to lengthy discussions of troop formations and assignments. Yet, when almost any text turns to the necessary qualities of a leader, it demands an amazing compilation of talents. The leader must be a brave, strong, farsighted, just, self-controlled man who comprehends history, geography, psychology, weapons, tactics, and drill. Surpassing Cicero's ideal orator, who understands all civilized arts, the στρατηγός knows them as well as inhumane ones. The only limit to the number of traits a theorist requires is imposed by his own imagination. Despite the awesome number of desirable skills found in manuals, several reappear frequently. Milton not only as-

[15] Rubens portrays Mulli: Achmat as an Eastern warrior (Figure 4). The pasha looks cautiously over his right shoulder at horsemen galloping on a wooded plain; his left hand lifts his sword for action (Museum of Fine Arts, Boston).

signs typical talents to Satan but also uses them—as he does the traits expected of soldiers—to measure the devil's behavior according to a nontheological standard.

Usually, a war book enumerates the faculties of a successful officer. Sometimes, the list emphasizes virtues appropriate to peace as well as war. For instance, Thomas Digges takes a deep breath and requests that the complete general be "religious, temperate, sober, wise, valiant, liberal, courteous, eloquent, of good fame, and reputation."[16] Similarly, Sutcliffe wants "iustice, liberalitie, courtesie, clemencie, temperance, and loyaltie" (*Practice*, p. 40). Another theorist will surprise us by mentioning martial talents and then glide to more pacific traits.

> The highest office of all is that of a Generall, who as hee is aboue the rest in authoritie and power, so ought hee not only to know perfectly the dueties of every officer, but also to excell them all in religion, wisedom, experience, policie, gravitie, secrecie, counsell, modestie, temperance, valour, magnanimitie, vigilancie, care[,] constancie, liberalitie, and resolution, with all other good partes incident to a perfect man of warre. (Achesone, *Garden*, p. 24)

A reader must remind himself that these are the qualifications for a soldier and not a saint. Indeed, the vocabulary of hagiographical writings often surfaces in war texts. Achesone follows the passage just quoted with an exhortation, familiar in sermons, that the general's "vertuous lyfe and carriage [should] bee a paterne, light, and lanterne vnto the whole numbers of the companies to imitate." (Barry uses "apateerne[,] lighte and lanterne of all the army" in *A Discourse*, p. 166.) Commanders are repeatedly urged to be examples for their men in more than bravery. Military manuals assumed, as did mirrors for magistrates, that the behavior of the leader would affect his men. He was thus advised to be "courteous and affable," "faithful of their words," "temperate, sober & chast," "*without envie*," and "*temperate in diet*" (Bernard, *Bible-Battells*, pp. 104-109).

---

[16] Quoted from *Stratioticos* (1590), p. 305. In Webb, *Elizabethan Military Science*, p. 55.

War experts commonly employ two images to describe the moral leader: tower and lantern. Francis Markham summarizes the conventions when he says the *"Colonell"*

> ought to be a man . . . so farre transcending all others which are of any Ranke below him, that as a *Pharohs* Tower, he should be a Lanthorne to guide euery wandring Souldier to the perfection of his duty. (*Epistles of Warre*, p. 162)

Thus seventeenth-century readers of *Paradise Lost* were prepared to hear that the leader of Hell's army "Stood like a Tow'r" (1. 591) or that *"Satan* with vast and haughty strides advanc'd, / Came tow'ring, arm'd in Adamant and Gold" (6. 109-10). Readers were less prepared for the way Satan degrades the tower reference, perhaps, but had to agree that he uses his position to lead others astray. His personal example sets the northern angels "wand'ring" (2. 523) and his disguise as a "Serpent" with "rising folds, that tow'r'd" (9. 495-98) eventually forces Adam and Eve to depart from Paradise "with wand'-ring steps" (12. 648). Satan-as-lantern also degenerates. He is a false light who hates the "full-blazing Sun" of Heaven (4. 29) and can only cast fitful gleams from volcanic "flames" (1. 222) or a moon-like shield (1. 287). He burns "like a Comet" (2. 708), inspiring his subordinates to operate in artificial light (2. 269-70). Even though Satan insults the tower-lantern tradition, he does establish an ethical norm for those he commands.

The ideal general needs to be more than a Christian prince, certainly, but even handbooks that keep their sights on his function in war often play down soldierly abilities and emphasize scholarly ones. "To no one," says Castiglione, "is learning more suited than to a warrior; and I would have these two accomplishments conjoined in our courtier" (*Courtier*, p. 73). A century later, Robert Ward enunciates a course of study that would have appealed to men as diverse as Machiavelli, Milton, or Uncle Toby.

> A Captaine ought to be well seene and read in all the Liberall Sciences, to be acquainted with History, and to

have what speculative knowledge that may bee to joyne
with their practice, all kinde of Stratagems should be famil-
iar with him, and nothing should be wanting that might
make him an accomplisht Souldier. . . . Hee must be a
good Enginiere, to know how to rayse all kinde of Workes
and Trenches, and how to place his men upon the Flankes
to scowre the Bulworkes by the lyne of Levell. (Ani-
ma'dversions, p. 201)

Ward advises readers who wish to oversee the bloody incivility
of human combat to acquire "great knowledge, by reading, and
practice" (Anima'dversions II, p. 3). He leaves little room for
mere physical display; rather, Ward continually praises the
mind as the one indispensable muscle that study should
toughen. In his view, there "be five things required in a Gen-
erall; knowledge, valour, foresight, authority, and fortune"
(Anima'dversions II, p. 2), only the second of which may be
termed a physical capability.

Lying behind Satan's curious boast of superior intellect is this
tradition of the learned commander who (as the familiar icon
shows) can be "portraited with a Booke in one hand, and a
Sword in the other" (Anima'dversions II, p. 3). Both Edmunds
and General Monk repeat exactly the same words about a good
leader's mental ability:

I take the office of a chiefe commander [says Edmunds], to
be a subiect capable of the greatest wisedome that may be
apprehended by naturall meanes, being to manage a mul-
titude of disagreeing mindes, as a fit instrument to execute
a dessigne of much consequence and great expectation, and
to qualifie both their affections and apprehensions accord-
ing to the accidentes which rise in the course of his
directions; besides the true iudgement, which he ought too
haue of such circumstances as are most important to a for-
tunate end, wherein our prouidence cannot haue enough
either from learning or experience, to preuent disaduan-
tages, or to take holde of opportunities. (Observations
1604, p. 6; also compare Monk, Observations, p. 150)

The general whom text books praise plays down warlike interests to philosophical ones. His indispensable learning embraces the entire corpus of Western wisdom, including facts about the East, too (as Barriff's *Mars* indicates). "Wherefore," says Sutcliffe, with characteristic practicality, "seeing so many vertues are required in a captaine, and so small faultes lay him open to the enemy: it is no maruell, if perfect Generals be so rare, and hard to finde" (*Practice*, p. 46).

Attributes: Spear, Sword, Helmet, Height

When describing Satan as a perfect military leader, Milton, like the theorists, places most of his emphasis on the fiend's inner qualities. Yet, so powerful is the tradition of an armed general, that he does not neglect first to furnish Hell's marshal with an impressive shield,

> like the Moon, whose Orb
> Through Optic Glass the *Tuscan* artist views
> At Ev'ning from the top of *Fesole*,
> Or in *Valdarno*, to descry new Lands.
>   (1. 288-91)

The comparison of a shield to the moon, found in Homer and Spenser, is particularly significant if Milton has in mind the circular Roman *clipeus*. Early illustrators of *Paradise Lost* regularly pictured Satan with a round shield[17] or at least "Ouall . . . like vnto an egge" (Edmunds, *Observations 1600*, p. 90). Familiar to any reader of classical literature, it had been adapted from the Greek hoplite's ἀσπίς[18] and appeared on coins, reliefs, and statues. Satan is obviously to be thought of as a Graeco-Roman warrior during most of his appearances. Furnished with his gigantic shield, he both anticipates and imitates the heroes who garner so much praise in pagan literature. Until we meet those

[17] See the many reproductions in Marcia R. Pointon, *Milton and English Art* (Manchester, 1970).

[18] Herodotus uses ἀσπίς for the Egyptian asp, still another possible connection between Satan's shield and an archetypal "serpent."

who have conquered him, he seems to fulfill the requirement
that epics deal with victorious fighters. However, the common
secondary meanings of the word *clipeus* cooperate to diminish
Satan's pose as soon as we meditate upon them. Perhaps Milton
uses his command of Latin to degrade the shield by means of
Joycean connotations. It was proverbial to say *clipeum post
vulnera sumere*, to do something when already too late for
meaningful action. Certainly the fiend's plan to revenge himself
on God by a paramilitary maneuver misses the significance of
his past failure and fall. Other linguistic reverberations of
clipeus help to shake the figure of a heroic devil even before we
witness his defeat in Book 6. The word referred to the sun,
whose "beams" (4. 37) torment Satan, to meteors, fit meaning
for one who "like a Comet burn'd" (2. 708), and to the dome of
Heaven itself, his home forever lost. The historical *clipeus* was
brass—similar to Hell's roof, of which "three folds were Brass"
(2. 645)—but the word came to mean the images of gods or
notable men engraved particularly upon gold or silver surfaces,
often shieldlike in shape. Satan's ridiculous boast that he is as
worthy of elevation as the Son, God's true image, begins his
fatal machinations.

Milton vilifies Satan's shield by means even more direct than
word play. Any shield associated with a "spotty" moon seen at
"Ev'ning" from Italy surrenders much of its immense circular-
ity to overtones of imperfection in Heaven, darkness and, even
for our sublunary planet, a nation too often identified with fick-
leness and ignorant repression. Milton introduces Galileo as an
admirable figure to displace Satan since the scientist represents
"a culture quite different from, and implicitly superior to, . . .
military heroism."[19] Possibly, we can overlook these verbal
dents in Satan's shield, but we cannot ignore its demonstrated
uselessness. Like a cardboard stage property, it fails to protect
him from Abdiel's blow (6. 192-93). It also fails during his duel
with Michael. The rebels use shields, ironically, to carry their
wounded leader "Back to his Chariot" (6. 338). Whatever ini-

---

[19] J. B. Broadbent, *Some Graver Subject* (London, 1960), p. 72.

tial admiration we feel for the Fiend's shield should evaporate
when the Son rides triumphantly "O'er Shields and Helms, and
helmed heads" (6. 840) and when in Hell "down thir arms, /
Down fell both Spear and Shield" (10. 541-42).

Similarly, Milton attaches so many qualifications to the
devil's spear that it can never prove his heroism.

> His Spear, to equal which the tallest Pine
> Hewn on *Norwegian* hills, to be the Mast
> Of some great Ammiral, were but a wand,
> He walkt with to support uneasy steps
> Over the burning Marl.
>
> (1. 292-96)

Commentators on this simile have already pointed out that the
wielder of a corresponding spear in Homer, Virgil, Dante,
Tasso, Ariosto, DuBartas, and Cowley is less frequently a hero
than a monster like Polyphemus or Goliath, anti-Christ or the
"wild wood man." In a military discussion, one should add that
Satan furnishes an unreliable model for young soldiers, since he
misuses his weapon. Here, and later (6. 195), he employs it as a
crutch to keep from collapsing. The spear's uselessness in
Paradise Lost draws attention to the gap between Satan's ap-
pearance and his performance. Even Minos, the degenerate king
of Crete, had a spear that never missed its mark.

The mutations of Satan's spear suggest an instability of form
that characterizes evil in general and Satan in particular. At one
point, it "seem'd both Spear and Shield" (4. 990). Milton may
allude to hybrid weapons such as bow-and-spear that theorists
dreamed up. Although Satan's instrument is vaguely menac-
ing, it is not used. At another point, the spear recalls that
"Rod" (1. 338) by which Moses controlled the locust plague of
Egypt. (The true Moses does not utilize his rod until Book 12.)
Satan completes his metamorphosis into a "stripling Cherub"
(3. 636) on the way to earth by carrying a "Silver wand" (3.
644). The original spear thus converts from tree to rod to wand,
appropriate tools for Satan in his roles of soldier, sorcerer, and
pilgrim. A Freudean might argue that the Fiend gives several

indications of phallic anxiety. The cannon he invents to assult
Heaven may represent an early effort to compensate for politi-
cal impotence. At any rate, the longer Satan is away from
Heaven, the more his "spear" shrinks, suggesting, perhaps,
that God requires from all creatures more than a simple mili-
tary identity.

Satan may bear the wand to remind himself that he is an
officer and should have some badge of office. Styward gives a
military reason for the ambiguous prop: "euerie souldier shall
haue uppon his outermost garment some speciall signe or token
wherby he maie be knowne. . . . [A]nd if there shall be anie
found without the said signes and tokens, he shall bee used as
an aduersarie or enemie" (Pathwaie, p. "61," misnumbered for
p. 62). Satan chooses a *vitis*, or swagger stick such as Roman
centurions carried. Pliny explains that the *vitis* symbolizes just
punishment (*Natural History* 14. 19): perhaps Satan is trying
to preserve his own military character in a universe which has
so far frustrated him. Although he is a spy in disguise, his
baton clearly identifies him as a leader, albeit unrecognized, of
troops bent on chastising their oppressor. Uriel seems unaware
of a long tradition in European art that says anyone carrying
such a staff is a military supervisor, no matter what his other
garments proclaim. The plastic arts before Milton had used this
devise to designate soldiers. An early example is the tomb carv-
ing of Marcus Favonius Facilis, who died c. A.D. 49 (now at the
Colchester and Essex Museum), but later ones abound. Italian
condottieri regularly carry *bastoni di comando*, and Milton
could hardly have missed their presence during his Italian jour-
ney (Figure 22). Two companion frescoes at the Duomo in
Florence, one honoring the English mercenary John Hawkwood
by Uccello and the other by Castagno repaying Niccolò da To-
lentino, may have suggested his epithet "Silver" since they
both are painted in a kind of blanched grisaille. Bandinelli
memorialized the warrior ancestor of the Medici, Giovanni
delle Bande Nere, with an ugly statue then at the Palazzo Vec-
chio. Now moved in front of the Medici church San Lorenzo,
Giovanni guards an even more striking illustration of how a

bastone automatically connoted martial vocation. Inside the chapel, Michelangelo distinguishes two young men, both of whom are dressed in armor: he sculpts Giuliano with the rod to indicate he follows a *via activa* and thus complements the meditative role of his relative Lorenzo. Everywhere Milton turned during those touring years, he would have noted what Uriel does not: warriors carry wands. Bas-reliefs of Colleoni the soldier of fortune by Amadeo in Bergamo and of Roberto Malatesta by an unknown Italian (1484, now in the Louvre) imitated the iconography of statues such as those erected for Colleoni in Venice by Verrocchio and for Gattamelata in Padua by Donatello.

Perhaps Milton attaches this particular symbol to Satan with no little malice. Most contemporary English portraits of soldiers show Royalists proudly wielding their swagger sticks. Admittedly, some Parliamentarians affected the prop, Fairfax, for example, or Nathaniel Fiennes in the Mirvelt portrait at Broughton Castle or even Oliver Cromwell as portrayed by Robert Walker (Figure 23). But aristocrats such as Sir Richard Willys or John, First Baron Byron of Rochdale, in two of Dobson's pictures, more typically stare out at us (Figure 24). They copy their lieges: Charles I routinely carries a staff whether he is painted by an unknown contemporary (Figure 25) or by the famous Van Dyck (*Equestrian Portrait*, 1636, now at London's National Portrait Gallery). Likewise the young Prince Charles is dignified at Edgehill by Dobson as a baton-holding field commander (Scottish National Portrait Gallery, Edinburgh).

There is a final reason to reject Satan's "wand": those foreigners who took one up were often as loathsome to Milton as were the Royalists at home. Rubens may idealize Marie de' Medici by awarding her a *baton de maréchal* in one of twenty-one canvases for the Luxembourg Palace, but a seventeenth-century Briton would see her less as the conqueror of Juliers than as a fat, arrogant, French Catholic schemer (The Louvre now displays this series). The same reaction would probably be forthcoming from any Englishman who noted the people whom Velásquez poses with a *bastón*, Philip IV, for instance (Prado,

Madrid; Pitti Palace, Florence, Figure 26; Frick, New York), or Spínola, who brought about *The Surrender of Breda* from its heroic, Protestant Dutch defenders (now at the Prado). Whatever might have been Milton's most immediate association with the "Silver wand," Roman, English or continental, its physical presence reminds us how Satan's spear metamorphoses in a sinister way.

Pejorative associations similar to ones that Milton imputes to the spear cluster in a popular geography of his boyhood. Concerning "Denmark, Sweden & Norway," Archbishop Abbot writes,

> There is no great thing to bee noted in these Countries: but that . . . from all these countries, is brought great furniture for war, or for shipping. As masts, cables, steele, sadles, armor, gunpowder & the like. And that in the seas adioyning tō these partes, there are fishes of much more mōstrous shape, then elsewhere are to be found.[20]

This schoolboy lore probably surfaces when Satan, the northern chief, appears in the same milieu with "*Leviathan* . . . slumb'-ring on the *Norway* foam" (1. 201-203), a ship's mast and a giant spear, "great furniture for war." And, if all these negative connotations do not diminish Satan's weapon for us, the narrator affirms that God's "Golden Sceptre" also can metamorphose itself, not into a decorative wand, but "an Iron Rod to bruise and break / [Satan's] disobedience" (5. 886-88). If a shaft must be transformed during war, there is more sense to have it promoted from symbol to weapon than, as the devil's spear, vice versa. No matter what possibilities the weapon may have, it accomplishes nothing. Unlike Ithuriel's spear, whose "Celestial temper" forces Satan to end his assault on the sleeping Eve (4. 810 ff), this one is merely decorative.

Two final arms simultaneously describe and degrade Hell's champion. Satan's sword is an expected accessory. Yet it differs

---

[20] [George Abbot,] *A Briefe Description of the Whole Worlde*, 3rd ed. (London, 1608), Sig. D1ᵛ.

significantly from the blades wielded by other heroes, Siegfried's Nothung, Roland's Durandal, or El Cid's Colada and Tizona: we hear of Satan's only because it breaks in combat with Michael (6. 324 ff). The last item of Satan's military regalia, his helmet, also disappoints one who compares it to those in, say, the *Iliad*. It has none of the artistic elegance of the Emperor Maximilian's parade helmets. Rather, it claims attention solely for one bizarre detail: "on his Crest / Sat horror Plum'd" (4. 988-89). Milton neglects entirely the odd tale he used elsewhere concerning Pluto's magic helmet that confers invisibility upon its wearer.

Even the simple matter of Satan's height, appropriate detail for one obsessed with upward mobility, becomes a booby trap. When the narrator says that Satan "above the rest / In shape and gesture proudly eminent / Stood" (1. 589-91), he gives what appears to be a formulaic description of heroes: they are physically larger than their followers. Indeed, the devil in his capacity as Heaven's rebel had already been imaged as tall. "J. A. Rivers" (actually John Abbot) describes how Satan treacherously finds

> New complices to act a dririe plot·
> So now seditious *Lucifer* ha's got
> Whole multitudes to second what he saith,
> As Impious Angels violate their faith,
> Turne to a Creature theire chiefe leader, and
> Amazed at his eminencies stand:
> For Lucifer had such similitude
> With God, that he, next him was the first good.
> No Cedar in Mount Libanus so tall,
> No Beech as hee: he far surmounted all.[21]

Yet, if we think exactly which generals overtopped their followers, we realize that the "tall leader" reference contains an im-

---

[21] *Devout Rhapsodies: In Which is Treated, Of the Excellencie of Divine Scripture* (London, 1647). Quoted in Joseph Frank's fascinating work *Hobbled Pegasus: A Descriptive Bibliography of Minor English Poetry, 1641-1660* (Albuquerque, N.M., 1968), p. 179.

portant qualification. Those commanders noted for their height include Hector, Turnus, Nimrod, Goliath, Saul, Capaneus, and Mago, brother to Hannibal:[22] every one of these men failed in his futile campaign against some divinely-led opponent.

Furthermore, Satan attains his greatest physical stature when he is about to fight "th' Angelic Squadron bright" (4. 977) in Paradise:

> On th' other side *Satan* alarm'd
> Collecting all his might dilated stood,
> Like *Teneriff* or *Atlas* unremov'd:
> His stature reacht the Sky.
>
> (4. 985-88)

Milton allows us to be overawed by this colossus for only a moment. At the final instant, Heaven removes its permission for epic encounter between the gigantic fiend and the surrounding good angels, who have drawn up "Thir Phalanx" "in mooned horns" that bristle "With ported Spears." Cancellation of the duel between combat ready opponents does not impugn the governing authority, as it does in *Richard II*. Rather, Satan diminishes himself when he churlishly "fled / Murmuring, and

---

[22] Hector: *Iliad* 13. 754. Turnus: *Aeneid* 7. 333. Nimrod: David Lyndsey, *A Dialogue betweene Experience and a Courtier* (London, 1566):

> This Nemrod was a mighty man,
>
> . . .
>
> He was a Giaunt stoute and stronge,
>
> . . .
>
> Ten cubits in height he did pas [.]
>
> . . .
>
> This Nemrod was the principall man,
> That first Idolatry began.
>
> (Fol. 27ᵛ).

Goliath: 1 Sam. 17:4. Saul: 1 Sam. 9:2. Capaneus: Statius, *Thebaid* 4. 165-66. Mago: Silius Italicus, *Punica* 3. 238. Frank S. Kastor has an epigrammatic point: "Satan's stature is largest in heaven (planetary); smaller, but still massive in hell (mountainous); and smallest on earth (man-sized)." " 'In His Own Shape': The Stature of Satan in *Paradise Lost*," *ELN*, 5 (1968), 267.

with him fled the shades of night" (4. 1014-15). Here Milton brilliantly employs several traditions in order to reduce the devil. "Murmuring" should remind us (as it did Dryden in "Absolom and Achitophel") of the rebellious Hebrews in Exodus; the whole phrase should also recall the last line of the *Aeneid*, where Turnus' life flees indignantly with a moan (*gemitu*), and provide yet another link between Satan and the defeated Turnus. Finally, hasty departure from a field of honor, no matter what the cause, violates a common military code. Sir William Segar sums up the rule:

> hee who runneth away, and abandoneth the Lists or field where the fight is performed, ought to lose the victorie, and be adiudged as vanquished, and this is the most base and dishonorable sort of vanquishment.[23]

Thus, superficial grandeur evaporates from Satan's size as it has already disappeared from his shield, spear, sword, and helmet. Viewed correctly, this universal dragon is no more than a puff adder.

Actions

Satan's actions belittle him even more than accouterments and size when juxtaposed to military clichés. Recalling to his assembled troops the rumor he heard in Heaven about "new Worlds" (1. 650 ff), he says, "Thither . . . shall be perhaps / Our first eruption." Raphael admits to Adam that it had been his assignment to guard against "such eruption bold" (8. 235). The word "eruption" illuminates several truths about the fiend.

---

[23] [Sir William Segar,] *The Booke of Honor and Armes* (London, 1590), p. 28. Apparently duels were common in the late sixteenth and early seventeenth centuries. On 15 October 1613 James I issued "A Proclamation Prohibiting the Publishing of any Reports or Writings of Duels." It compared God and the King to the "Sunne and Moone." Since both deity and sovereign dislike "mens arrogant conceits of their own valour," duels should stop. "The best remedy against all sinnes and offences is forgetfulnesse." Satan typically disregards this law also.

It reminds us that he is a volatile creature who resembles Mount Aetna in eruption (1. 233 ff). It also associates him with putrid matter expelled from a boil since he is later compared to a "Comet" whose "horrid hair / Shakes Pestilence."[24] These connotations not only debase Satan—even his followers have no admiration for volcanic ejecta or plague sores' suppuration—but also conflict with a neutral military denotation. As used by Caesar and others, *eruptio* means sortie from a besieged place. Although English tactical authors and Satan understand this to be the primary meaning of the word, there was in Milton's time a shift of emphasis. The *Oxford English Dictionary* gives the full range of martial significances: "the sallying forth of armed men from a stronghold, or of *a horde of barbarians from their own country*" (*s.v.*, 3, my italics). Thus, in the matter of defining his own action Satan, spokesman for "barbarous Sons" of "the populous North" (1. 351 ff), reproduces his habitual blindness. By taking part of a truth and acting upon it, he deceived himself into revolt, now feels revenge is possible, and later will think satisfaction gained after misleading Eve.

Satan's inability to see the universe except as a battlefield reappears in the passage where he inspects his troops: "Thir number last he sums" (1. 571). As noted before, "number" sounds like *numerus*, a post-Augustan army unit often recruited from semicivilized tribes. But here again Satan's military action smashes any propriety his census may have. In one of his very few appearances in the Old Testament, "Satan stood up against Israel and provoked David to number Israel" (1 Chron. 21:1). Admittedly, Yahweh had earlier authorized Moses to count his people for military purposes (Num. 26). It is

---

[24] 2. 708-11. Editors link the comet reference to Virgil's Aeneas and Tasso's Argantes. Perhaps even closer than these is the distraught Hannibal in Silius' *Punica* 1. 460. He retreats like a madman, his plume streaming out behind him like the tail of a malign comet. William B. Hunter, Jr. provides useful information on astronomical events in "Satan as Comet: *Paradise Lost* II. 708-711," *ELN*, 5 (1967), 17-21. Both poets and scientists disliked "Amazing Comets, threatning Monarchs might," as Samuel Daniel calls them in his list of portents before the fall of Richard II. *The First Fowre Bookes of the Civile Wars* (London, 1595), Fol. 15ᵛ.

also true that Satan counterfeits Moses at times—with his "potent Rod" (1. 338) he resembles the powerful Hebrew whom Botticelli paints confounding rebels among the Hebrews (1482, in the Sistine Chapel). But Yahweh later threatens David with famine, flight, or pestilence and indicates a new attitude toward enumeration. Milton's Satan characteristically abides by the rule appropriate to a nomadic chieftain rather than to the king of a settled state. He is neither Moses nor David, but his census imitates an exercise allowable only for a primitive society. When Satan attempts to copy the great temple David plans immediately after his abortive numbering, he raises Pandaemonium. With its roof of "fretted Gold," Pandaemonium is a sinful place. Satan loses sight of the Holy Spirit who prefers "Before all Temples th' upright heart and pure" (1. 18). He foolishly raises a "Temple" (1. 713), thinking, perhaps, to avert punishment for having numbered his subordinates. If Milton means us to see Satan as an infernal David, then we also should perceive how he already is as hungry, driven, and sick as any creature can be. If Satan understood the temple to be a magic talisman which would avert the consequences of his census, then he again fails, prisoner of set methods and blind to the ethical import of physical deeds.

Oratory

When Milton turns from Satan's equipment and actions to the Fiend's mental capacity, he emphasizes one talent out of many possible ones: oratory. Far from being an incongruous or an "arty" activity, the ability to speak well is essential to a commander. Machiavelli summarizes the opinion of almost all military writers when he explains why the ancients felt

> it was requisite that the excellente Capitaines were oratours: for that without knowyng how to speake to al the army, with difficultie maie be wrought any good thing: the whiche altogether in this our tyme is laide aude. . . . [F]or that this speakyng taketh awaie feare, incourageth the

mindes, increaseth the obstinatenes to faight, discouereth
the deceiptes, promiseth rewardes, sheweth the perilles,
and the waie to auoide theim, reprehendeth, praseth,
threateneth, filleth full of hope, praise, shame, and doeth
all those thynges, by the whiche the humaine passions are
extincte, or kendeled: wherefore, that prince, or cōmon
weale, whiche should appoincte to make a newe power, and
cause reputacion to their armie, ought to accustome the
Souldiours thereof, to heare the capitain to speake, and the
capitain to know how to speake unto thē.[25]

For those commanders who lack silver tongues to effect these
vital results, Garrard and Hichcock offer a sample address. Its
dignified beginning probably has little in common with actual
words flung at human troops, but it illustrates the high stand-
ard after which officers were supposed to strive:

My louing friends, fellowes, and companions in Armes,
wee bee gathered togither for the seruice of God, his holie
Church, our Prince and Countrie, and for that none
through ignorance shall perish or run in daunger of the
lawes of the field, you shal from time to time by mee . . .
bee instructed by woords or deedes in such points. (*Arte of
Warre*, p. 84)

Satan's magnificent speeches need no ghost writer. They run
the prescriptive gamut from praise to blame and are uniformly
impressive. They seem to fulfill all the canons of superb camp
rhetoric. Certainly, their magisterial tone would satisfy Di Por-
cia when he says,

The oration of the capitayne, setforth and spoken, wyth
weyghtye sentences, & apte wordes, is moche cōmendable,

[25] *The Arte of Warre*, tr. Peter Whitehorne (London, 1560), Sig. R1[r,v]. I use
Whitehorne here (and only here) rather than the Farneworth and Ellis transla-
tion because of its rhetorical vigor. Machiavelli's words reappear in William de
Bellay, *Instructions for the Warres*, tr. Paule Ive (London, 1589), p. 148. A
useful background and structural study by Ezio Raimondi is "Machiavelli and
the Rhetoric of the Warrior," *MLN*, 92 (1977), 1-16.

and verye requisyte. For weyghtye and fete wordes shal
make hym praysed of al men and taken as the very ymage
of vertue, & wysdome. . . . [T]heyr wordes ought to be
seasou[n]ed wyth sagenesse and grauitie, and estemed as
the oracles of the goddes. (*Preceptes*, Sig. H₁ ʳ·ᵛ)

Even when Satan's language seems crude, it receives protection
from war experts. The vicious gloating that the rebels' can-
nonade inspires (the loyal angels "dance . . . / Somewhat ex-
travagant and wild." 6. 615-16) parallels grim humor in books
like Markham's *Epistles of Warre* (A "Scholler . . . may be able
to dance a *Lavolta* to the tune of the Cannon," p. 2).

Satan's manner of (apparently) delivering "oracles" deserves
notice, but so does his matter. Perhaps he is goaded into talking
so much since (as Richard Bernard recalls), "the Lord himselfe
spake to his Generals, exhorting them not to fear". (*Bible-
Battells*, p. 192). Theorists agreed that a leader must speak with
authority to beaten troops: "resolute men giue courage to their
souldiers, and restore battels almost lost" (Sutcliffe, *Practice*, p.
39). Satan's optimistic picture of "the Glorious Enterprise" (1.
89) complements the dictum of Styward: "the Generall com-
forting the souldiers easilie maie perswade euerie one of them
to despise all perils, & to attend to *the glorious enterprise*"
(*Pathwaie*, Sig. Bᵢᵢʳ, my italics). Although exiled to the place
where "hope never comes" (1. 66), Satan still obeys Xenophon:
"For putting enthusiasm into the soldiers, nothing seems to be
more effectual than the power of inspiring men with hopes"
(*Cyropaedia* 1. 6. 19). Satan chooses the ringing "All is not
lost" (1. 106) as his thesis. He annihilates facts consistently to
make his orations remarkably coherent. He does not term the
late defeat a disaster but, from his first utterance to Beelzebub,
a fortunate incident that leaves them "in foresight much ad-
vanc't" (1. 119). He claims their uprising "emptied Heav'n" (1.
633), although we later learn only one-third of God's angels
succumbed to his incitation. Other lies support his buoyant as-
sertion. It was not his rebels who "shook" (1. 105) God's
throne; only the Son's chariot with its "rapid Wheels" (6. 711)

can shake Heaven. Nor did God's "Ministers of vengeance" (1.
170), the many "swift pursuers" (1. 326) whom Satan conjures
up to frighten his men, throw them from Heaven; rather the
Son clearly was "Sole Victor from th' expulsion of his Foes" (6.
880). Repeatedly, Satan manipulates *res* as well as *verba* so that
an auditor may assent more easily than question.

A brilliant extension of the commander-as-orator *topos* fur-
ther complicates our response to Satan. Milton stresses the
self-control that Satan must exercise before he addresses his fol-
lowers. The fallen leader speaks glibly to Beelzebub, "though in
pain,/ Vaunting aloud, but rackt with deep despair" (1. 125-26).
The depression of his troops "on his count'nance cast / Like
doubtful hue: but he his wonted pride / Soon recollecting, with
high words, that bore / Semblance of worth, not substance,
gently rais'd / Thir fainting courage, and dispell'd thir fears" (1.
526-30). When they have obediently assembled, Satan attempts
to speak three times, "and thrice in spite of scorn, / Tears such
as Angels weep, burst forth: at last / Words interwove with
sighs found out thir way" (1. 619-21). On the plus side of the
ledger is Satan's valiant self-mastery. He exemplifies the popu-
lar Renaissance maxim, "He that orders others, must first order
himselfe" (Leighton, *Speculum*, p. 36. Compare di Porcia, *Pre-
ceptes of Warre*, Sig. B$_{ii}$^{v}: "For he that shall rule other[s], con-
uenient it is that he know to master hym selfe."). Like Henry
V, the ideal warrior-king, his "passion is as subject / As are our
wretches fettered in our prisons" (*Henry V* 1. 2. 242-43). Even
more than the disciplined "Gentlemen of the Artillery Garden"
whom Barriff praises, Hell's commissar "can / Govern a little
world" (*Mars*, p. 8) of private feeling. He resembles admirable
heroes who suppress their emotions when serving a larger
cause. Romulus chokes back tears at Remus' death to set a pub-
lic example (*Fasti* 4. 845). Like sad Aeneas withstanding the
pleas of Anna (*Aeneid* 4. 448-49) or like Hercules submitting to
the death of Pallas, Satan "stifles a great sigh in his heart and
sheds tears in vain" (*Aeneid* 10. 464-65). His struggle with per-
sonal feeling would win respect from any war writer. Robert
Ward encourages the ideal leader to remain hopeful whether

"fortune is come to the height or Brumall Solstice of her frowning":

> a Generall therefore plunged into the lowest deep of disasters, must beware he sinke not to the nethermost hell of despaire, from whence is no redemption; but let him reserve himselfe for better fortunes. (Anima'dversions II, p. 20)

If we look for a real-life counterpart to Satan, the calm leader of a desparate campaign, we probably should point to Oliver Cromwell. Milton's long eulogy in The Second Defence sounds remarkably like these phrases and emphasizes the same accomplishment of becoming "commander over himself" (C.E. 8. 215).

Satan's competent lies and complete self-command press us to find facts supporting the narrator's disapproval. An interesting quandry of A.J.A. Waldock and John Peter,[26] who see little evidence to substantiate the speaker's allegation about Satan's villainy, recurs when the fiend lies. He is, after, "a liar and the father of lies" (John 8:44). Milton's contemporaries often linked Satan to lying and drew political conclusions. While Milton was at work on Paradise Lost, Thomas Bancroft finished Time's Out of Tune. His "Satyre VI. Against Lying" springs from the untruths told by "Royalists" and "the parlying party." Both sides in "this blood-drenched age" spout as many "hateful lyes / As Hell and Heresie could ere devise." The tellers act

> As they had serv'd a Prentiship in Hell.
> Surely Hell propagates apace by lyes
> (The Devils progeny) sith to devise
> Prodigious falsities, is now become
> As frequent as to fornicate at Rome.[27]

[26] Paradise Lost and Its Critics (Cambridge, 1962); A Critique of Paradise Lost.

[27] Time's Out of Tune; Plaid Upon However. In XX Satyres (London, 1658), pp. 36-37.

Such behavior endangers the entire country since, if untruth prevails, "this Isle would ever bleed, / The work of war would forward go in haste, / Mischief would like *Aegyptain* hail lay waste / All in its ways" (p. 41). Bancroft tries to avert this cataclysm by exhorting his countrymen that prevarication hurts both conscience and country:

> The Prince of wandering shades, with specious lyes
> (Such as some Oracles) doth still disguise
> His black designs, and as his Imps, applauds
> Such as by slippery windings and sly frauds
> Do act the Serpent: double tongues (aswell
> As cloven feet) are cursed marks of Hell.
>
> (p. 41)

Bancroft unites Miltonic words ("wandering . . . frauds") and sounds (the serpentine sibilants) to common English ideas ("cloven feet") so that no moral person can approve of mendacity.

However, this truth of religion clashes with the military truth of *salubria mendacia*. "Deceit is necessary," explains Onasander, "when a big battle has arisen" (*General* 23. 1). Speaking through Darius, Herodotus accords this doctrine of the life-giving lie, a staple of military advisors like Frontinus and Polyaenus, a sophistic rationale:

> If a lie is necessary, why not speak it? We are all after the same thing, whether we lie or speak the truth: our own advantage. Men lie when they think to profit by deception, and tell the truth for the same reason—to get something they want, and to be the better trusted for their honesty. It is only two different roads to the same goal.[28]

Homer seems to admire Odysseus' lies and Herodotus speaks favorably of the deceits by Themistocles and Queen Artemisia at Salamis (*Histories* 8. 75, 87-88). We are once again placed in

---

[28] *Histories* 3. 72. Tr. Aubrey de Selincourt (Baltimore; 1954), p. 106. Polyaenus begins his work by recounting the deceptions that deities like Bacchus, Pan, and Hercules used. The archetype of lying, he implies, is found near Olympus.

the difficult position of evaluating tactics that are, at the same time, approved by martial and classical standards but condemned by faith. Here, as elsewhere, we experience an uncomfortable double vision when we are forced to view the same activity through the eyes of a military man and the eyes of a moralist.

Or consider Satan's self-assurance. He subdues his passions so he can deliver magisterial speeches to persuade his army that it acts with probity. For millennia military psychologists urged leaders to state specific grounds for declaring war. Only in a just cause, they reasoned, would troops develop that zeal which insures success. Much of Satan's rhetoric attempts to inspire popular certainty of rectitude. As usual, his words sound like those used in martial manuals. Leighton furnishes a list of motives that the general should use to "perswade" his troops before an engagement. The major stimuli include, "the goodnesse of the cause"; "the preservation of them and theirs; for goods, liberty, wiues and children"; "hope of glory, and promise of reward"; "the impossibility to escape the enemie"; "the cruelty and inhumane condition of the enemy" (*Speculum*, pp. 180-82). These ideas reappear in almost all of Satan's addresses to the rebel forces.

While animating his army, Satan does more than employ random clichés. He tries to argue a legal question: is his crusade justified? A long series of precedents seems to bolster his defense and to award his undertaking a certain respectability. Since law conserves previous definitions, the mid-seventeenth century classified social turmoil in much the same way as Raban Maur during the ninth century:

There are four kinds of war, namely Just, Unjust, Civil and More-Than-Civil. A Just War is announced and waged either to recover lost things or to expel an enemy. An Unjust War is one which arises from madness, not from some legitimate cause. . . . No war can be called "Just" unless it is waged for the purpose of punishing a foe or pushing out an invader. . . . A Civil War is one which involves sedition or riots between citizens. . . . A More-Than-Civil War is one fought between citizens who enlist their kinsmen. (*De Universo* 16. 20)

Except for Hugo Grotius' concern with national states, the three bulky volumes *De Iure Belli ac Pacis* offer identical formulations.[29] And military writers naturally make it their business to outline conditions for a just war that decent leaders must satisfy. Garrard and Hichcock give the simplest guidelines: "That warre is iust, which a Prince commaunds, for to recouer that is lost, or to defende iniuries and wrongs offered to him by others" (*Arte of Warre*, p. 352). Satan carefully chooses his words so that they furnish unimpeachable reasons for aggression. For example, his opening address to the Great Consult bristles with traditional phrases. He says he was created leader through "just right and the fixt Laws of Heav'n" (2. 18). Thus, he and his followers may with full integrity "now return / To claim our just inheritence of old" (2. 37-38). Anyone with a minimal competency in legal language must admit that Satan fulfills the stipulations of Garrard and Hichcock. He has been personally injured by God's decision to promote Christ. As Bernard explains, "Reproches offered and injuries done to principall men in a State is just cause of warre" (*Bible-Battells*, p. 43). Satan's war is partly personal, then: "to get . . . possession of a Crowne justly claymed; as David did" (p. 45). But God has not simply stolen Satan's "just right"; he has also filched from Satan's followers their "just inheritance." *Recuperatio*, the recovery of stolen property or honor, commonly excused a declaration of belligerency. Markham defines as blameless any campaign that seeks "to regaine those Rights and Dominions, which (formerly being giuen from God) haue been iniuriously taken and withheld from the true and lawfull owners" (*Epistles of Warre*, p. 10). Edmunds echoes the other analysts when he declares, "Reparation of honour is a chiefe point in the cariage of an army" (*Observations 1600*, p. "96," misnumbered for p. 98).

[29] *De Iure Belli ac Pacis Libri Tres*, 1625, ed. P. C. Molhuijsen (The Hague, 1919).

Satan cunningly weaves together these two excuses for war that lawyers traditionally accepted as valid. No one in a rationally administered world may steal another's liberty or his honor with impunity. Whether Satan lectures on hierarchy or angelogenesis, he dwells on God's alleged abuses against freedom and dignity. Book 5 and later (if we straighten out the chronology) Book 1 repeat the same accusations. Speaking to the first point, he poses as a political conservative who mistrusts the innovative "new Laws" (5. 679-80) promulgated by Deity, since they supposedly constrict freedom in Heaven. In Book 1, he continues to present their "Glorious Enterprise" (1. 89) as a just resistance to God's tyrannic order that all Heaven "deify his power" (1. 112). When speaking to the matter of honor, Satan proudly asserts that their "being [is] ordain'd to govern, not to serve" (5. 802). In Book 1, he vehemently restates this high opinion of the rebels' innate nobility: "who overcomes / By force, hath overcome but half his foe" (1. 648-49). Satan's repeated rationales place him in a tradition of admired heroes who fight for the liberation of a noble people. Moses, Harmodius and Aristogeiton, Vercingetorix, and the Dutch *Gueux* furnish unimpeachable models for instigators of legitimate rebellion. Satan arouses his subjects by regularly imputing to God the character of a despot who glories in stealing his subjects' freedom and good name. His first speech to Beelzebub initiates this accusation against the one "Who now Triumphs, and . . . / Sole reigning holds the Tyranny of Heav'n" (1. 123-24). Subsequent references to God reinforce the element of tyranny by implying that he rules only temporarily: God becomes the one "Who *now* is Sovran" (1. 246, my italics).

At the level of verbal consistency, Satan's allegation of unmerited rule does legitimatize revolt. Milton himself formulates the clearest of many statements concerning the duty of subjects to rebel against illegal rulers. Characteristically, he unites precedents from Christian and classical history:

The true and proper ground of our obedience has no connection whatsoever with slavery. . . . He [St. Paul] does

not [in Romans 13], therefore, condemn a war taken up
against a tyrant, a bosom enemy of his own country, and
consequently the most dangerous enemy possible. [There
follows a list of commendable tyrant killers: Samson, Re-
hoboam, Alexander, Constantine.] (Def 1. 3. C.E. 7. 165)

. . . .

It is evident that the most excellent of the Romans did not
only kill tyrants however and whenever they could, but
like the Greeks before them thought the deed most
praiseworthy. (Def 1. 5. C.E. 7. 329)

Except for ardent Royalists speaking to the specific issue of
Charles' deposition, most writers accept Milton's opinion.
Bacon supports him, fancifully but traditionally, when he urges

that the cause of the war be just and honorable; for this
adds alacrity both to the soldiers, and the people who find
the supplies; procures aid, alliances, and numerous other
conveniences. Now there is no tyranny, but which a people
are dispirited, benumbed, or left without life and vigour,
as at the sight of Medusa.[30]

The entire topic of Satan's articulate jingoism may encourage
in us a kind of paralysis. We are asked to judge his words by
two previously compatible standards, the martial and the ethi-
cal. He is, to be sure, of "good perswasion," one of those who
"knowe howe to speake wel,"[31] a leader who has "a sweet vaine
in speech."[32] But whether or not we approve of this facility de-
pends how we see him: is Satan a "Chief of many Throned
Powers, / That led th' imbattl'd Seraphim to War" (1. 128-29)
or one of God's creations who chose to fall (3. 100 ff)? The epic
forces us to decide which standard, soldierly or theological,
applies. Otherwise Satan (in Landor's words),

[30] "Perseus, or War" from The Wisdom of the Ancients. In Lord Bacon, The
Moral and Historical Works, ed. Joseph Devey (London, 1890), p. 217.
[31] Barnaby Rich, A Path-Way to Military Practise (London, 1587), Sig. E1ᵛ.
[32] Robert Barret, The Theorike and Practike of Moderne Warres (London,
1598), p. 29.

If he sometimes appears with the gloomy grandeur of a fallen Angel, and sometimes as the antagonist of Omnipotence, is often a thing to be thrown out of the way, among the rods and foolscaps of the nursery.[33]

Paradise Lost offers the same Hercules' choice for Satan as T[homas] M[ay]'s *A Continuation of Lucan's Historicall Poem* does for the victorious-but-villainous Caesar. Having defeated Pompey, Caesar sadly wonders whether he is now at the precarious top of Fortune's wheel:

> But lest his sadnesse should too much dismay
> The Souldiers hearts before so great a day,
> He recollects himselfe, and with fain'd cheare,
> And forced lookes, taught to dissemble feare,
> Thus to his army speakes.[34]

Caesar harangues his troops and himself seizes weapons, simultaneously inspiring and despairing, outwardly proficient but inwardly without hope.

Armed with military information, though, one can show that Milton does not allow Satan's excuses for revolution to remain very convincing. There are several indications that we should despise Satan's oratory even before Book 6 disproves his lies. The narrator assures us that a follower who can "make the worse appear / The better reason" (2. 113-14) mirrors a facile captain who uses "high words, that bore / Semblance of worth, not substance" (1. 528-29). Our own memory of military history likewise urges us to condemn Satan's words. As admirers of Greece, which nursed civic liberty, we should mistrust a commander who weeps before addressing his troops: the closest analogue to Satan's outburst is that of the barbarian Xerxes (Herodotus, *Histories* 7. 45-46). As heirs to free-born Romans, we should be repelled by the infernal host's response to his *contio*, their pugnacious *vápna-tak* in Book 1 (663-69). By reject-

---

[33] "The Abbe Delille and Walter Landor." In *The Complete Works of Walter Savage Landor*, ed. T. Earle Welby (London, 1938), 7: 240.

[34] *A Continuation of Lucan's Historicall Poem* (London, 1630), Sig. H7ᵛ.

ing the speech, we can share the relief of Roman soldiers as they stare at some Gaulish prisoners whom Camillus has stripped:

> These are the creatures who assail you with such terrible shouts in battle, and clash their arms and shake their long swords and toss their hair. Behold their lack of hardihood . . . and gird yourself to your work. (Appian, *Roman History* 4. 8)

And as mature readers who approve of self-control in commandants, we nonetheless understand, as Montaigne does when thinking of Julius Caesar, that a resolve to wage unending war against an omnipotent power indicates a kind of vainglorious insanity, "a determined resolve to lose his life, to avoid the shame of being vanquished."[35] Whatever topical utility Satan's rhetoric has, it finally fails by both Christian and camp tests. It is impractical for a protracted campaign because it does not separate fact from fiction, necessity from dream, capacity from bravado. Although exciting, it brings its auditors far from any possibility of dealing with essentials. They hear only of malleable accidents and secondary attributes that may be denigrated without furthering the cause of emancipation.

The difficulty we experience when evaluating Satan's rhetoric finally derives from the composite nature of the speaker. Normally, Satan's speeches would typify one of two antithetical characters. The first is a concerned commander who skillfully encourages his army to better its condition and gives little thought to his own profit. This altruistic professional steps from war books and acts with integrity. The second orator misleads an entire army so he may satisfy a personal grudge. With admirable felicity, Milton intertwines the two traditions. Consequently, Satan's harangues oscillate between propriety and misfeasance because they emanate from one creature who is both (in the words of Garrard and Hichcock) "diuell" and "soueraigne":

---

[35] "Julius Caesar's Methods of Making War," in *The Complete Essays of Montaigne*, tr. Donald M. Frame (Garden City, N.Y., 1960), 2: 449.

Subtile enimies approue to corrupt souldiers with giftes, and the diuell to entrap them with the sweete intising baites of lewd libertie. But since the reward of truth is euerlasting life, & the untrue and dissembler looseth the same in continuall darkenesse, I trust none of our countrimen will learne the one for the other, [or] will be false to his soueraigne. (*Arte of Warre*, p. 31)

Failure in Book 6

After Satan's speeches have had ample airing, Book 6 completes the process of vanquishing the demon-soldier with a double-pointed sword of ethical and martial censure. We have heard his lies and possibly assented. Now we finally see him commanding troops in battle. During his previous accounts of the war in Heaven, Satan has conditioned us to expect a glorious pageant whose bravery and intelligence would perhaps not excuse him from the charge of rebel, but at least would prove his genius as a warrior. If we have responded to Milton's method of making us choose between moral and military efficiency, then we may fear to read this book. It is by far the longest expansion of a few lines in Revelation and obviously occupies a central place in the epic. But, mercifully, it does not rip us apart by demanding that we choose between two standards of conduct. Instead, all references cooperate to rout Satan's pretensions. His soldierly behavior underscores, not contradicts, his reprehensible stupidity as a rebel from God's decent fellowship. An odd combination of historical references to other wars, sardonic puns, awkward duels, and visionary triumph cooperates to disarm the braggart soldier.

Clearly, war and ethics are key issues. But just as clearly, Satan cannot separate one from the other. The first rousing speech he delivers from his palace in Heaven shows that he consistently mixes the two categories. "Will ye submit your necks, and choose to bend / The supple knee," Satan demands of his followers, or will they "cast off this Yoke?" (5. 786-88). His

vocabulary is only partially theological. Jerome Zanchy's popu-
lar *Confession of Christian Religion* declares,

> euerie soule, that is, euerie man, none except, and there-
> fore also euerie inferior power, must be subiect to the
> higher and greater power: . . . For it is Gods will that they
> should al kisse the Sonne: and bowe their neckes vnder the
> yoake of his discipline.[36]

Although Satan and Zanchy share words like "Necks" and
"Yoke," the Fiend's harangue is largely military It suggests a
new kind of society that can combat humiliation: "Orders and
Degrees / Jar not with liberty" (5. 792-93). Even in an exhorta-
tion that pretends to discuss political issues, Satan betrays his
obsessive urge to be a general. Every schoolboy knew that
beaten armies in the Roman world were sent under the *jugum*,
or symbolic "Yoke" improvised from three spears. To avoid
such disgrace, men who wished to preserve their "liberty" will-
ingly accepted *ordo*, or placement in an armed company, and
gradus, or posture characteristic of combatants. (Among
others, Leighton also links order and degree in a military con-
text. *Speculum*, p. 46.) While Abdiel attempts to lead the de-
bate from army words used by Caesar, Cicero, Livy, Ovid, and
Tacitus, to the moral question ("Shalt thou give Law to God"),
he picks up the notion of just leadership: God "form'd the
Pow'rs of Heav'n / Such as he pleas'd, and circumscrib'd thir
being" (5. 822-25). In other words, the convenor of a militia
("Pow'rs") legitimately assigns duties and limits responsibility.
But such logic cannot deter Satan. He crows, "Our puissance is
our own, our own right hand / Shall teach us highest deeds, by
proof to try / Who is our equal" (5. 864-66). The rebel here im-
itates numberless human mercenaries who will come after him
by asserting that "Beseeching or besieging" (5. 869) have no
essential difference. (Leighton accuses militant "*Iesuits*" of
trusting "*more to the prey then to their prayers*" in *Speculum*,

[36] *Confession of Christian Religion* (Cambridge, 1599), p. 248, an anony-
mous translation of *De Religione Christiana* (Neustadt, 1585).

p. 201.) He can satisfy his anger most easily by waging war. Like Shakespeare's King John, Satan looks to combat for the solution of moral questions:

> Cousin [the Bastard], go draw our puissance together.
> France, I am burned up with inflaming wrath,
> A rage whose heat hath this condition,
> That nothing can allay, nothing but blood. . . .
> . . . To arms let's hie!
>
> (King John 3. 1. 339-47)

Casuistry for Satan almost invariably precedes fighting.

Many readers recognize that Satan's battle for Heaven is both prototype and epitome of all earthly wars. Book 6 conscripts military vocabulary from various eras and parades it relentlessly: "dislodge" (6. 7, 415), "Quadrate" (62), "shout / Of Battle,"[37] "edge of battle" (108; compare *acies*, front line), "hand" (231; compare *manus*, squad, corps), "Cubic Phalanx" (399) (Figure 27), day "Scouts" (529; compare the ἡμερο-σκόπος of Aeneas Tacticus 6. 1), "Battalion" (534), "quit of all impediment" (548. i.e. *expeditus*, without *impedimenta*, baggage), "hollow Cube" (552), "impal'd" (553) and "posture" (605). Like this vocabulary, the actions remind us that we are simultaneously previewing and reviewing sublunary conflict. When Satan duels with Abdiel and Michael, he reminds us of classical bouts complete with taunts and weapon play. There are numerous historical analogues when music accompanies the good angels' "perfet ranks" (71), when Messiah enjoys a "Triumph" (886), when Satan invents cannon or when all engage in weltering melees. If, as has been argued, the three days summarize classical, modern, and cosmic wars,[38] then Satan loses everywhere at the very activity by which he chooses to

---

[37] 6. 95-96, 200. Aelian, *The Second Part*, tr. John Bingham (London, 1626), p. 85 mentions a "Greeke ἀλάλαγμος [sic], in Latine *clamor*. in English a shout of the whole Army."

[38] Stella P. Revard, "Milton's Critique of Heroic Warfare in *Paradise Lost* V and VI." Michael Lieb gives an interesting analysis of Satan's failure in *The Dialectics of Creation* (Amherst, Mass., 1970), pp. 81-124.

define himself. Wounds do not kill (344), cannon does not an-
nihilate (606), armor only hinders (656). While some of his
techniques are successful in earthly conflict, such ploys as chal-
lenging an opponent to single combat or concealing cannon be-
hind lines of troops are inefficacious against the one entity in
our universe which is "Supreme . . ., / First, Highest, Holiest,
Best" (723-24). Everyone except Satan knows that "God *is the*
Lord *of* Hoasts, *and the* God *of* Battels,"[39] determiner of vic-
tory, bestower of triumph. The loss reduces Satan to, at best, a
survivor. Book 6 pulverizes his potentiality for widespread de-
struction and leaves him as a furtive guerrilla who wages hole-
and-corner attacks, mean in scale and shabby in concept. Mil-
ton's version of the war for Heaven completes the deflation of
the Fiend from self-proclaimed crusader to publicly observed
failure.

Like all activites in *Paradise Lost*, this demonstration of Sa-
tan's military impotence is set in a matrix of ethical concerns.
God's first speech reviews the issues that will be decided at the
forthcoming trial by combat. He arrays words like "Truth" (32,
33), "word" (32), "stand approv'd in sight of God" (36),
"friends" (38), "reason" (41, 42), "Right" (42, 43), "Law"
(41, 42), and "merit" (43) against their Satanic opponents: "re-
volted" (31), "Arms" (32), "violence" (35), "foes" (39), and
"force" (41). The bivalent possibilities of our universe emerge
throughout the book. Merit versus ambition, right reason and
law versus force—these are the alternatives in a system that al-
lows free choice between supreme good and lesser values.

Satan's decision to war against the Almighty sounds at first
hearing (but only at first hearing) like the moral commitment of
some respectable Puritan apologist. For example, in 1649
Royalist ministers proposed two laws that forbade rebellion.
Charles I immediately approved them. One affirmed,

---

[39] George Wither, "For Victorie." In *The Hymmes and Songs of the Church*
(London, 1623), p. 213. H. H. Scudder gives several real life parallels to Satan's
trick of hiding his cannon. See "Satan's Artillery," especially the quotations
from Davila's *Historie of the Civill Warres of France* and Wilson's *History of
Great Britain.*

For subjects to bear arms against their Kings, offensive or
defensive, upon any pretence whatsoever, is at least to re-
sist the powers which are ordained of God; and though
they do not invade, but only resist, St. Paul tells them
plainly, they shall receive to themselves damnation.

To this repressive dictum John Selden replies at some length.
His discussion concludes: "To know that obedience is due to the
prince, you must look into the contract betwixt him and his
people. . . . Where the contract is broken, and there is no third
person to judge, then the decision is by arms."[40] Such reason-
ing untangles any lesser relationship; for the primal contract
between God's creations and God himself, archetype of all
earthly princes and plenipotentiary for whom kings merely
substitute, such verbiage cannot apply.

Nevertheless, Book 6 invites us to accept the battle as one
that will prove by ordeal what Satan's talk could not, whether
he or the Son should rule Heaven. The rebel cannot claim Sel-
den as his attorney since the revolt rests on very shaky legal
ground. We need little judicial training to recognize that
Satan—despite his elaborate claim of legitimacy—neglects most
requirements for *justum bellum* that were available in the Ren-
aissance. He contradicts Aristotle since Satan's war is not one of
self-defense, is not to establish rule over those who would ben-
efit from a new regime, and is not to enslave those who have
demonstrated that they would benefit from tyranny (*Politics*
1333b38 ff). Contrary to stipulations such as those laid down by
Cicero, Satan neither formally demands reparation from God
for his alleged injury nor initiates hostilities by a public declara-
tion (*De Officiis* 1. 11. 36). And contrary to almost every code
promulgated by theorists as diverse as Augustine, Aquinas,
Suarez, Belli, Gentili, Ayala, and Grotius, Satan does not se-
cure his king's permission to fight (civil war is commonly said
to be the most reprehensible), does not present sufficient cause

[40] See the full discussion of "War" in *The Table Talk of John Selden*, ed.
Samuel Harvey Reynolds (Oxford, 1892), pp. 190-93, which includes the words
of King Charles.

for non-negotiable conflict and, because of his warped spirit, does not act with right intention ⟨On all counts, Satan stands guilty of breaking standard laws and, worse, consistently perjuring himself The defeat that Satan suffers in Book 6 thus eliminates in general terms both the martial and ethical bases upon which his earlier propaganda had been based.⟩

Strategy of "Force or Guile"

In one very specific way, the loss of Heaven involves a debate that had exercised moral and military philosophers. Satan introduces the terms of this *paragone* when he sums up his situation:

> Since through experience of this great event
> In Arms not worse, in foresight much advanc't,
> We may with more successful hope resolve
> To wage by force or guile eternal War
> Irreconcilable to our grand Foe.
>
> (1. 118-22)

His thoughts immediately polarize about the time-battered axes of a human commander, "force or guile." When taking stock of the resources left to him, Satan divides them into "Arms" and "foresight." Once again he arranges phenomena into traditional military categories. Although Satan aspires to be a commandant more successful than God, his mind operates as mechanically as that of Taine's drill-sergeant. He exhibits "the tension of external adaptability with internal rigidity"[41] and never learns the vanity of words that float free from objective realities. The labels he idolizes are those that hide uncomfortable facts. He does not mention "God," for instance, as if withholding *nomen* will annul *ens*.[42] Although it was normal to

[41] Thomas Kranidas, *The Fierce Equation: A Study of Milton's Decorum* (The Hague, 1965), p. 123.

[42] It is something of a tradition to refuse a name for someone you hate. Deiphobus does not refer directly to Helen, cause of his death, in *Aeneid* 6. 511. Nor does Horace mention Cleopatra in the ode celebrating her defeat at Actium

plan terrestrial strategy on the bases of force or guile, Satan's campaign against Deity is abnormal and demands extraordinary thought. But his "eternal War" calls forth from the fiend only tired platitudes about military conduct that reveal how much Satan is a prisoner of formulas.

Milton concentrates so pointedly upon these particular resources because they were two of the most important categories of thought in our Western tradition. They annoyed Milton, but he had to deal with them. Ever since Polyphemos' brothers stood outside his cave and asked, "Is someone trying to kill you by trickery (δόλῳ) or by force" (βίηφιν, *Odyssey* 9. 406), writers had weighed these options. Whether an author selects one or the other tactic depends upon his evaluation of man's essential nature. If we are primarily mind, then fraud is vital (albeit dangerous) during conflict; if humans are predominantly body, then force is the weapon of choice. *Dolos* and *bia* or their equivalents form an unsavory partnership in literature after Homer and before military theorists seize upon them in the Renaissance.

While the early debate was largely a Roman one, there were thinking men before Virgil. In Hesiod's *Theogony*, Zeus defeats tricksters like Cronos as well as brutes like the Titans, thereby reassuring readers that law inevitably triumphs over deceit and raw power. Sophocles bases much of *Philoctetes* upon their merits and Xenophon has the young Cyrus grudgingly accept them both as necessary weapons (*Cyropaedia* 1. 6. 27-43). But, quite obviously, they invade more of Virgil, Milton's only ancient rival in epic ratiocination. Aeneas' comrade Coroebus cynically demands, "During war, who would ask 'trickery' or 'bravery' " (*dolus an virtus. Aeneid* 2. 390) and presents alternatives with which the author wrestles. Certainly, Virgil admits the stratagem of the Trojan horse brings low those whom Ajax, Achilles, and a thousand ships could not conquer (2. 195-98). Sometimes, as with the harpy Celaeno, Aeneas finds it

---

(*Odes* 1. 37). Nor can the damned call God by name in Dante's *Inferno*. "Charles I" does not name Cromwell, Pym, or Fairfax in *Eikon Basilike* either.

wiser to abandon weapons and employ prayers (*armis . . . votis*. 3. 259-61). Othertimes, he assures a stranger like Charon that he has foresaken all means of assault, both *insidiae* and *vim* (6. 399-400), in order to secure trust. The last third of Virgil's epic considers this deceit / valor topic. For example, Mezentius, the fiery atheist, wins not by stealth but by strength of arms (*furto . . . fortibus armis*. 10. 734-35) and Turnus scoffs at Drances. A prototype of Belial, Drances jabbers on in wordy speeches while war requires action.[43]

Although Virgil frequently refers to guile and power, he leaves unanswered the question of which is preferable. True to his own humaneness, he knows that they coexist in the dark work of war but sponsors other values. He urges us to set aside any hasty approval for either Ulysses, the ready liar (*fandi fictor*. 9. 602), or Turnus, the headstrong brawler who vows to fight by day and not use Greek treachery by night (9. 150 ff). Virgil offers Aeneas as a model for men in society to emulate since the ancestor of all Romans combines justice with military ability (11. 124-26), piety with martial skill (11. 289 ff). Mental and physical perfections must unite so that civilization can triumph. As Lucretius knew, any animal who wishes to survive must possess cunning and hardihood (*dolus aut virtus*. *De Rerum Natura* 5. 858). But for men, especially Romans chosen to war down the arrogant and legislate to a world community, the negative alternatives had limited utility, and then during war, a tragic aberration in the continuum of our lives. Even when demanded by fate, a decision between *dolus* or *virtus* lacks decency. Virgil recognized their utility but resented their presence. They showed human capacity for a stumble down what later writers called the ladder of being. As Cicero says,

> Injustice fights with two weapons, force and fraud [*aut vi aut fraude*]; fraud suggests the mean little fox; force, the lion. Both are unworthy of man, but fraud is the more detestable. The most criminal injustice is that of the hypo-

[43] For a suggestion that Belial is based upon Drances, see E. C. Baldwin, "An Instance of Milton's Debt to Vergil," *JEGP*, 7 (1908), 85-86.

crite who hides an act of treachery under the cloak of virtue.[44]

Most Romans, perhaps aware of their own empire's awesome capacity for destruction, warned against pure strength or untempered intellect. Each had fearful consequences when met in some rebel with a depraved soul like Catiline (Sallust, *Conspiracy of Catiline* 5. 1). And one without the other unbalances the possessor. Horace warns, brute force (*vis*) bereft of wisdom (*consili*) falls of its own weight (*Odes* 3. 4. 65-67). At the other extreme, cunning alone is deplorable. Livy pictures some old senators in 172 B.C. when they reflect that earlier, more decent generations had won wars without *insidias*.[45] As an armchair general, Livy admits the advantage of both expedients, but as a moralist he usually associates them with enemies. For instance, Livy justifies a slaughter of Sicilians in 214 B.C. since the Roman commander knows that Hennians are people "from whom we may fear force or fraud" (*aut vis aut fraus*. 24. 38. 7). Later, in 210 B.C., the Carthaginian Hanno becomes jealous of his subordinate, the Numidian Muttines, and sums up personal envy in military terms: "neither armed force [of the Romans] nor any of their stratagy could interdict" Muttines (*ni aut arte ulla*. 26. 40. 4).

Silius Italicus echoes Livy's disdain for the two choices since he knows that "war calls for strategy: valour is less praiseworthy in a commander."[46] A good warrior like Xanthippus combines sword work with stratagem (6. 307). However slight the grasp on poetry Silius may display, he understands Roman morality. He dislikes treachery and associates it with the Cartha-

---

[44] *De Officiis* 1. 13. Tr. George B. Gardiner in *The Basic Works of Cicero*, ed. Moses Hadas (New York, 1951), pp. 19-20. There is a similar distinction made by Aristotle in *Nichomachean Ethics* 7. 1.

[45] 42. 47. 5 ff. Diodorus Siculus 30. 7. 1. tells how the Roman envoys outwitted Perseus and reported their triumph to the Senate. While some new members were elated, older senators were displeased. Romans should not copy Carthaginians. The high-minded sons of Romulus should not overcome with knavery but with bravery.

[46] *Punica* 5. 100. Loeb *Silius*, 1: 240.

ginians. After one battle Hannibal escapes from Fabius by tying torches to the horns of cattle. The *Punica* condemns rather than commends this trick, saying that the victor of Trebia and Trasimene has degenerated into a mere escape artist (7. 311). Silius blithely neglects to mention that the Roman victor Scipio Africanus the Younger had, like Gideon and Hannibal, also frightened his foe at night by a similar ruse with torches (Appian, *Roman History* 8. 15. 101), a convenient lapse of military memory for one composing moralized history.

A fear of frenzy underlies the Roman hesitancy about *dolus an virtus*. Citizens of *Roma Aeterna* prided themselves (at least officially) on their self-restraint. Polybius appreciated the rigid discipline that became a commonplace when discussing Rome's militia. Although guile and outright daring differ greatly, an irrational experience like war could make one forget their disparity. Significantly, Ovid picks up their opposition when recounting conflict or love, two exciting but dangerous activities. In the thirteenth book of the *Metamorphoses*, Ajax contends bitterly with Ulysses for possession of Achilles' armor. Embodying raw force, Ajax gives no credit to a man of "deceits and duplicity" (*furtisque et fraude*, p. 32). Ulysses' reply predictably degrades *vis*. "If," he says in a memorable adunaton, "I should stop working for your victory, Simois will flow backward and Mt. Ida stand without foliage and Achaians will aid Troy sooner than stupid Ajax's talent be of real advantage to the Greeks" (324-27). Ulysses' concluding remarks justify his credo that "a fighter is lower than a thinker" (354). Crafty Ulysses wins this debate and Ajax kills himself. Since Ovid inherited the tale, and since he was not overly concerned with ethical presuppositions, the reader should not impute irony to the scene—Ulysses, after all, is not favorable to the ancestors of Rome—but rather note that an *agon* of cunning versus strength occurs after a bloody war and before a suicide.

Similarly, Ovid uses the opposition in a tale of seduction. Inflamed by lust for Cydippe, Acontius threatens her, "if arts don't win, I'll resort to arms" (*artes . . . arma. Heroides* 20. 47). She picks up the choices in her reply: "If I could be won by listening to your wooing, why did you wish to force me rather than convince me" (*cogere . . . persuadere*. 21. 131-32). Highly charged scenes allowing sententious oratory attract Ovid, but he is, finally, enough of an antique Roman to know that at the dark end of time, during the Iron Age, modesty and truth and fidelity deserted earth. In their place, he says, came duplicity, double dealing, trickery, and violence (*fraudesque dolusque/ insidiaeque et vis*. *Metamorphoses* 1. 127-32).

If Romans were pressed to choose one of the two, they felt obliged to select open war. Tydeus stands "like a strong tower" against fifty ambushers. With justifiable ebullience he brags that his courage alone overcame "violence (*vim*), night treachery, weapons, deceit (*dolos*)" (Statius, *Thebaid* 3. 341 ff). In his *Gallic War*, Caesar indulges in romantic primitivism at least twice. He quotes Divico, leader of the Helvetians, who promises to stand up to Caesar since his people have learned from their ancestors how to fight with bravery rather than tricks and schemes (*virtute . . . dolo aut insidiis*. 1. 13). Similarly Vercingetorix, Caesar's most gallant opponent, promises to wrest power from the Roman by victory, not treachery (*victoria . . . proditionem*. 7. 21). Although the *Commentaries* are notable for saying what Romans wished to hear from their representative on the frontier of civilization, these two foreigners sum up the best that Rome preached: war is necessary; dissimulation and courage are weapons; both are used; but it is preferable to employ open bravery alone.

The Middle Ages agreed with this noble prescript. St. Jerome sets his eyes on heavenly things and calls *dolus an virtus, quis in hoste requirat "sententia saecularis"* (*In Ezekiel* 17. 19). By and large, the *agon* was translated into its most positive form: is body or mind more efficacious in securing an upright life? Seen primarily as agents for good, they reappear in various forms. Discussions of the *via activa* versus the *via contemplativa*, Leah or Rachel and Martha or Mary betray the ancient rivalry. Surviving well into the Renaissance, the positive aspects of force and fraud animate Michelangelo's tombs for the Medici at San Lorenzo in Florence and the many pictures of

Hercules' Choice. Milton's own "L'Allegro" and "Il Pensoroso" descend from the debate. So do the *topoi* assembled by Ernst Robert Curtius: young heroes or old, strong or wise rulers, chivalry or scholarship and (to give a pedigree for Rubens' picture that opened this book) Mars or the Muses.[47] Until the late Middle Ages, *fortitudo* and *sapientia* were generally free from their military connotation. Chaucer's Knight is "worthy" and "wys"—brave and (not tricky or sly but) prudent (*Canterbury Tales*, "General Prologue," 68).

The fourteenth century, however, contains linguistic evidence that a new worldliness was creeping into Western thought. Dante restates the categories of Aristotle and Cicero without any hint they are valuable military devices that should be given some credit. Prosaically but pointedly, Virgilio explains the arrangement of Inferno to Dante the pilgrim:

> Every kind of wickedness that gains the hatred of Heaven has injustice for its end, and every such end afflicts someone either by force or fraud [*o con forza o con frode*]; but because fraud is a sin peculiar to man it is more offensive to God, and for that reason the fraudulent have their place lower and more pain assails them. All the first circle is of the violent.[48]

About the time of Dante's birth, though, Laȝamon proves that the cyclopes' alternatives had arrived on English soil without their continental moral associations. Merlin cheers up King Arthur, who is worried about moving colossal stones from a far country, by praising the hero who has been sent: "Hit wes ȝare iqueðen þat betere is liste þene ufel strenðe" (*Brut* 8589-90: It was formerly said that his cunning is better than evil strength). The Wife of Bath recognizes their efficacy when she chortles about her five husbands,

> And thus of o thyng I avaunte me,
> Atte ende I hadde the bettre in ech degree,

---

[47] *European Literature and the Latin Middle Ages*, tr. Willard R. Trask (New York, 1963), pp. 167-79.

[48] *Inferno* 11. 22-28. Tr. John D. Sinclair (Oxford, 1948), p. 145.

> By sleighte, or force.
> (*Canterbury Tales*, "Wife's Prologue," 403-405)

Not two centuries after Dante, a fellow Florentine, perhaps listening more to the plump Wife than Beatrice, describes the qualities of an ideal prince and prepares the way for Milton's Satan. Machiavelli revives the animal metaphor of Cicero but empties it of morality:

> So you must know that there are two ways to fight, by laws and by force [*leggi . . . forza*]. The first is man's, the second the way of wild animals. But since this first method often is not enough, you must repair to the second. Therefore a prince should understand how to use both beast and man. . . . One without the other is not permanent.
>
> Obligated as a prince is to know the beasts, he should imitate the fox and the lion. The lion, you see, cannot protect himself from traps and the fox is defenceless against wolves.[49]

Machiavelli offers to Milton's great-grandparents the same traits that Cicero had thought "unjust" and that Dante had called "sins"—only he christens them *virtù* that will protect the wielder against *fortuna*. More's *Utopia* spells out how the verdict had changed from Roman and medieval condemnation to Renaissance approval. After a look backward to absolute morality ("War, as an activity fit only for beasts and yet practiced by no kind of beast so constantly as by man, they regard with utter loathing"),[50] More previews the coming ethics of expedience:

> If they overcome and crush the enemy by stratagem and cunning, they feel great pride and celebrate a public triumph over the victory and put up a trophy as for a strenuous exploit. They boast themselves as having acted with valor and heroism whenever their victory is such as no animal as man could have won, that is, by strength of intellect; for, by strength of body, say they, bears, lions,

---

[49] *Il Principe*, Chap. 18, my translation.
[50] Thomas More, *Utopia*, ed. Edward Surtz (New Haven, 1964), p. 118. The next quotation is from p. 120.

boars, wolves, dogs, and other wild beasts are wont to fight. Most of them are superior to us in brawn and fierceness, but they are all inferior in cleverness and calculation.

Whatever lies behind this new approval of chicanery, whether exaltation of mind, distaste for animalism, revaluation of earthly life, or simple thrift during war, the previous strictures fade. Although classically educated and religiously principled, More reanimates for his reader the worst that the ancient world offered as moral guidance. Instead of resurrecting a dictum from some rational saint, he dignifies the memory of a scoundrel like Lysander who, as Plutarch paints him, was "unscrupulous, cunning, a trickster in war. . . . He ridiculed anyone urging that Herakles' descendants should not use deceit [δόλου] in war: "Patch a skimpy lion's skin with a fox's" (*Lysander*, 7).

Understandably, military writers in the later sixteenth and seventeenth centuries discuss force (or might, strength, etc.) and fraud (or policy,[51] sleight, cunning, stratagem, and the like) as their own possession. The oppressively moral Leighton dictates: "let this position take place without controversie, *That stratagems are both lawfull and necessary*; neither doe they (being lawfully used) deserue the name of deceit" (*Speculum*, p. 133). Sutcliffe praises cunning in a general. He "cannot without some griefe remember" how the French succeeded in capturing parts of Normandy "not with dint of sword, nor open force, but with secret practices" (*Practice*, p. 30). Taught by realpolitik, he concedes,

> Many doe more matters by sleight, then by force. Charles the fifth of France did more represse the force of the English nation by practice, then by force. The Lacedemonians when their leaders preuailed against their enemies by counsell and stratagemes, sacrificed an oxe; when by open force, a cocke onely. (p. 39)

[51] A specialized study of this word by N. W. Bawcutt is "Policy, Machiavellianism, and the Earlier Tudor Drama," *ELR*, 1 (1971), 195-209.

No matter what a man's civilian desires, his survival in war depends upon fact. Thus, without railing at universal injustice, Sutcliffe calmly states that "places are taken either . . . by intelligence, and trechery, or els by force" (p. 242). With a burst of British decency, Sutcliffe attempts to hedge about the seamy use of *dolus*:

> whatsoeuer tendeth to deceiue, and abuse the enemy, or to incourage, & giue aduantage to our own souldiers; the same ought wise leaders to deuise, & practice. Prouided alway, that they neither breake othe, nor promise nor offend against piety, or the lawes of nations. Let such vile facts be practiced of Turks, & Spaniards. (p. 196)

Late Renaissance war writers accept policy with disheartening ease. Richard Bernard begins *The Bible-Battells* by piously reminding his readers of their recent escapes from foreign domination: "Miraculous deliverances *we haue had. . . . And what still maintaines it?* Power or Policie *of man? No, no such thing; but the hand of the* Almightie" ("To the Reader"). Once launched upon his treatise, however, Bernard goes beyond Machiavelli. "Courage and strength hath gotten many a glorious day," he notes, "but policie hath the preheminence" (p. 103). One who wishes to fight a good fight should not neglect

> To vse stratagems, so did *Iosua* ; yea the Lord himself . . . : by stratagems *Hannibal* and *Scanderbeg* preuailed mightily, for inventing whereof they both were very subtle. But stratagems must bee such as are not to the breach of oath, against godlinesse, against the law of nature and nations. (pp. 197-98)

Likewise Henry Hexham, having observed the face of war in Holland, agrees with Machiavelli: a general "may vanquish, aswell by *Policie* . . . as by *force*, by pulling on the *Foxes* skin, aswell as the *Lyons*."[52] Perhaps Robert Ward, that most literate

---

[52] *The Second Part of the Principles, of the Art Militarie Practized in the Warres of the United Provinces* (London, 1638), p. 12. Subsequently cited in the text as *Principles II*. My sons Matthew and Eric generously treated me to a

of commentators, best proves how late Renaissance writers for-
got ethics when they discussed tactics. He inserts into his chap-
ter on valor a jingle—

> A Souldiers honour shines as bright
> In politique Conquest, as in bloudy fight.
> (Anima'dversions, p. 180)

and appends a catalogue of "Politique Stratagems" since they
"haue been the immediate means next under the providence of
God, to gaine victories enervating and weakning an enemy" (p.
321). The long advance of that grim duo, force and fraud, ends
at Milton's own doorstep. His friend Henry Lawrence urges
men to thank God's angels for helping the Puritans win their
Civil War. These holy agents, Lawrence reminds us, "by
stratagems, and methods, as well as by fine force, contributed
exceedingly" (History, Sig. *₂ᵛ). Encouraged by humanists and
pragmatists, unwearied by Roman or Christian jibes,
"methods" and "fine force" had reason to expect a cordial re-
ception from Milton.

Milton knows how much pressure this tradition exerts. Yet
very early he displays an out-of-fashion strictness by associat-
ing both *dolus* and *vis* with *caedes* (murder) and the Titans' re-
volt (El 5. 39-40). He also imagines a lurid horde surrounding
Dolus in "The Fifth of November": "Murder, double-tongued
Treason, . . . Discord, . . . Calumny, . . . Fury, . . . Fear, . . .
Horror" and Roman Catholic envy (139-56). *Prolusion* 1 has a
similar gaggle of night-crawlers. Obviously, Milton responds to
melodramatic passages in writers like Cicero and Valerius Flac-
cus rather than to encomia of craft's utility in the military
writers we've just noted. Even after Milton cons martial texts in
the forties, he still treats force and fraud as an abomination. It is
a two-handed engine used, so far as he can see, only for destruc-
tion. His political writings often conjure up the unholy pair,

---

movie one rainy afternoon and showed me that this tradition persists. In Walt
Disney's *The Mark of Zorro* (1958), the hero calls himself "fox" (*zorro*) since
his enemy has the strength of a lion. Here, too, cleverness triumphs, but in a
good cause.

usually in passages such as this which recounts the "blessings" of life under Charles:

> This with the power of the Militia in his own hands over our bodies and estates, and the Prelats to enthrall our consciences either by fraud or force, is the sum of that happiness and liberty we were to look for. (*Eikon* 27. C.E. 5. 288)

The two appear here and elsewhere as servants of military and ecclesiastical tyranny, fit inhabitants of a bygone iron age. *Eikonoklastes* also reanimates them in their animal shapes when it talks of declination from fighting to undermining, violence to craft, lions to foxes (18. C.E. 5. 235).

By the time of *Paradise Lost*, Milton's censure is more subtle. He skillfully weaves together Christian and classical strands so that his extended discussion of force and fraud both echoes and modifies prototypes. The narrator first introduces Satan as a trickster by using familiar Christian terms:

> Th' infernal Serpent; hee it was, whose guile
> Stirr'd up with Envy and Revenge, deceiv'd
> The Mother of Mankind; what time his Pride
> Had cast him out from Heav'n, with all his Host
> Of Rebel Angels.
>
> (1. 34-38)

These lines condition us to expect a completely orthodox devil. Words like "Serpent . . . guile . . . Envy . . . Revenge . . . Mother of Mankind . . . Pride . . . Heav'n . . . Rebel Angels" draw upon Genesis, Revelation, and a host of Biblical commentaries to lull us into pious anticipation of yet another sacred paraphrase. This first description gives little hint how much the secular motif of "guile" will emerge since the vocabulary is so traditional. Listen to a translation of Augustine on the Fall:

> That proud and therefore envious angel . . . fell from the spiritual Paradise, and essaying to insinuate his persuasive guile into the mind of man . . . chose the serpent as his

mouthpiece in that bodily Paradise . . . and first tried his
deceit on the woman.[53]

Augustine sounds much like the narrator of *Paradise Lost*. Yet
Satan's first words apprise us that pagan as well as Christian
terms will energize his new portrait: "O how fall'n! how
chang'd" (1. 84) conflates words from Aeneas when he recog-
nizes the gory shade of Hector and those of Isaiah when he pon-
ders the fall of Babylon's proud king.[54] As with the Proem, so
with the entire epic: secular ideas and Christian exist symbioti-
cally.

Satan's many subsequent references to the force and fraud
question have little biblical authority. Their very profaneness
reminds us how inappropriate they are for a being who was next
to pure godhead. The nervous stratagems of unhallowed strug-
gle should be superfluous to anyone who realizes his felicity.
Repeatedly we see that the discussion, so modish after
Machiavelli, is literally devilish. It degrades the mystery of
being an angel to another bout between Ajax and Ulysses, im-
portant, perhaps, in certain situations, but scarcely resplendent
with noumenal grandeur. Consider how Satan boasts of his in-
tellect. Their late defeat, asserts Satan, was the result of God's
strength alone:

> fardest from him is best
> Whom reason hath equall'd, force hath made supreme
> Above his equals.
>
> (1. 247-49)

But when Satan harangues the infernal army, he gives a differ-
ent excuse for the defeat. He whines that his vaunted "reason"
was unequal to the task of challenging God.

> what power of mind
> Foreseeing or presaging, from the Depth
> Of knowledge past or present, could have fear'd

[53] *The City of God* 14. 11. Tr. Marcus Dods (New York, 1950), p. 458.
[54] John M. Steadman, "The Quantum Mutatus Theme and the Fall," *Ameri-
can Notes and Queries*, 2 (1964), 83.

> How such united force of Gods, how such
> As stood like these, could ever know repulse?
> (1. 626-30)

His conceit demands that he find some warrant for their failure on the field. Yet he does not suspect that "knowledge" and "force" may be partial labels for a totality of divine efficacy. He separates them as if they were merely means to victory rather than attributes of an achieved phenomenon. Satan concludes that God has the more powerful brigades and feels compelled to prolong the war by trickery:

> our better part remains
> To work in close design, by fraud or guile
> What force effected not: that he no less
> At length from us may find, who overcomes
> By force, hath overcome but half his foe.[55]

This reliance upon the mind draws less from Renaissance idealism than from medieval Manichaeanism. Satan perceives a radical discontinuity between physical and mental operations. At this early point in the poem, we are likely to accept his dualistic pattern without question. But by the time we have learned from Raphael that all in our universe is some form of "one first matter" (5. 469 ff), we must reject Satan's simplistic and divisive model.

Since Satan does not intuit the truth immediately like an angel, he must search after it like a befuddled human. Already enslaved by his vaulting ambition, he bows his head to the common order of military texts concerning the need for a staff meeting to plan campaigns. One small leader may see farther, the theory goes, if he clambers upon the backs of guides: "A generall also ought to take the graue sage Councill and wise ad-

---

[55] 1. 645-49. There may be a nasty echo of Jesus' words to Martha in Luke 10:42: "But one thing is needful and Mary hath chosen that good part, which shall not be taken away from her." Note that Satan uses the word "fraud," which explained how Solomon was deceived (1. 401), and "guile," which the narrator used to describe Satan. These repetitions have a cumulative effect akin to that produced by refrains in other forms of verse.

vice, of his chiefes, and commandours" (Hexham, *Principles II*, p. 12). However, the Great Consult is as narcissistic a gesture as Eve's gazing into water, since Satan has decided in advance to carry on furtive guerrilla operations. (Previously "he assembl'd all his Train" in Heaven, "Pretending . . . to consult." 5. 767-68.) He speaks deceptively to his staff as if they still have the traditional option between weapons and wiliness:

> by what best way,
> Whether of open War or covert guile,
> We now debate.
>
> (2. 40-42)

Each speaker makes his recommendation. Moloch, the rash militarist, "is for open War" (2. 51 ff). Like Ovid's Ajax, he claims to be "unexpert" in "wiles" and scornful of those who "sit contriving." Belial opts out of the choice. He attempts to substitute an alternate mode of perceiving their experience. Like all his compeers, he does not understand the eternality of their situation. He speaks as if the rebellion were a disturbance with no permanent consequence. God, he asserts, may change his mind and thus they should not debate the force and fraud alternative. Sensibly enough, Belial claims that deity holds the initiative:

> War therefore, open or conceal'd, alike
> My voice dissuades; for what can force or guile
> With him, or who deceive his mind, whose eye
> Views all things at one view?
>
> (2. 187-90)

In concert with his master's grasp of partial truths, Belial justifies his sloth by mingling facts about God's omnipotence with a fly-eye fragmentation of faculties ("voice . . . mind . . . eye"). Mammon similarly diverts energy from a crusade against Heaven to a refurbishing of Hell. He carries to their logical conclusion both Belial's remarks and Satan's "Hail horrors" speech (1. 242 ff). Mammon inconveniently imitates Satan's previous bravado (1. 263: "Better to reign in Hell, than serve in

Heav'n") and further agrees with Satan that the mind may be used to deceive. But the objects of deception are not God or the loyal angels; they are the Fiend's own followers. Having won the applause of his fellow *legati*, Mammon seems to have destroyed the assumption that there are only two responses possible in their condition.

Satan's puppet Beelzebub must bring the consult to a consummation devoutly wished by both advisors and leader. He appeals to the devils' love of ease: "What if we find / Some easier enterprise?" (2. 344-45). He also reinstates the original alternatives of power and knavery, now attractively aimed at someone other than God.

> Thither let us bend all our thoughts, to learn
> What creatures there inhabit, of what mould,
> Or substance, how endu'd, and what thir Power,
> And where thir weakness, how attempted best,
> By force or subtlety.
>
> (2. 354-58)

As Hanford says, the conquest of God's creature would be "a revenge as fierce as Moloch's by means as safe as Belial's and with a possibility of profit more rich than contemplated by Mammon."[56] Although the new enemy is unknown, Beelzebub (and presumably Satan) minimizes the possible need for flexible strategy by initiating the campaign with camp-worn alternatives.

God recognizes the satanic dualism, knowing as well as we human readers that the devil travels toward man

> with purpose to assay
> If him by force he can destroy, or worse,
> By some false guile pervert.
>
> (3. 90-92)

Satan has plunged from God's realm, where success comes from obedience, into our own world, where one must constantly sift

---

[56] James Holly Hanford, *A Milton Handbook*, 4th ed. (New York, 1946), p. 199.

alternatives. Both Father and Son share knowledge that man will "Fall circumvented thus by fraud" (3. 152) and plan accordingly to redeem him. The two persons base their plan upon providence and not, as Satan's bustling, upon suppositions. As they talk, we should understand the inadequacy of Satan's categories. Instead of a world divided like Plato's apple into "force" or "guile," God indicates that will unites the cosmos. He repeats the familiar Christian belief in a complicated hierarchic relationship between God and right reason, reason and man, man and choice, choice and responsibility. Book 3 exposes the ignorant simplicity of Satan's schema. He operates as does caricature, by translating some incidental features of a system into the key that opens all. Satan's prescription for attack thus falls from its tenable place as a military tactic in Books 1 and 2 to its inadequate low in Books 3 and after. No longer can the choice between force and fraud be honored as a comprehensive masterplan. It is, finally, an expedient for local action that may temporarily menace, but cannot alter, the all-embracing system of God.

Milton is so intent upon exploding the damnable respectability his generation imputed to force and guile that he mentions them repeatedly. As narrator he reminds us the devil was an "Artificer of fraud" (4. 121), thereby conflating the biblical "father of lies" and classical "lie forging" (*fandi fictor* of *Aeneid* 9. 602) epithets. God, too, emphasizes Satan's mendacity when he commissions Raphael to warn Adam that man will be assaulted "By violence, no, for that shall be withstood, / But by deceit and lies" (5. 242-43). True to his errand, Raphael makes clear that the rebel is an opportunist without honor. He quotes Abdiel to Adam and undercuts whatever glory might have adhered to the revolt by naming it "this perfidious fraud" (5. 880). Abdiel also articulates the lesson of the civil war when he says,

> nor is it aught but just,
> That he who in debate of Truth hath won,
> Should win in Arms, in both disputes alike
> Victor; though brutish that contest and foul,

> When Reason hath to deal with force, yet so
> Most reason is that Reason overcome.
>
> (6. 121-26)

All these voices swell in a stereophonic chorus to alert readers who may have reserved some credit for Satan. In Heaven, right makes might. There is no divorce between decent thought and potent action. Despite the simplicity of this verity, Satan repairs to his "fraud" (6. 555) of a newfangled cannon to upset the system. Even here he is drably unoriginal. The rebel in John Davies' *Civile Warres of Death and Fortune* had already boasted, "Ile make my selfe a God, with Thunder-shot."[57] And John Smith had earlier advised a leader to hide "Fielde peeces" behind his "squadrons" (*Instructions*, pp. 77-78). Satan does not understand that no duplicity can topple absolute goodness. His troops partake of his ignorance as they stand

> Insensate, hope conceiving from despair.
> In heav'nly Spirits could such perverseness dwell?
> . . . .
> They . . .
> Stood reimbattl'd fierce, by force or fraud
> Weening to prosper, and at length prevail
> Against God and *Messiah*, or to fall
> In universal ruin.
>
> (6. 787-97)

The *furor* that simmered beneath the surface of Roman history here bursts out, at once recalling and condemning zeal in earthly wars.

Raphael attempts to inform Adam that any separation of divine efficacy into *virtus* and *sapientia* is dangerous nominalism. To some extent, he succeeds. Our general Father at least grasps the possible tactics to be used against him. For her part, Eve knows that they will be stalked by a "subtle or violent" (9. 324) foe and most dreads "His fraud" (9. 285). But, as war books

---

[57] *Civile Warres of Death and Fortune* (London, 1605), p. "193," misnumbered for p. 211.

continually iterated, theory without practice is vain in military operations. Accordingly, our Parents cannot match the incarnation of "meditated fraud and malice" (9. 55). Since the husband is "for contemplation . . . and valor form'd" (4. 297), the Adversary confronts Eve. With a cunning often present in cowards, he wheedles, praises, and lies so he finally wins a duel that she never realized was taking place.

Satan convinces himself that he chose the right strategy. By lying he won, apparently, without risking himself or his army. Like a citizen of More's *Utopia*, he brags to his men as soon as he returns, "Him by fraud I have seduc'd" (10. 485). No matter that it was Eve: Adam is masculine and does fall, whatever the proximate cause, and thus Satan almost justifies his barbaric yawp. His perversions of truth, so familiar to us, should be evaluated now lest we dismiss them with no appreciation of their meaning in the epic's plan. They demonstrate that Satan has not lost all power of intellect. Unlike the stupid demons in Dante, he has cunning that easily outpaces Geryon, that beaverlike epitome of fraud, or Dis, the robotlike incarnation of infernal force. Rather, Satan conforms to the general seventeenth-century estimation of fallen angels. As Edward Fowler claims in 1680,

> they are Spirits indued with great Strength and Power, with great Knowledge, Sagacity and quickness of Understanding, and with large Dominions, though Usurped, but have lost that integrity of Nature, and those good Principles, whereby they should govern themselves, and be determined in the exercise of their Power and Wisdom[.] 'Tis certain they would be nothing so michievous and wicked as they are, if with the loss of their *Moral* endowments, they had also been divested of their *Natural*: I mean their Strength and Power, their Knowledge and Acuteness of Understanding. . . . Their great Power and Knowledge [are] . . . estranged from Righteousness and Goodness.[58]

[58] *Libertas Evangelica* (London), pp. 35-36.

In his own dry way, Fowler reauthenticates Satan's credentials. Devils are strong and smart, but without proper direction for their assets.

Satan's residual intelligence chooses to pervert the facts that it does comprehend. When first spoken, his cozening words to Eve seem to be authorized by no less a theorist than Milton himself.

> Hardly any of the ambushes or surprise-tactics common in warfare can be carried out without the telling of a great many flagrant untruths which are specifically designed to deceive. . . . Stratagems are allowable, even when they entail falsehood, because if it is not our duty to tell someone the truth, it does not matter if we lie to him whenever it is convenient. (*CD* 2. 13. C.E. 6. 761-62)

As with most moral imperatives, however, Milton's statement depends upon seeing the entire world as he does. Satan perceives a fragmented universe of hostile inhabitants who live in discontinuous space and exist (like Robinson Crusoe) merely to exploit whatever presents itself. Such a universe exalts lying. But for Milton, misrepresentation must be necessitated by more than personal advantage. He follows his defense of prevarication with an important stipulation: "The scriptural texts which are cited condemning falsehood must be understood, then, to refer to that kind of falsehood which evidently injures our neighbor or detracts from the glory of God." In short, according to Christian doctrines, we may lie, if the auditor is not a neighbor—"one with whom we are at peace, and whose lawful society we enjoy"—and if the intent is not to defile the Deity. Although Eve is certainly not Satan's neighbor, he admittedly speaks to her for the intention of assaulting God.

For once, Milton's dislike of a war trick has the support of others. John Davies of Hereford writes in 1605 that "Lady Phusis" [nature] no longer meets "Lady Aletheia" [truth]. Phusis asks "Logus" [reason] where truth has fled. Logus replies,

> She [Aletheia] wonted was (said he) to neighbour mee;
> But since that *Fraus* and *Dolus* (wicked Twinnes)
> The World produc'd, I do her seldom see.[59]

In another poem of the same year, Davies exhibits an antiquarian rectitude when he envisions honest soldiers:

> They, with right Swords, do ballance kingdomes rights;
> (A glorious office they perform the while)
> . . . .
> Yet they gaine nought but blows, in blody fights,
> So, store [of blows] they get without, or fraude, or guile;
> The while the gown-mā keeps vnscarr'd his skin,
> And with his Pen (in peace) the world doth win.

These satiric defenses of abstract truth seem puerile next to Leighton's long explanation of permissible stratagems. Leighton's reasoning quite closely parallels that of Milton when he absolutely forbids an outright lie (*"an abomination in* [God's] *sight"*). But then Leighton drifts. We are to eschew *"Synons* cogging craft" since it would lower good Protestants to the level of "the new *Synons* of Rome; the *croaking frogges,* and other Papists, who are become . . . crafts-masters in shamelesse lying, and *hellish equivocation"* that *"haue brought many massacres, treasons, and outrages to passe.* They laugh it off, and answer with their Master, *That a man must put on the Fox skin, when the Lyons will not serue."* Like Kingsley attacking Newman, Leighton loses sight of logic while he imputes all prevarication to Rome's *"hollow* fathers, fogged up with deceit." At least he does reject it, "though it were to gain *Troy,"* and thus swims with Milton against the stream of modern military opinion (*Speculum*, pp. 134-37).

Milton accomplishes several goals by using force and fraud so often. He confesses that the *topos* is nearly obligatory in combat narratives. However, he adds to his own untraditional

---

[59] *Humours Heav'n on Earth* (London), p. 36. The next quotation is from his *Civile Warres*, p. 198. These two vigorous works are bound together and use continuous pagination.

antimilitary argument when he demonstrates that the rough-
and-ready field expediency Satan chooses is a debased parody of
divine faculties. The Deity calls Christ, "my wisdom, and effec-
tual might" (3. 170), thus defining the proper union. When the
devil contemplates "fraud," he dreams of stunted "wisdom";
when he considers "force," he thinks of diminished "might."
By separating the two from each other and scheming with their
most reduced states, Satan should warn us how much his mind
has deteriorated. He can offer only a disjunctive and reduc-
tionist formula to battle God's comprehensiveness. In effect,
Satan's adherence to this staple of martial authorities helps to
weaken the moral correctness that Milton's generation auto-
matically assumed for a contest between power and cunning.

Rashness

Satan impairs his reputation as war expert by perverting the
force and fraud choice that responsible teachers like Di Porcia,
Leighton, and Ward had carefully discussed (*Preceptes of
Warre*, Sec. 11; *Speculum*, p. 133; *Anima'dversions II*, p. 15).
He completes the demolition of his status by breaking a second
rule. Contrary to the advice of almost every theorist, the Fiend
risks his own "strength" and "art" (2. 410) on the "hazard
huge" (2. 473) of attacking Earth. After Beelzebub calls for vol-
unteers, his chief swiftly claims the assignment. Satan's lunge
for glory has only a marginal excuse from writers who counsel
quick action. The free-floating maxim that Bernard offers—
"make no delay vpon good resolved grounds to execute design-
ments" (*Bible-Battells*, p. 208)—emphasizes forethought as
strongly as haste. Satan's three-day struggle in Heaven first
boosted him to prominence in military operation, but this pre-
cipitate gesture demonstrates how much he has to learn. Roger
Williams castigates his kind of leader in *A Briefe Discourse of
Warre*: "These Coronells of three dayes, marres all the Armies
of the world."[60] Most generals possess some moral flaw, Wil-

---

[60] *A Briefe Discourse of Warre* (London, 1590), p. 8.

liams continues, but he grudgingly accepts a pattern to which Satan conforms:

> if iustice were executed to the vttermost, fewe great Captains should liue. The most great Captaines cannot denie, but their profession ouer-reacheth theselues, more than any other, because al their speaches, deedes, and mindes consists in ambition for honour, seking to ouerthrow al estates, to aduance their own, weighing no perill in respect of fame. (*Discourse*, p. 17)

Warriors serve such a vital function that society must overlook the majority of their personal deficiencies. Yet writers go on from this premise: the ruler is under a special obligation to preserve himself. Styward mingles contempt with fear as he describes a general who

> is so ignoraunt, arrogant, and couetous, that beleeueth not to doe anie thing honourablie, except hee fighteth himselfe is not to be thought, but rather presumptuous and foolish hardie, and he that will hazard his life to gette him a name of the multitude, whereby to putte those waightie affaires in perill, is uerie unmeete for such a charge. (*Pathwaie*, p. 138)

Even if Satan's other sins could escape whipping, his "foolish hardie" rashness must be condemned. He identifies his own personal vendetta as paramount and involves others to pursue it. Any war thinker would reject his facile excuse of "public reason just" (4. 389) since wounded vanity and fear of being supplanted goad Satan. Francis Markham patiently explains why an impetuous commandant must restrain his last infirmity:

> he ought to haue a principall regard of his owne safetie; for Generals when too freely they thrust themselues into dangers, are not carelesse of their owne but of the health of the Armie, and the trespasse is made against the publique, when any rashnesse hales the priuate into danger; let him

therefore only outbraue danger not wooe it. (*Epistles of Warre*, p. 200)

Although Satan's speeches promulgate an organic theory of society, his acts prove that he cannot subordinate himself to any external cause. When militarists debate "Whether a great Prince [should] make warre in person, or by his Lieutenant" (Rohan, *Treatise*, p. 180), they sometimes cite cases where "Generals and Princes themselues" "haue adventured their liues." Leighton (who is speaking) recalls the boldness of "*Saladine, Sultain* of Egipt" and "*Francis Sforcia, Duke of Millain.*" But such behavior is culpable: "to clear those attempts in such personages of temerity, will not stand" (*Speculum*, p. 122). Sutcliffe too calls the impulsiveness of a general "great temeritie" (*Practice*, p. 40). Even when a group's leader happens to be its best fighter, manuals like Gervase Markham's *Second Part of the Soldiers Grammar* warn such talented individuals "not . . . to imbarque themselues into the danger of the Warres."[61] Since the power of Hell is so completely vested in one individual, Satan's behavior jeopardizes an entire group. James I patiently explains to his son why kings cannot indulge in personal combat with the enemy. ΒΑΣΙΛΙΚΟΝ ΔΩΡΟΝ reasons

> that all Duell appeareth to bee vnlawfull, committing the quarrel, as it were, to a lot, whereof there is no warrant in the Scripture, since the abrogating of the old Lawe: it is specially most vnlawful in the person of a King: who being a publike person hath no power therefore to dispose of himselfe, in respect, that to his preseruation or fall, the safetie or wracke of the whole common-weale is necessarilie coupled, as the bodie is to the head.[62]

Satan's monomania overrides this caution from a fellow monarch, at once compromising his safety and the destiny of

---

[61] *Second Part of the Soldiers Grammar* (London, 1627), p. 9. (Cited as *Grammar II.*)
[62] ΒΑΣΙΛΙΚΟΝ ΔΩΡΟΝ (London, 1603), pp. 57-58.

his followers. Stubborn and solipsistic, he scorns God's law and war writer's repeated advice, "A Generall over an Army, must be . . . not rash in undertaking" (Ward, *Anima'dversions II*, p. 1).

Satan's disregard of this basic rule should be isolated from his local success. He does deal competently with threats like those of Death, Chaos, and Uriel. Likewise, he insinuates himself into Paradise by means of a fountain (9. 75), thereby imitating the suitable ruse of Cyrus, who "entred Babylon by the riuer" (Sutcliffe, *Practice*, p. 226 mentions other tricksters who "had good hap to enter Townes by wayes not suspect"). These and other small victories fuel the familiar debate: can morally vicious people be good commanders? Ovid is one of the first to claim that unjust rulers like Tarquin can be superb soldiers (*Fasti* 2. 688), and the Renaissance did not lack other set examples. Garrard and Hichcock stretch their point about the need for impartial army regulations by citing villains like Sardanapalus, Cyrus, and Cambyses, each of whom had been personally cruel but, when acting as judge in camp, displayed fairness and therefore won his men's respect (*Arte of Warre*, p. 32). Most theorists, however, could not tolerate the unnatural prospect of an infected tree bringing forth good fruit. Leighton belabors the monstrous assertion about Sardanapalus and Nero in *Speculum Sacri Belli* since bad leaders corrupt subjects. His words resemble those of Milton defining a true poet: "he must be a good man before he be a good and acceptable souldyer to God" (p. 24). Richard Bernard seconds this ethical prescription by admitting how some scoundrels may have been efficient soldiers but would have been better had they been true Christians: "Let not the roaring boyes, the Machavilian Athiests, the prophane *Esaus*, the drunken sonnes of *Bacchus*, the blasphemous swearers, nor the filthy Adulterers laugh at this" (*Bible-Battells*, p. 79). Both these war writers and Milton share the assumption that good and evil, no matter how mixed in practice, are mutually exclusive entities. No one can mingle them, not even a fallen angel who vows to interchange them ("Evil be thou my Good," 4. 110). Polluted fountains and degenerate creatures, according to this postulate, cannot nourish those who turn to them. When we wedge Satan between the obvious facts that he risks himself and that he is evil, we have sufficient intellectual leverage to crush his preeminence in war.

Picturability

If so many martial commonplaces prove that Satan fails, then why do readers view him as heroic? I suggest part of the answer is visual. *Paradise Lost* pictures Satan as a defeated soldier, but one who still leads. Whether or not Milton read technical treatises on painting, Leonardo's advice about the proper way to portray losers in battle is instructive:

> You must make the conquered and beaten pale, their brows raised and knit, and the skin above their brows furrowed with pain, the sides of the nose with wrinkles going in an arch from the nostrils drawn up . . . , and the lips arched upwards and discovering the upper teeth; and the teeth apart as with crying out and lamentation.[63]

Superficially, Satan conforms to this precept:

> his face
> Deep scars of Thunder had intrencht, and care
> Sat on his faded cheek
>
> (1. 600-602)

Yet, having aroused the reader's expectation for a conventional description of the common subject, "A Beaten Warrior," and having perhaps reminded himself of academic battle scenes such as Vasari's in the Great Hall of the Palazzo Vecchio at Florence, Milton shocks us. Care does sit on his Devil's pale cheek,

> but under Brows
> Of dauntless courage, and considerate Pride
> Waiting revenge: cruel his eye, but cast

[63] Leonardo Da Vinci, *The Notebooks*, ed. Jean Paul Richter (1884, rpt. New York, 1970), 1: 302-303.

> Signs of remorse and passion to behold
> The fellows of his crime.
>
> (1. 602-606)

This fiend is neither a woolly monstrosity, incapable of arousing much besides disgust, nor is he merely a failed fighter who could, at best, educe some pity. Rather he is commanding. Defeat, care, courage, pride, vengefulness, cruelty, remorse, passion—all announce their presence on his visage. Obviously, literature can impute more traits to a character than can a plastic art. Yet the reader capable of receiving eidetic information thinks he has been invited to view a commonplace subject and then realizes he has been introduced to a very complex subject. Although Satan has been beaten, he manages to control both his men and, during public appearances, himself. He is light years away from the static beasts in Italian art, more palpable than the abstract creature of biblical detestation and a paradox to art experts who expect a vanquished general to lose all control.

Whether Satan is alone or in company, his complicated expressions legitimatize his role as chief. After meditating on the sun,

> each passion dimm'd his face,
> Thrice chang'd with pale, ire, envy and despair,
> Which marr'd his borrow'd visage. . . .
> . . . Whereof hee soon aware,
> Each perturbation smooth'd with outward calm.
>
> (4. 114-20)

Satan tames these powerful emotions, any one of which would incapacitate a human, so that he may continue his intelligence gathering. Following a tradition of baroque expression, perhaps, Satan ogles, glares, and grimaces when struck by novelty. Seeing Adam and Eve embrace, he "turn'd / For envy, yet with jealous leer malign / Ey'd them askance" (4. 502-504). He replies to Abdiel's challenge "with scornful eye askance" (6. 149), thus duplicating in open his wonted private contortions. (Satan here may not be losing control so much as he may be following the advice William Segar gives to a duelist in *The Booke of Honor*, Book 5, second page: "He should be of bold aspect, rather inclined to seuertitie than softness: which countenance the *Swisses* and *Turkes* doo much affect.") Usually, though, Satan controls his personal expression so that viewers have no hint that his appearance and nature are not congruent. To Nisroch, who asks for a better weapon to assault God, Satan answers "with look compos'd" (6. 469), although he logically should be bursting with eagerness to reveal his new invention, the cannon. Despite seeing Eve and being momentarily dissuaded from his military purpose—Satan "for the time remain'd / Stupidly good, of enmity disarm'd, / Of guile, of hate, of envy, of revenge" (9. 464-66)—he overcomes his "abstracted" state: "then soon / Fierce hate he recollects, and all his thoughts / Of mischief, gratulating, thus excites" (9. 470-72). Although victimized by violent internal pressure, the king of Hell subdues his features so that they further his desired image.

Satan cooperates both with dictates of art and the demands of military writers who tell a true leader to check inappropriate expressions that might jeopardize effective rule. The Lord of Praissac explains why Satan's victories over his own features may arouse our respect: "Good successes or bad should not make him [a perfect general] change countenance, but to receiue both modestly, without discouering the passions of his soul by his countenance" (*The Art of Warre*, p. 149). Other war advisors agree. Barry even suggests that a sentry will be more effective if, when he receives no answer to his challenge, he displays "furiouse" faces (*A Discourse*, p. 50). Satan's self-management makes him the direct ancestor of England's great commander, Sir Thomas Fairfax. Joshua Sprigge evaluates this "Captain-General of all the Parliaments Forces" at the end of *Anglia Rediviva* by noting, "He never discovered passions abroad in counsels or actions, what he had at home in himself, he (not others) knew; and this was of advantage, both to what was advised and what was done."[64] Ostensibly, Hell's

[64] *Anglia Rediviva* (London, 1647), p. 321.

"Captain-General" lives up to his boast that soldiers create themselves. Since the governance of Heaven, which is based on reality, denies him celebrity status, Satan casts himself as the leading warmaker in a drama he hopes to direct. He knows, as does Matthew Sutcliffe, that in *"warres . . . souldiers are the principall actors"* (*Practice*, Sig. C2ᵛ).

Satan's final appearance on the infernal stage recalls his theatrical behavior. He again dominates his followers as they crowd about him eager to hear of his guerrilla campaign. As usual, he manipulates them: "with hand / Silence, and with these words attention won" (10. 458-59). In his own mind, he is completing for his crew the mission to which "His count'nance . . . allur'd them" (5. 708-709). Satan also feels he is finally duplicating the "calm aspect and clear" (5. 733) that identifies the Son's public posture. But this memory of Satan as a poised orator is only the penultimate one. Milton emphasizes Satan's climactic loss of self-control. Instead of the "high applause" he had anticipated from his troops for his "performance" (10. 505, 502), Satan hears a curious hissing sound.

> he wonder'd, but not long
> Had leisure, wond'ring at himself now more;
> His Visage drawn he felt to sharp and spare,
> His Arms clung to his Ribs, his Legs entwining
> Each other, till supplanted down he fell
> A monstrous Serpent on his Belly prone,
> Reluctant, but in vain: a greater power
> Now rul'd him, punisht in the shape he sinn'd,
> According to his doom: he would have spoke,
> But hiss for hiss return'd with fork'd tongue.
> (10. 509-18)

With superb visual irony, Milton shatters the icon that he has carefully sustained throughout the preceding portions of his poem. He completes a great artistic circle to relieve anyone who feared that Satan's guises as a sea serpent "Prone on the Flood" (1. 195) and a snake in the Garden were only temporary and his generalship permanent. Satan ends where he began, deep in

Hell. *Katabasis* follows *anabasis*, impotence trails impertinence and unmasking comes after acting. Milton rips from Satan's viperish face the mask of self-control that he had assumed. God allowed him to control his tears and emotions temporarily, but Satan was always a reptile. When his career ends in Book 10, the role of commander has fulfilled our visual expectation, reminded us that evil is mutable and yet not contradicted Satan's essential character as abhorred serpent. If we pay proper attention to the sequence of attitudes that Satan exhibits, then we can correctly say he degenerates visually as well as morally.

IV

WAR IN UNEXPECTED PLACES

Once a reader hears how many changes Milton rings upon the theme of war in *Paradise Lost*, he is prepared to read the epic backward. Knowing how many allusions to reprobate spirits are martial, he can examine other passages that seem untouched by Milton's vigorous quarrel with militarism.

Book 1: The Bee Simile

A good example is the famous bee simile that concludes Book 1. This comparison between Satan's soldiers milling about Pandaemonium and a swarm of spring bees should affect everyone, especially those who have been sensitized to the war motif. Awaiting the Great Consult, the warrior angels

> Thick swarm'd, both on the ground and in the air,
> Brusht with the hiss of rustling wings. As Bees
> In spring time, when the Sun with *Taurus* rides,
> Pour forth thir populous youth about the Hive
> In clusters; they among fresh dews and flowers
> Fly to and fro, or on the smoothed Plank,
> The suburb of thir Straw-built Citadel,
> New rubb'd with Balm, expatiate and confer
> Thir State affairs. So thick the aery crowd
> Swarm'd and were strait'n'd.
>
> (1. 767-76)

Since the tone of Book 1 has been so martial, this simile seems to right an artistic imbalance. Milton apparently allows us some respite from war by furnishing a glimpse of pastoral tranquility. Most readers who discuss these lines agree with a proposition of Boileau concerning the function of similes. Addison popularizes the French critic's theory in *Spectator* No. 303 (16 February 1712):

> "Comparison," says he, "in Odes and Epic Poems are not introduced only to illustrate and embellish the Discourse, but to amuse and relax the Mind of the Reader, by frequently disengaging him from too painful an Attention to the principal Subject, and by leading him into other agreeable Images."

Using this standard, Addison pronounces the bee simile to be one of the epic's "great Beauties."[1]

Subsequent commentators almost uniformly agree with Addison. A cento of modern judgments could be woven together, but it would be a straw opponent. Clearly, there is truth to the claim that the simile confers on the demons a "sociable or industrious innocence,"[2] and that it "almost pit[ies] the devils' vain busyness."[3] Certainly, "the transformation to bees adjusts [Milton's] colossal fiends to the focus of human attention."[4] The "hiss" of these reduced rebels reminds us we are "hearing serpents and ephemeral locusts, not angels, and watching unnatural distentions and collapses rather than substance."[5] Any new critic can say with confidence that the bee simile grants some relief from the preceding reference to "mortal combat" (1. 766) and showy jousts. Its translatable meaning seems to be that winged creatures, bees or angels, enjoy leisurely amity at certain seasons, even "spring time" when kings usually go forth to war. We can comprehend the number ("populous . . . clusters . . . thick . . . crowd . . . swarm'd"), their urban setting ("smoothed Plank . . . suburb . . . Citadel") and civilized concerns ("State affairs") without annotation. There is value to such straightforward analyses.

[1] Reprinted in *Milton: The Critical Heritage*, ed. John T. Shawcross (New York, 1970), p. 173.

[2] Peter, *A Critique of Paradise Lost*, p. 40.

[3] Broadbent, *Some Graver Subject*, p. 102.

[4] B. A. Wright, *Milton's 'Paradise Lost'* (London, 1962), p. 103.

[5] Jon S. Lawry, *The Shadow of Heaven* (Ithaca, N.Y., 1968), p. 138.

Yet military data suggest a new explanation of how the bee simile calms us. Given the temper of Milton's age and a large body of unexplored analogues, I can only conclude that we are once more in Addison's debt when he comments on *Paradise Lost*: "The clean current, tho' serene and bright, / Betrays a bottom odious to the sight."[6] Specifically, any annotated edition of the poem will suggest bee "sources" in Homer or Virgil or the Barbarini *stemma*. For years historical scholars have pawed over the lines like bears in search of honey. Their results are fascinating, but even the most thorough cataloguer admits Milton does something unprecedented: "One may look in vain through previous epic writing for the fellow to Milton's bee-simile."[7] Both context and text demand that we look outside the patrimony of earlier epic to read the comparison correctly.

Whatever peace is extracted from the text comes by way of certain sociomilitary associations that were almost automatically linked to the word "Bees" during the Renaissance. Three ideas about entomology were as common then as the facts about busyness, honey, and wax that survive to our own day. First, the begetting of bees is mysterious. Aristotle dwells upon this puzzle for a whole chapter in his *Generation of Animals* (3. 10) and suggests the most common explanation, parthenogenesis. Perhaps the tradition of self-propagation among bees underlies a curious statement that Satan makes to his followers in *Paradise Lost*. They are not beholden to the Deity for their birth since, he claims, angels are "self-begot, self-raised / By our own quick'ning power" (5. 856 ff). He bolsters his un-

---

[6] Quoted in Shawcross, *Milton*, p. 106, from "An Account of the Greatest English Poets" (3 April 1694).

[7] James Whaler, "Animal Simile in *Paradise Lost*," *PMLA*, 47 (1932), 534-53. While I admire Whaler's list of parallels (and do not duplicate it) and agree that Milton's passage has no one source, I completely differ from his interpretation. He says the central concern of the simile is to reduce the angels' numbers and movement so "the reader or auditor . . . may observe great events in miniature, serene spectator of processes and perturbations he is relieved from sharing" (pp. 551-52). As I soon explain, I think Milton aims to keep us nervous. His own unrelenting battle against the insanity of all war leads him to stimulate our watchfulness, not tranquilize it.

grateful charge by asking an odd question: "who saw / When this creation was?" His general drift is that all his followers are gods. But the specific way he phrases his impious conundrum, hitherto adumbrated by only a few theologians,[8] echoes Aristotle's familiar dictum, "Never has any [bee] been observed in the act of reproduction" (Generation 3. 10. 20), which Pliny (among many others) repeats: "Sexual intercourse has never been observed between them."[9]

A second belief about seventeenth-century bees hovers even closer to the concern for military matters in Paradise Lost: they live in an efficiently organized community ruled by a king. "The king bee," says Aelian, "is concerned that his hive be governed like this: some bees he details to bring water; others he commands to shape honeycombs within the hive; still a third group he orders to procure food from outside" (On Animals 5. 11). The belief was widespread: Saint Ambrose uses almost identical words (Hexaemeron 5. 21). Although personally chary of analogues to human life from the liber naturae, Milton recognized the hold such parallels had upon his contemporaries. Edward Symmons expresses A Loyall Subjects Beliefe from Oxford in the turbulent year 1643:

Concerning Monarchy, I do believe, that of all Governments it is the best, and most perfect; it being most oppo-

[8] The first line of Arius' heretical creed hints at Satan's blasphemy: "We acknowledge one God, who is alone ingenerate, alone eternal, alone without beginning." In Early Christian Doctrines, tr. J.N.D. Kelly (London, 1965), p. 227.

[9] Natural History 11. 16. 46. Before asserting that "Bees were never yet seen so to joyn together," Edward Topsell challenges self-proclaimed experts in natural history: bees "couple together . . . privily and apart by themselves, which whether it proceed of modesty, or be done through the admirable instinct of Nature, I leave to the dispute and quaint resolution of those grave Doctors, who being laden with the badges and cognizances of learning, do not stick to affirm that they can render a true reason even by their own wits, of all the causes in nature, though never so obscure, hid and difficult." The History of Serpents (London, 1608), p. 642. St. John Cassian knows "bees have no normal generation," but adds they must arise from specially picked flowers that breed them spontaneously. On the Incarnation 7. 5.

site to *Anarchy*, most agreeing to well ordered nature (as
appears among planets, birds, beasts and bees) [,] the most
ancient and Noble, from the beginning of Nations, yea of
families, whereof there is still an Image in every well
guided house where one is chiefe.[10]

Milton feels obliged to scold Salmasius for claiming that apian
royalism justifies human monarchies (*Def. 1. 5.* C.E. *7.* 279).
Sure that animal paradigms are wrong, he even undercuts the
myth about ants used by democrats. It assumed *The Schoole of
Beastes* (as Peter Viret called his book) had lessons for human
society. Ants "haue no king nor Prince"; "there is among
them, the order and fashion of a common wealth."[11] Despite
the lure of this analogy, Milton questions it by mentioning
"The Parsimonious Emmet, . . ,. / Pattern of just equality
perhaps" (*Paradise Lost 7.* 485-87, my italics). Yet, for artistic
presentation, there is force to his frequent assertion that Satan
is a "great Sultan" (1. 348) or "great Emperor" (1. 378) who
sits "High on a Throne of Royal State" (2. 1). Just as one
"truth" of bee lore supports the strange claim of angelic self-
production, so this second renders more palpable the presence
of infernal tyranny. Satan founds his pretension to leadership
on a universal premise: every hierarchy must have one pri-
mate. As the Adversary usually does with facts, however, he
insists that he alone is their interpreter. Everyone in Milton's
audience could have recognized traces of royalist apologetics in
the Devil's position. Griffith Williams defends Charles I and
prepares the way for Satan the king bee:

And indeed it is concluded by the *common* consent of the
best *Philosophers* that the Lawes of *Nature* lead us to a
Monarchie, as when among all creatures both animate and
inanimate, we do always find *one* that hath the prehemi-
nence above all the rest of his kinde, as among the *Beasts*
the Lion, among the *Fowles* the Eagle, among *Graines* the
Wheat, amongs *Drinkes* the Wine, among *Spices* the

---

[10] *A Loyall Subjects Beliefe* (Oxford, 1643), p. 7.
[11] *The Schoole of Beastes* (London, 1585), pp. 24, 11.

Baulme[,] among *Metalls* the Gold, among the *Elements*
the Fire, among the *Planets* the Sun.[12]

Perhaps Milton's simile gives Satan and Charles their due as
tyrants when it dwells upon observations of nature that had
recently been interpreted by authorities whom the Puritans
hated.

A third entomological "fact"—this one purely military—
illustrates again how various strands of popular science
strengthen the epic's fabric. A bestiary of the twelfth century
glides from the second observation about bees to this last one:
"They have kings. They have armies. They go to war."[13] Ac-
cepted by audiences long after the time of Milton and em-
phasized by natural historians, the warfare instinctively waged
by bees complicates our apparently one-dimensional simile. No
matter what momentary pacificity the soldiers crowding around
Pandaemonium may exhibit, a complete reader must quickly
recall the bees' quarrelsome disposition. They were regularly
associated with war's frenzy. Three out of the four biblical ref-
erences to *deborah*, the bee, link it to armies of bumptious
enemies like Amorites and Assyrians (Deut. 1:44; Ps. 118:12;
Is. 7:18). Similarly, classical authors, Columella, for example,
say bees "wage something like civil war among themselves and
foreign wars, you might term them, with other swarms" (*De
Re Rustica* 9. 9, 5-6). Prosaic nature books such as Charles But-
ler's *The Feminine Monarchie, or a Treatise Concerning Bees*
become eloquent when speaking of the bees' fighting. Butler is
usually quite utilitarian, outlining all that a beekeeper needs to
know about their anatomy, hives, honey, and illnesses. But a
peculiar energy vivifies his account of how bees repel would-be
robbers:

[12] *Jura Majestatis* (Oxford, 1644), p. 21.
[13] Tr. T. H. White, *The Bestiary* (New York, 1960), p. 153. This same
phrase occurs in several authors: Isidore of Seville, *Etymologiae* 12. 8. 1; Hugh
of St. Victor, *De Bestiis* 3. 38; Raban Maur, *De Universo* 8. 7. Macrobius
praises Virgil for calling bees *"quirites"* since, as these authorities knew, bees
have communities which make war (*Saturnalia* 6. 6). Because of their civic and
military organization, Eustathius aptly calls them *"animalia urbana"*
(*Hexaemeri Metaphrasis* 8. 4).

When the theeues hauing first made an entrie begin to
come thicke, and the true Bees perceiue themselues to be
assaulted by many, they suddainely make an outcrie: and
issuing out of their holds by troopes presently prepare
themselues to battaile. Some keepe the gates: some as
skout watches fly about: some runne in againe to see what
is done there: some begin to bussel with the enemie: and
that with such a noise and dinne, as if the drum did sound
an alarme. Besides which base sound you shall eftsoones,
in the heate of the battaile, heare a more shril and sharpe
note, as it were of a flute, . . . Which I am out of doubt is
tuned by their generall commander, encouraging them to
fight for their Prince, their liues, and their goods.[14]

The aggression that bees display toward their own kind also
extends to human victims. Aelian cites an old history of Crete
that records how bees so harassed the inhabitants of Rhaucus
that they were obliged to build an entirely new city (*On Ani-
mals* 17. 35). The bees' military propensities—"all of them live
like soldiers in a camp" (Varro, *De Re Rustica* 3. 16. 9)—helped
humans once during war: defenders of Themiscyra released
swarms of them into the tunnels that Lucullus' sappers had dug
under their walls in 72 B.C. (Appian, *Mithridatic Wars* 12. 11.
78). Even Gervase Markham, a naturalist who focuses upon the
utility of bees, must admit that, once a human being has
aroused them, "they are curst and malicious, and will sting
spitefully," thus summarizing the complex assertions that an-
cient and modern observers felt to be true.[15]

Since bees were so belligerent to other bees and to humans,
they earned a reputation as harbingers of war even when they
were not actually fighting. Pliny stands alone when he suggests
that some bees omens may not indicate disaster (*Natural His-
tory* 11. 18. 55). Almost universally, people equated the pres-
ence of bees with unsavory military acts such as rebellion. Cic-
ero illustrates his assertion that hordes of slaves in the midst of

[14] *The Feminine Monarchie* (Oxford, 1609), Sigs. I1ᵛ-I2ʳ.
[15] *Cheape and Good Husbandry* (London, 1614), p. 151.

a republic are dangerous by mentioning them. If swarms appeared on a stage or in the auditorium, Romans would rightly be alarmed. How much more worried should they all be by the sinister crowds of unwilling servants (*De Haruspicium Responsis* 12. 25). Other writers assert that bees foretell a defeat in normal war. Roman losses to Hannibal at Ticinum, Trasimene, and Cannae were prefaced by bees as was Pompey's calamity at Pharsalus. Yet a third group of writers bridges the gap between history and religion by associating bees with war in poetry. Virgil describes a swarm that infested the sacred laurel in King Latinus' courtyard (*Aeneid* 7. 64 ff), Lucan mentions the bees on Pompey's standards (*Pharsalia* 7. 161), Silius Italicus reminds us that they predicted Cannae (*Punica* 8. 635-36) and Claudian ruefully admits they warned only the percipient about the gloomy end of fifth-century peace (*De Bello Gothico* 238). Rightly interpreted, each of these signs forecasts a fatal conflict. The ancient world so routinely linked bees to civic and military contention that Julius Obsequens, a fourth-century A.D. epitomizer, regularly punctuates his handbook of sinister portents with bee references. Sandwiched between meteors, talking oxen, two-headed babies, and sweating statues, bees appear in 118 B.C., 104, 102, 92, 50, 42, every time prophecying doom (*De Prodigiis* 95, 103, 104, 113, 125, 130, 132).

Medieval authors, too, trust the bee as a war omen. Bartholomeus Anglicus[16] sees fit to mention it. Polydore Vergil draws upon material from the tenth century when he claims Rollo, a Dane fighting in England, dreamed of a swarm that flew noisily to France, there feasting on blossoms and wandering freely. This vision Rollo rightly interpreted as meaning his soldiers would defeat the French (*Anglica Historia* 5).

Likewise, the Renaissance believed that bees mean war. There was little reason for doubt. Homer's first simile in the

---

[16] *De Proprietatibus Rerum*, tr. John Trevisa (London, 1535), *passim*. See especially 12. 4: "They have an host and a king, and move war and battle." Also 18. 12: "And no creature is more wreakful, nor more fervent to take wreak than is the Bee when he is wroth."

Iliad likens soldiers to bees (2. 87-90) as does the chorus of old watchmen who open Aeschylus' *Persians* with a comment on

> . . . all our horse with frequent tramp,
> And all our footmen from the camp.
> Even as Bees on busy wing,
> Swarmed out with the king:
> And they paved their briny way
> [With Xerxes' bridge from Asia to Thrace].[17]

Imaginative writers like Tasso[18] and John Lyly[19] follow these poetic leads. Modern naturalists like Thomas Hill,[20] Edward Topsell[21] and Thomas Mouffet[22] repeat the traditional lore about bees and combat, thereby demonstrating the slow growth of observational science and pertinacity of an arresting assertion.

Whatever Milton or modern readers think of the popular errors that bees are autogenerated, have kings, and wage war, they cooperate with so many points that the epic has taken pains to stress about fallen rebels that they must be taken seriously. Long before Milton, Origen attacked the pagan Celsus

---

[17] In *The Lyrical Dramas of Aeschylus*, tr. John Stuart Blackie (London, 1906), p. 305. The Greek lines are *Persai* 126 ff.

[18] *Jerusalem Delivered* twice compares the activities of human armies to the behavior of bees: 3. 1. 8; 11. 48. 3.

[19] Fidus lectures Euphues and his companion Philautus about the admirable organization of bees. He then glides to their military appearance: bees "keepe watch and ward, as lyving in a campe to others." *Euphues*, ed. E. Arber (London, 1868), p. 262.

[20] *A Profitable Instruction of the Perfect Ordering of Bees* (London, 1608), p. 21: "Bees sometimes minding to fight, do hastily burst out of the hiues, and (as were in ciuill batels among themselues) do fight like strangers one against the other, & smite eagerly in their fight one at another."

[21] *The History of Serpents*, especially pp. 642-43: each "Souldier" is said to have a "Sword or Spear." More important, Topsell lists many military disasters which the presence of bees had foretold (pp. 644-45).

[22] Probably the father of "Little Miss Mouffet," Thomas published *Insectorum sive Minimorum Animalium Theatrum* at London in 1634. An English version appeared in 1658 as *The Theater of Insects*. Like Topsell, Mouffet notes the first "use" of bees to be prophets of defeat in war (*Theater*, p. 905).

for a stubbornly simplistic observation of bees that cast doubt
on Christian intelligence.

"Bees, indeed, [says Celsus, trying to diminish humans to
the level of animals] have a sovereign, who has followers
and attendants; and there occur among them wars and vic-
tories, and slaughterings of the vanquished, and cities and
suburbs. . . ."

Now here [replies Origen] he did not observe the differ-
ence that exists between what is done after reason and con-
sideration, and what is the result of an irrational nature,
and is purely mechanical. . . . But we ought to admire the
divine nature, which extended even to irrational animals
the capacity, as it were, of imitating rational beings,
perhaps with a view of putting rational beings to shame.
. . . Perhaps also the so-called wars among the bees convey
instruction as to the manner in which wars, if ever there
arise a necessity for them, should be waged in a just and
orderly way among men.[23]

Although not overly fond of Origen, Milton amplifies a favorite
point in his epic by making a similar equation: fallen angels
equal bees. Both groups operate by primitive instincts that pre
clude rational choice. Thus, their accomplishments as city-
builders or as soldiers merit no praise. As Virgilio explains to
Dante, bees merely illustrate primal impulse (*prima voglia*)
realized in action (*Purgatorio* 18. 58-60). Early Greek psychol-
ogists had already used bees as stock examples of φύσις not
λόγος,[24] of instinct, not thought. Later, ecclesiastical writers
who make it their business to read lessons for man from God's
second scripture say that the bees' birth, organization, and ac-

---

[23] *Contra Celsum* 4. 81-82 in *The Writings*, tr. Frederick Crombie (Edin-
burgh, 1872), pp. 247-48. Milton's own thoughts on a just war are found in
C.D. 2. 17. As *PL* 6 shows, he realized that war was sometimes necessary.

[24] Sherwood Owen Dickerman collects ancient references to ants, bees, spi-
ders, and swallows to illustrate how these creatures were offered as proof of
instinct in lower animals, not reason. See "Some Stock Illustrations of Animal
Intelligence in Greek Psychology," *TAPA*, 42 (1911), 123-30.

tivities are unconnected to reason. One saint agrees with another in saying that bees act like robots. With only minor variations, the same description of these "mindless creatures" (as Basil calls them in *On the Hexameron* 8. 4) comes from Gregory Nazianzen (*Oration* 28. 25) and John Chrysostom (*Concerning the Statues* 12. 2) as from the proto-saint Marcus Aurelius (*Meditations* 5. 6).

So Milton's simile linking soldiers and bees contains an impurity for a conditioned reader: Hell's perfect militia is really an assemblage of zombies led by some equally irrational king. Certainly the evidence warrants such a conclusion. Yet any hostile army is frightening. How does Milton allay this fear? The consolation may spring from a final act of bee culture. Until mid-nineteenth century, the domed straw "skeps" (as hives were called) underwent routine dismantling in late summer. The keeper either killed or drove off a majority of the swarm with sulphur fumes. This common practice reassures anyone who applies it to Satan's minions: there will be a final assertion of God's power over even the most awesome hordes, a judgment when fine palaces and soldierly skill count for nothing. The fate of earthly bees intimates that Satan's bees are not immortal. Certainly Christ the "gardener" of John 20:15 will know how to treat them at the end of days.

At last, then, the simile does calm readers. After they have followed it through a long but probably inevitable path of Renaissance associations, it reveals its benign sting, a surprise that depends upon noting both the antimilitary tone of *Paradise Lost* and the contents of popular science that any "Peasant" (1. 783) might know.[25]

Both surface statement and *significatio* in *Paradise Lost* so

[25] Folklore familiar to such a peasant regularly associated bees with death. See E. and M. Radford, *Encyclopedia of Superstitions* (New York, 1949), *s.v.* bees. Milton's references to bees in his other works confirm that he too was familiar with the usual commonplaces. Bees extract "liquid" from "the Bloom" (*PL* 5. 24-25); they carry honey on their thighs and sing (*Il P* 142-43); female workers feed male drones (*PL* 7. 489-92); they produce an "industrious murmur" (*PR* 4. 247-49); they are selective, like biased readers (*Eikon* 21. C.E. 5.

often involve military matters that resolutely eirenic readers must be deprived of success when seeking to penetrate the epic's center. Conscious ignoring of war words can only prevent Milton from educating them about true valor in a world besieged by multiple enemies. Unlike, say, Shakespeare, he usually rejects a reference that is only locally efficacious. Rather, he aims at a unity of message and vehicle. This complexity is largely absent from the Elizabethan didacticism of Canterbury when he lectures Henry V:

> Therefore doth Heaven divide
> The state of man in divers functions,
> Setting endeavor in continual motion.
> To which is fixed, as an aim or butt,
> Obedience. For so work the honeybees,
> Creatures that by a rule in nature teach
> The act of order to a peopled kingdom.
> They have a King and officers of sorts,
> Where some, like magistrates, correct at home,
> Others, like merchants, venture trade abroad.
> Others, like soldiers, armed in their stings,
> Make boot upon the summer's velvet buds,

---

253); they adhere to a law that transcends the authority of their kings (Def. 1. 2. C.E. 7. 87); their community may be described as a commonwealth (Def. 1. 5. C.E. 7. 281); they hate beetles (ibid.); there is a possibility that they teach us something about politics (Pro 7. C.E. 12. 283). While these statements vary widely in seriousness, they at least touch upon many seventeenth-century clichés.

The custom of destroying bee colonies with smoke underlies a request to Jupiter in John Ogilby's Aesopicks, 2nd ed. (London, 1673). A bee gives honey to the king of gods and prays,

> Let not base Villagers our Stocks destroy,
> And what you so are pleas'd to like, enjoy;
> Who drown whole Nations, or with stifling Smoke
> Establish'd Kingdoms in a Minute choke.
>
> (p. 56)

Jupiter prudently refuses to give "deadly Poyson" to the bees' "little Darts" and decrees that bees with "Malice to our Minion" man will lose their stingers.

Which pillage they with merry march bring home
To the royal tent of their Emperor.

(1. 2. 183-96)

Here the learned archbishop does all the work. He spells out the
political lesson of the bee, demanding only that the reader listen
and assent, not (as in Milton) probe, remember, and apply on
his own. Division of labor under an absolute ruler may be desir-
able in fifteenth-century kingdoms of imagination, but, con-
sonant with the negative associations of bees' birth, rule, and
war making, is in Milton's Hell somewhat sinister. There the
mindless functionalism has no redeeming self-awareness and
guarantees ultimate annihilation.

This way of reading Milton's unprecedented bee simile comes
full circle. Initially, the reference may have soothed us by its
apparent idyllicism. Just as any value can be measured only
after it has been compared with its opposite, so the relaxed
amiability outside Pandaemonium momentarily offers a spring
scene that anyone would prefer to Satan's army. Yet pugnacity
inevitably accompanied a mention of bees. The soothing "hiss
of rustling wings" merely counterpoints an ominous bass note
of bellicose buzzing. When a reader recalls how these small in-
habitants of the natural world practice unworthy human ac-
tivities such as fighting, he once more plunges back into Hell,
that prison that allows no escape from the belligerent feelings
for fallen angels or readers. Finally, the simile's other associa-
tions reassert that truculent militarism is a sign of stupidity
which will be punished.[26]

We can only surmise what effect his novel antiwar lesson had
on readers inclined to admire martial activity. While unusual
for the Renaissance, it expresses one of Milton's deepest convic-
tions. Life holds employment more worthy than being a "Cap-
tain or Colonel, or Knight in Arms." As Christ rebukes Satan
after the latter has tempted him to seize power, "that cumber-

---

[26] Jason P. Rosenblatt, "Milton's Bee-lines," *TSLL*, 18 (1977), 609-23, fol-
lows the association of honey and eloquence and comes to a roughly similar
conclusion.

some / Luggage of war" is "argument / Of human weakness
rather than of strength" (*Paradise Regained* 3. 400-402).

Book 4: The Failure of Pastoralism and Militarism

Book 4 may also be reread with profit for its military signifi-
cance. Satan accepts his evil inclinations and invades the Gar-
den. There, after he observes its beauty, eavesdrops on Adam
and Eve, and maneuvers himself next to our sleeping Mother,
guardian angels from Gabriel's "night-watch" (Argument) ap-
prehend him. As the book ends, the demon retreats from this
exquisite corner of Eden. Previous studies rightly point to the
pastoral conventions that Milton uses to describe Paradise.[27]
During the first 775 lines, idyllic tropes predominate. Except for
the anxious but short dialogue between Uriel and Gabriel (4.
561-88), we hear mostly of "Nature's whole wealth" (207).
This happy collocation of phenomena enchants every sense.
Here, tumbled into our mental laps with ravishing profusion, is
a "various view" (247) for eyes that usually see little to interest
them, "delicious taste" (251) for numbered palates, roses
"without Thorn" (256) that we can safely touch, "murmuring
waters" (260) and bird song to caress ears that seldom hear har-
mony, and—a special delight for those who ordinarily live in
the miasma of human towns—"the smell of field and grove"
(265). These sensory references in the first three-quarters of
Book 4 join with many literary allusions and appeal to some
eternal instinct that generates pleasure when a *locus amoenus* is
described. To stroll from Alcinous' orchard to seventeenth-
century gardens exhilarates anyone and tempts him to dally
with some false surmise: wouldn't a tranquil world be wonder-
ful?

Unlike most painters who ease the entry into a timeless world

---

[27] So many fine treatments of the pastoral theme in *Paradise Lost* exist that I
must here reject the advice of Hedda Gabler's pedantic husband concerning
footnotes ("One can never have too many"). Having said this, I admit I have
enjoyed the general studies of John Armstrong, Joseph Duncan, Harry Levin,
and A. Bartlett Giamatti.

of sensory and psychological joy, Milton does not neglect realism. A dangerous serpent insinuates himself into the picture. Especially during the last quarter of Book 4, Satan's soldierly presence forbids us to desert reality for a soothing realm of tensionless gratification. Although Satan infests Paradise only temporarily, he makes us understand how delicate is "the happy Garden" (*Paradise Regained* 1. 1). His raid limits our imaginative tenure in Paradise just as it shortens our Parents' actual stay. Martial references once more put everyone's comfort to flight. By weaving a somber thread of war in his Poussin-like tapestry, Milton forces us to choose between two modes of perceiving ourselves in relation to the external world. The first and more attractive alternative is pastoral. Its premises are almost irresistible, but its consequences seem too dangerous, finally, for adequacy. Militarism, while harsh and life-denying, appears to be the more mature attitude since it is the means by which Satan nearly corrupts Eve and by which he is driven away from her. It is time to examine this problem of self-definition in Book 4. Choice faces angels and humans, civilians as well as soldiers. Specifically, every character somehow fails to be thoroughly aware of himself and his setting. Many notable gaps separate each speaker's words from the reality that they should recreate. Such inexactness may not jeopardize an arcadian shepherd, but can be fatal to anyone in a combat zone.

Since a state of war exists, one may first question the behavior of Deity. His character in Book 3 is certainly not pastoral. He controls Heaven, a spiritual *plataea* almost bare of material or linguistic ornaments. There he successfully exercises suasion without stage properties like Pandaemonium or rhetorical tricks like similes. As Salkeld reasoned, "The diuine essence doth represent it selfe vnto itself" (*Treatise*, p. 129 margin). God's flat and nonpastoral words resemble those of an ideal soldier who makes each utterance count. However, an inspector general observing God's behavior outside Heaven would have to award him a low proficiency rating because he seems oblivious to even the most elementary precautions. Before the opening of Book 4, God has entrusted the key for Hell's gate to Sin, a most untrustworthy sentinel. Aeneas Tacticus warns all commanders who are responsible for defending endangered cities:

> No chance persons should be appointed keepers of the gates, but only discreet and sagacious men always capable of suspecting anything brought into the city; and besides they should be well-to-do and men who have something at stake in the city . . . ; but not men who, because of poverty, or the pressure of some agreement, or from other stress of circumstances, might . . . be persuaded by anyone . . . to revolt. (5. 1)

If Milton's allegory (you enter Hell by Sin) is read as straight narrative, one may speculate that his love of symmetry here forced him to impute unsound tactics to the Father so that Sin could foreshadow Eve's insubordination: both females disobey an order from the commander of our universe. But other assertions indicate that Milton means God to be remiss in other military particulars. He does not provide Uriel, his second guardian, with passwords or tokens of recognition, two essential tools that traditionally maintained security. (Aeneas Tacticus stresses their necessity in his twenty-fourth and twenty-fifth chapters, but Deity forgets or rejects the advice.) In fact, God's memory is remarkably short since the first medal given to all ranks of an English army, the Dunbar Medal awarded to those who helped Cromwell defeat David Leslie on 3 September 1650, pictures on its obverse the triumphant leader with a motto, "The Lord of Hosts." This phrase, at once pious and pugnacious, was (as the legend further states) the "Word at Dunbar."[28] Apparently the rawest recruit knows more about field words than the Lord in *Paradise Lost*.

Divine strategy amounts to noninvolvement. Only God's subordinates meet Satan. Since the good angels are conspicuously free, they do not have to share praise for accomplishment with their leader. Thus, when they apprehend Satan, credit for

[28] The medal is pictured by Peter Young in *The English Civil War Armies* (Reading, Eng., 1973), p. 6.

their alertness does not revert to Deity. And even when God cancels the duel between Satan and his pickets, he obscures a question that the last quarter of Book 4 has built up: will the devil's individual prowess defeat good angels or not? Rather than enter the arena of martial proof, God seems to reject all military conventions.

While God, who knows what is to happen in the Garden, avoids acting on his foresight as a prudent defender should, Adam and Eve cannot act. They are unaware of the approaching military assault and behave as if all phenomena in the perceptible world were pastoral extensions of themselves: placid, appreciative, and cooperative. The narrator stresses how they understand themselves to be placed in a benign hierarchy. It encompasses humans and creator ("Hee for God only, shee for God in him." 4. 299), humans and animated nature ("About them frisking play'd / All Beasts of th' Earth." 340-41) and humans in relation to the vegetable realm ("thir sweet Gard'ning labor." 328). So far as our Parents know, they have only two responsibilities toward external reality. These extend horizontally and vertically. On the terrestrial plane, both realize that they must "not . . . taste that only Tree / Of Knowledge" (423-24) and are obliged "To prune these growing Plants" (438-39); their spiritual duty directs their attention upward: "wee to him indeed all praises owe" (444). Adam and Eve acknowledge these responsibilities since they think themselves encapsulated in a finite world with clear boundaries. The Creator of this pleasant place makes seemly requests from them that harmonize with their environment.

Our Sires' nonmilitary views of themselves in relation to each other, nature, or God seem to be rewarded during the brief idyll of this book because nothing menaces them in the world they perceive. Whether they look down, around, or upward, they find simulacra that confirm their unthreatened "reality." When Eve is born, she stares down "with unexperienc't thought" (457) at her own reflection. This joyous act rewards her "soon with answering looks / Of sympathy and love" (464-65). When she notices Adam, she learns that she is "Part of [his] Soul . . . / [His] other half" (487-88). Acquiescing to her new role, Eve discovers that Adam shares her instinct to adore something. In our world, they look to each other and are fulfilled with "connubial Love" (743); in the large universe, they gaze with "adoration pure" (737) up to nature's glories and base their evening prayer upon them. Every reflection from pool, partner, or distant planet reinforces their enviable state of willing reliance.

Milton does not allow us to forget this characteristic reduplication. Even Satan, who first sees the Garden and its inhabitants, puns significantly when he spies them "Imparadis't in one another's arms," creatures of *"Eden"* who "enjoy thir fill / Of bliss on bliss" (4. 505-508). ("Eden" was said to be Hebrew for "pleasure, bliss.") The perfect lovers, Adam and Eve form a microcosm of the world they perceive. Milton gives a physical sign of their emotional union when, within the space of a few hundred lines, he speaks four times of their being "hand in hand" (321, 488, 689, 739). Words like "mutual" and "wedded" reemphasize their secure unanimity. The lovers experience some moments of imaginative criticism (Eve knows that without Adam nothing in the Garden is "sweet." 656), but generally anticipate no surprises. At most, our Parents foresee the arrival of children, "a Race" (732) that will see what they see and do what they do. Unlike us, they feel themselves bound to a wheel of mythic time that will revolve them, endlessly and benevolently, through similar settings and experiences.

Sadly, however, their placidity is possible because their vision is partial. They do not know of Satan yet, the missile that will explode the world of mirrors and imaginary wheel of time. Despite his capacity for destruction, he also views the universe incompletely. Satan stresses the innate hostility of all creatures rather than their instinctive amiability. Instead of benignly mingling "I" and "Not-I" as Adam and Eve do, Satan always acts like a warrior in alien territory. Wary of real involvement, suspicious of sympathy, the devil reminds us of Xerxes and Lucan's villainous Caesar,[29] two solipsists whose fascination with

[29] Two interesting pedigrees for Satan are suggested by: William Blissett, "Caesar and Satan," *JHI*, 18 (1957), 221-32; and Manfred Weidhorn, "Satan's Persian Expedition," *N & Q*, 103 (1958), 389-92.

total ruin rudely contradicts the attitude of our Parents. Although Satan operates in the same physical ambiance as Adam and Eve, he perceives it very differently. Satan clearly clashes with his setting: Eden may be rural, its inhabitants amicable and their emotions altruistic, yet he acts as if they dwell in some hostile city that he must besiege and despoil. Obeying his chosen role, he resents the charm that Paradise radiates to other creatures. The perpetual outsider, he seems to have learned nothing from his experience in Heaven's blissful fields since he now attempts to blast those of Earth. Why does he remain so relentlessly out of harmony with his surroundings, a cancerous cell which ravages its host?

Satan's understanding of time and space differs radically from our Parents'. Thus he cannot see Paradise as they do. His very presence in Book 4 is legitimatized, not by the raptures of pastoralism or the requirements of theology, but by the advice of military councillors: "The general," says Onasander, "should skillfully inspect the camp of the enemy" (10. 16). Like any warrior, Satan assumes that past, present, and future are malleable entities subject to some alteration by personal initiative. Rather than allow himself to be rolled through time like Adam, he continually tries to alter the sequence or significance of events. He calls his past defeat in Heaven, an egregious rout to any impartial spectator, a "dubious Battle" (1. 104). There is no durational aspect to truth so far as Satan knows. Present for him is the nodal point at which one has the duty to rearrange past so it can lead to some desired future. When he plans to "seek / Deliverance for us all" (2. 464-65), he sums up his inability to live in present time. For him, the vital moment will always be that future when revenge for past affronts will erase their reason for being remembered.

Satan most clearly illustrates his anxiety in both past and present when he claims to the potential rebels that no one can remember a "time when we were not as now" (5. 859). Since they are ignorant of any past moment of generation, they owe no fealty to God in the future. This argument implies that events are radically discontinuous unless proven to be related.

Because none of the malcontents can recall some specific instant during which God impressed upon him an obligation to repay the gift of existence, then no debt can exist. Adam accepts time, looking gratefully to his own past. His very first speech (4. 411 ff) bases his present happiness upon the admission that some "Power / . . . made us" and now requests only unanxious dependence. Our Sire's earliest and only response to the external world is this appreciative acknowledgment of being joined to a wholly Other. He is thoroughly at ease in the medium of time, a fish in water, so to speak, while Satan flounders in the same inevitable category.

Humans and Devil also evaluate place differently. Where Adam finds only continuous space, symmetrical and harmonious, Satan's experiences have taught him that there are markedly dissimilar environments in the universe. His anguish at losing Heaven, his nausea when acquiring Hell, his startled envy on seeing Earth, all combine to instruct him how some territories are more worth having than others. He entertains no pastoral illusion since he is one whom "wounds of deadly hate have pierc'd so deep" (4. 99). The Fiend's estimates of relative land value are more broadly based than those of Adam; they seem to express a more sophisticated grasp of territoriality. As any campaigner, he assumes that different realms have different rulers who must be dealt with in different ways. During his wide travels, he alters his own behavior in order to pass safely through places that are governed by Sin, Chaos, Uriel, and our Parents. (We scarcely need remind ourselves how uniformly respectful Adam is to one ruler.) Since Satan believes that no region should be neutral, he readily claims a most unattractive district—"thou profoundest Hell / Receive thy new Possessor" (1. 251-52)—and contemplates acquiring Earth.

Satan's fascination with private ownership partly governs a statement about "the full-blazing Sun, / . . . high in his Meridian Tow'r" (4. 29-30). Students of Milton recognize the allusion to *Culex* 42, a minor poem attributed to Virgil. Students of folklore recognize one of many allusions to the *daemonio meridionalis*, that noontide horror who surfaces in Mediterra-

nean and English superstition. Most important, students of
Satan the empire builder recognize the first of several allusions
in this book to the way in which territory is guarded. Here he
resents the Sun, perhaps thinking "Tow'r" an appropriate sta-
tion for any watchman who intends to protect his property.
(Christ was regularly imaged as a tower, a fact that should gall
Satan even more since the Son has already wrested one king-
dom from him.) Later, the first spy sneers at the meager pre-
caution against invasion that he finds on the perimeter:
Paradise is "Ill fenc't for Heav'n to keep out such a foe / As now
is enter'd" (372-73). Although Adam and Eve are "Lords of all"
(290), their defenses bring forth his scorn. He thinks like a sol-
dier, amazed that such a desirable realm is so laxly patrolled.
Nothing prevents Satan from "sly circumspection" (537). Un-
challenged as it is, "his roam" (538) illustrates two features of
his character. First, it fulfills the prescriptive meaning of שׁוּט ,
a possible root for his name which means "rove about, in-
spect."[30] Second, it reminds us that he volunteered to explore
unknown areas for the sake of tactical advantage. The consum-
mate "discoverer," Satan knows he "must walk round / This
Garden, and no corner leave unspi'd" (528-29). His inspection
reveals nothing that any competent military scout would inter-
pret as a formidable barrier. Excepting only Adam, the Garden
appears to have no combatants whom an attacker might fear.
Thanks to Satan's martial training, the time seems right and the
terrain vulnerable to an assault.

　　Such conclusions may indicate tunnel vision to a pastoral
commentator. Yet Satan defines himself as a conqueror. He
views Earth as a prize whose winning will somehow discomfit
God. He continues to be the same inflexible opportunist we
have met elsewhere. Before arriving on Earth, Satan has given
ample evidence that he considers antagonism his only posture
in any realm. He confronts Sin, Chaos, Uriel, and the sun with

---

[30] Forms of the verb are common. See 2 Sam. 24:2, 8 and Job 1: 7, 22. Riv-
kah Schärf Kluger rejects this older etymology in *Satan in the Old Testament*,
tr. Hildegard Nagel (Evanston, Ill., 1967), pp. 29-31. She prefers the modern
derivation from a word meaning "accuse."

animosity. Dressed (as Sin notes) "in those bright Arms" (2. 812) that are required equipment for one who anticipates a hostile reception, Satan's prophecy of universal enmity fulfills itself. He skirmishes with Death and nervously bargains with Chaos. When he apostrophizes the sun, emblem of Messiah, "with no friendly voice" (4. 36), he emanates the same truculence.

Satan is always ready for combat. During his deception of Uriel, he sheds his armor and appears as "a stripling Cherub" (3. 636). Yet he fights by lying. The fiend admits how slavishly he heeds military advice. Frontinus 3. 2. 7 teaches him that the most dangerous weapon of a commandant's arsenal is an agent in disputed territory who pretends to be an ally of the enemy; Sutcliffe urges "discouerers" to disguise themselves lest they be captured (*Practice*, p. 116). Following these dicta, Satan easily penetrates the cordon sanitaire surrounding Earth. He lies about his intention, of course, but his behavior is consistent with the previous misrepresentations to Sin and Death ("I come no enemy, but to set free / From out this dark and dismal house of pain, / Both him and thee." 2. 822-24) and to Chaos ("I come no Spy, / With purpose to explore or to disturb / The secrets of your Realm." 2. 970-72). These two self-definitions at least blended fact with camouflage; the request that Uriel direct him to Earth so he "may praise" (3. 676) is as deceitful as Herod's request that the Wise Men lead him to Jesus so he "may come and worship him" (Matt. 2:8). The nearer Satan approaches our interdicted planet, the more dissembling he becomes.

His false lineaments are part of his tactic as potential victor, certainly, but readers who concentrate upon them are forced to make a choice between behavior that is either militarily effective or morally decent. On the martial side of this debate is a certain integrity to Satan's pickeering. At each stage of his exploration, he has selected a guise appropriate to the field situation. When he bounds from Hell and courses to our world through space, a possibly hostile environment, he is a fully-armed warrior whose "bright Arms, / . . . temper'd heav'nly" (2. 812-13) are coterminous with his intention. Approaching the outer defence of our sun, he becomes a "stripling Cherub" to avoid identification. He still retains a "wand" to satisfy the long tradition in European art that says an unidentified figure with a baton should be understood as a soldier. That Uriel does not recognize the symbol equated by Romans, Europeans, and Englishmen with militarism is especially disheartening because Satan seems to have given him a chance to pierce through the pilgrim mask. Once arrived in the Garden, Satan quite sensibly abandons the roles of warrior angel or devout cherub. He reconnoiters his targets in that wildlife area by assuming several animal disguises. Like any terrorist, he tries to blend into the native population. Even after Ithuriel and Zephon penetrate his cover as a toad, Satan continues to act as a frightening creature. He lies vigorously to his interrogators and, when that ruse has failed, reverts to the first role of soldier by offering to fight them openly.

On the whole, Milton means us to judge Satan's military behavior as exemplary. The dissembling of deep agents or evasions of a skillful marauder were recognized by Milton's audience to be effective wartime maneuvers that should be applauded. People as dissimilar as Spartans and Hebrews appreciated exactly the kind of machinations that Satan here employs. Polyaenus tells of many humans who wore disguises; Jael, Rahab, Eglon, and Judith helped various Hebrew struggles by lies. Elizabeth and the Cromwells spent lavish sums to support the secret services under Walsingham and John Thurloe. According to Pepys, Oliver Cromwell allowed £70,000 per year for intelligence gatherers who insinuated themselves into the most dangerous locales.[31]

[31] Under 14 February 1668, Pepys reports that "Secretary Morrice did this day in the House, when they talked of intelligence, say that he was allowed but 700L. a-year for intelligence; whereas in Cromwell's time he did allow 70,000L. a-year for it; and was confirmed therein by Colonell Birch, who said that thereby Cromwell carried the secrets of all the princes of Europe at his girdle." Under 27 December 1668 he tells how one spy in Holland regularly picked the pocket of a prominent Dutch official so the English King "hath always had their most private debates . . . brought to him in an hour after." *Memoirs of Samuel Pepys, Esq.*, ed. Richard Lord Braybrooke (London, n.d.), pp. 487, 555.

Even by modern standards, Satan could be praised. The recent Code of Conduct that all United States military personnel were obliged to memorize explains many of Satan's deeds in Book 4. The code reads in part,

> I will never surrender of my own free will. If in command I will never surrender my men while they still have the means to resist. . . . If I am captured I will continue to resist by all means available. I will make every effort to escape and aid others to escape. . . . When questioned, should I become a prisoner of war, I am bound to give only name, rank, service number, and date of birth. I will evade answering further questions to the utmost of my ability.[32]

Satan adheres to this code on Earth as he did in Heaven and Hell. His consistency may seem foolish to moralists, but militarists no doubt find it admirable. Satan calls from his own depths "courage never to submit or yield" (1. 108), even when faced by Gabriel and an entire "Angelic Squadron" (4. 977). He tries several ways to evade his captors' inquiries about his presence in the Garden: "Who would not, finding way, break loose from Hell" (889) is a credible private excuse; "my afflicted Powers / . . . settle here on Earth" (939-40) is an unimpeachable reason for a commander. An arbiter who calibrates his judgmental apparatus by martial measurements from any era will find that Satan is a nearly faultless operative.

But Satan's shifts may just as legitimately be appraised by ethical standards. A moralist can say that the same ruses proving Satan's soldierly steadfastness really demonstrate a moral decline. C. S. Lewis' familiar expression of a fall theory springs to my mind:

> From hero to general, from general to politician, from politician to secret service agent, and thence to a thing that peers in at bedroom or bathroom windows, and thence to

---

[32] *The Armed Forces Officer*, Department of Defense Pamphlet 1-20 (Washington, 1965), p. 25.

a toad, and finally to a snake—such is the progress of Satan.[33]

According to this mode of evaluation, Satan's grandeur oozes away each time he acts. The metamorphoses that a military historian might accept as proof of intelligent field resource here give evidence that the fiend's will is perverted: he not only blasphemes but also voluntarily slithers downward to lower genera. Speech and semblance cooperate in this book to convince Christians that the Father of Lies degrades everything he touches, including himself. To this method of reading there is also much merit.

First, Satan's animal transformations do not put him in vital contact with natural sources of pleasure and enlightenment. Where Adam and Eve found joyful lessons of humble gratitude, Satan perceives creatures whose exterior he must imitate. Again a literalist, he assumes that only the outside of an object affects an observer's comprehension. His arrogant lack of curiosity is commendable if he is no more than a crusader who never loses sight of his goal. If, on the other hand, he is as intelligent as he claims, he shows remarkably little interest in alternate forms of life. They all repel him and exacerbate his self-pity. To accomplish his revenge for not being elevated to the summit of Heaven's hierarchy, he must parody the Incarnation, allow himself to be "constrain'd / Into a Beast" and lament, "O foul descent" (9. 163 ff). He is (to paraphrase Keats) that slave of thought who snobbishly denies himself the blissful sensation of taking part in a sparrow's existence as it picks about the gravel.[34]

There is even more reason to castigate Satan if we move beyond this Romantic criticism and abide by Renaissance dicta.

[33] *A Preface to Paradise Lost* (London, 1942), p. 99.

[34] Keats' letter concerning "Negative Capability" to his friend Benjamin Bailey may be found in *Prose of the Romantic Period*, ed. Carl R. Woodring (Boston, 1961), p. 523. Satan's literalism leads him to a serious underestimation of what his punishment will be. He boasts to his troops in Hell: "I am to bruise [man's] heel; / His Seed, when is not set, shall bruise my head: / A World who would not purchase with a bruise" (10. 498-99). He never seems to grasp metaphoric implications.

Changes of shape abet his campaign but disconcert those who fear mutability. He assumes many identities during the expedition to Earth: warrior, pilgrim cherub, metaphoric "Wolf" (4. 183) and "Cormorant" (196), various "fourfooted kinds" (397) such as "A Lion" (402), "a Tiger" (403) and "a Toad" (800). Each guise augments his potentiality as an opponent, but both folklore and religion mistrusted shape shifters. Whether metamorphoses were accidental or willed, they occurred in eerie regions of magic and alchemy. Looming behind Satan is Proteus, the unpredictable wizard who furnished Milton's age with two contradictory sets of credentials. Early humanists saw him as a symbol of man's admirable ability to make himself. Pico della Mirandola supports his assertion that humans have a unique talent for self-development by equating Proteus with the man resolutely ascending toward perfection.[35] Following this tradition, Juan Vives tells how a man successfully relies "upon a very wise mind" and fools the immortal gods into thinking he is "that multiform Proteus."[36] These authors praise a certain uncircumscribed force in humans. Ernst Cassirer explains its appeal: "This protean nature is elevated above the transitoriness of natural existence, because it manifests no mere being acted upon, but an activity, the sum-total indeed of human action."[37] Reformation thinkers disagreed. They saw praise for Proteus as an unwelcome revival of Pelagianism. Drawing on an old equation found in Boccaccio's *Genealogy of the Gentile Gods*, Erasmus encourages his readers to use their minds since these noble organs may "bind fast that Proteus" of degrading passion.[38] Even such limited possibility of perfection angered Luther, who thunders that Erasmus himself is a devious liar, Proteus incarnate.[39] And poets quickly seized upon the wily transubstan-

[35] "Oration on the Dignity of Man." In *The Renaissance Philosophy of Man*, ed. E. Cassirer et al. (Chicago, 1963), p. 225.

[36] "A Fable about Man." In *Renaissance*, ed. Cassirer et al., p. 389.

[37] E. Cassirer, "Giovanni Pico della Mirandola," *JHI*, 3 (1942), 334.

[38] *The Enchiridion of Erasmus*, tr. Raymond Himelick (Bloomington, Ind., 1963), p. 76.

[39] *The Bondage of the Will*, tr. J. I. Packer and O. R. Johnston (Westwood, N.J., 1957), pp. 68, 145.

tiator as a symbol—alchemists already used him to represent mercury, volatile but everpresent—because of his second set of attributes. In *The Faerie Queene*, Archimago uses "his mighty science" to transfigure himself so that he may spy unobserved upon Red Crosse and Una; he took "As many formes and shapes . . . / As ever Proteus to himself could make" (1. 2. 10). Later, Proteus himself appears as an "old leachour" (3. 8. 36) who attempts to rape Florimell:

> To dreadfull shapes he did him selfe transforme,
> Now like a gyaunt, now like to a feend,
> Then like a centaure, then like to a storme,
> Raging within the waves: thereby he weend
> Her will to win unto his wished end.
>
> (3. 8. 41)

In Satan's opinion, his self-mutations deserve the glory awarded to Proteus in the older tradition; in our eyes, however, such admiration would be perversely anachronistic: "This face-changing Proteus" (*CD* 1. 5. C.E. 6. 229) is now known to be an unsavory creature whom no sane person would accept. Gabriel helps us to sort out the proper interpretation when he commands Satan, "avaunt" (4. 962), a word to exorcise demons rather than address noble fighters. But Satan has so completely hypnotized himself that the order does not slap him into self-awareness. He replies as a warrior, not a warlock, and accuses Gabriel of being only a "Proud limitary Cherub" (971), that is, *miles limitaneus*, some common soldier assigned to garrison duty on a frontier who forgets how mean his station is. (Francis Markham defines "*Limitanei*" as "all those souldiers, who liued vpon the Marches or Frontiers of Countries bordering vpon the enemy, and were to withstand all maner of assaults and forraine Incursions." *Epistles of Warre*, p. 162.) Although Gabriel has bested him in a military encounter, Satan scorns the soldier who turns only one face to an adversary.

Despite the negative associations of shape shifting, Satan can persist in his delusion that it is part of a military campaign. The Renaissance did not specify degrees of regularity for combatants, but the current international definition can puncture the devil's pretense. To qualify as a bona fide "irregular soldier," one must "have a fixed distinctive insignia recognizable at a distance."[40] Satan's swagger stick was a temporary and ambiguous badge; the animal disguises violate this stipulation. The legal guerrilla is "commanded by a person responsible for his subordinates." Here, too, Satan fails to conform: he revolted from his own superior in Heaven, abandoned his offspring, Death, and shares credit with no one. His preference for guile rather than open force eliminates still another characteristic of a true irregular since the partisan must carry "arms openly." Finally, Satan does not "conduct operations in accordance with the laws and customs of war." At best, he uses certain tricks mentioned by military writers, but his deceits avoid meaningful confrontation. Perhaps Milton sensed how useful this modern description of unconventional operatives would be since he twice excludes Satan from normal war epithets. The fiend is called a "Thief" (4. 188, 192) and thus branded an outlaw by any standard.

Satan's obsession with his role may cause him to shrug off connotations of Proteus or terrorist, but he cannot deny that his tactics fail. Ithuriel discovers him waging psychological war against Eve and ends his career as agent provocateur. Satan springs up indignantly, forcing God's guards to recognize "the grisly King" (4. 821) of Hell. He pays a double price for such eminence: he must abort his mission. Also, his transformation from toad to monarch permits a simile that further debases him. He explodes from spy to czar,

> As when a spark
> Lights on a heap of nitrous Powder, laid
> Fit for the Tun some Magazin to store
> Against a rumor'd War, the Smutty grain
> With sudden blaze diffus'd, inflames the Air.
> (4. 814-18)

[40] These four prerequisites are summed up in *Guerilla Warfare and Special Forces Operations*, Department of the Army Field Manual 31-21 (Washington, 1958), p. 5.

Englishmen no doubt flinched at this hint of Guy Fawkes' scurrilous plot. Like Francis Herring, they remembered "The Powder-plot" as "Treasons Master-peece," a vile scenario manipulated by England's *"Proteus,"* Guydo *"Fauks* that curst incarnate *Deuill."*[41] A wider audience of Europeans probably remembered the lament of many war theorists that artillery had imposed a vulgar impersonality upon modern battles. Although a Catholic monk or Satan himself was reputed to have invented gunpowder, many people in the late Renaissance recognized its utility. They had to reconcile their distaste with their practicality. John Smithe fights a notorious rear guard battle to eliminate firearms, blaming self-indulgence and drunkenness for having made Englishmen "seek to abolish and extinguish the notable exercise and use of our longbows."[42] The hateful Spaniards are the most proficient musketeers, but even "their bullets do work as much effect against the moon as against the enemy that they aim at." Smithe resented the emphasis that Roger Williams places on guns in *A Briefe Discourse of Warre*. Whatever the truth of Smithe's charges that his countrymen were degenerating, his technical accusations against muskets were rebutted by Humfrey Barwick's *A Breefe Discourse, Concerning the Force and Effect of all Manuall Weapons of Fire, and the Disability of the Long Bowe* (London, 1594?). Yet a quarter century later, W[illiam] N[eade] still railed against the "most deuellish Inuention of Gunpowder" made by "Bertholdus Swart, the Franciscan Fryer." *The Double-armed Man* won Charles I's approval by picturing Neade's "New Inuention" that would obviate artillery: a stalwart man in armor aims a

[41] [Francis] Herring, *Mischeefes Mysterie: or, Treasons Masterpeece. The Powder-plot*, tr. John Vicars (London, 1617). Stella P. Revard make some interesting comments in "Milton's Gunpowder Poems and Satan's Conspiracy," *MS*, 4 (1972), 63-77. *Mischeefes Mysterie* contains several similarities to *Paradise Lost*: "Pluto" copulates with "Romes Strumpet" who bears the viperish "Treason." When his mother complains about the enmity of Britain, Treason flies off to Fawks' "faithlesse brest." Luckily, *"Iehouah"* sees all the tricks of that "crafty *Hunter Sathan"* and saves his people "from the gaping *Whale."*

[42] *Certain Discourses . . . Military* (London, 1590), pp. 61-62.

longbow cleverly attached to the midsection of a pike.[43] As late as 1629, F[rancis] Malthus attempts to dignify the parentage of explosives. The title page of Malthus' *A Treatise of Artificiall Fireworkes Both for Warres and Recreation* (London) shows Jupiter and Minerva cooperating to produce cannon, limpet bombs, and stage dragons which could breath fire. A few years later, John Babington's *Pyrotechnia or, A Discourse of Artificiall Fire-Works* (London, 1635) goes to elaborate lengths as it pictures the desirable role of gunpowder in pageants or civic celebrations. But the old suspicion remained and could not with any finality conceal the normal abhorrence of "nitrous Powder" used in war. Anyone who had fought must have groaned with Leighton, "What universall hurt and damage brought he to all Christendome, that taught the Great Turke the use and making of Ordinance?" (*Speculum*, p. 44).

Much of the force of Book 4 arises from a similar strain upon allegiances. Satan and our Parents perceive the same universe in markedly different ways. Readers must choose between the representative of Pandaemonium and the inhabitants of a "blissful Bower" (4. 690). The narrator conditions us to dislike Satan: he wishes for a "warning voice" (1 ff) so "our first Parents" may defend themselves against "The coming of thir Secret foe." We cannot extend approval to both pastoral and military modes because they are mutually exclusive. Satan teaches us this sad truth when he admits he might have sought "League . . . / And mutual amity" (375-76) with humans if he were not a devotee of "public reason just" which "compels" him to treat them as hostiles. Just as he had chosen to be "far" (103) from God, he now opts for separation from our surrogates and their bucolic world. Thus Milton opposes garden to battle field and shows how each area blinds its occupants to a larger world that God offers those who are not prisoners of narrow literary preconceptions.

[43] *The Double-Armed Man* (London, 1625), Sigs. B1^r and C3^v.

V

CONCLUSION

Paradise Lost has denigrated military affairs so thoroughly that it may surprise us to read how Michael, God's faithful retainer, appears before Adam dressed like a soldier:

> th'Arch-Angel soon drew nigh,
> Not in his shape Celestial, but as Man
> Clad to meet Man; over his lucid Arms
> A military Vest of purple flow'd
> Livlier than *Melibaean*, or the grain
> Of *Sarra*, worn by Kings and Heroes old
> In time of Truce; *Iris* had dipt the woof;
> His starry Helm unbuckl'd show'd him prime
> In Manhood where Youth ended; by his side
> As in a glistering *Zodiac* hung the Sword,
> Satan's dire dread, and in his hand the Spear.
>
> (11. 238-48)

By continuing to juxtapose historical references to epic statements, one can suggest several reasons why Michael's "military Vest" is "purple." Yahweh's soldiers about to destroy Nineveh are clothed in "scarlet" (Nahum 2:3); Xerxes' formidable army includes some who paint half their bodies with vermilion (Herodotus, *Histories* 7. 69). Interesting as such annotation is, however, it may lead away from Milton's main point. He pictures Michael as the fighter "In time of Truce," finished with preliminary battles, prepared for subsequent ones, but now intent upon civilized discourse. Like a graduate from the academy in *Of Education*, Michael is secure in his roles during peace and war. Easily outscoring Satan for obedience and amiability, Michael also defeats him in army skills: his "Vest," "Helm," "Sword" and "Spear" surpass the moon-shield and tree-spear of Hell's champion. Michael can speak "as Man . . . to . . . Man" or act as warrior to instill "dire dread." (For this mission to Adam, God had ordered Michael, "all terror hide." 11. 111) He typifies the successful soldier who has a valid identity during any social condition. Since Milton individuates him, Michael appeals more than the depersonalized "*Locusts*" (1. 341) who slavishly obey Satan. Like the awesome Ninevites whom Nahum calls "great grasshoppers" (3:17), these soldiers willingly detach themselves from their rightful commander to assist Satan's mutiny. Their chosen role as outlaws gained a temporary stability since they observed certain martial conventions. But Michael's behavior corrects the malevolent ignorance that Satan encouraged and allows the reader to draw away from the details of *Paradise Lost* to appreciate some overall patterns concerning obedience and independence.

Michael readily obeys his legal superior, thereby proving himself to be a good soldier and a moral creature. No army can function unless its members admit the necessity of circumscribed duties. The "chiefe Magistrate," as Gr[iffith] Williams teaches, is obliged by his office either "to make and continue peace . . . or to make iust warres, when there be iust occasions offered."[1] And subordinates must confirm their magistrate's projects by "not murmuringe nor speaking ill of any Officer . . . nor of any that serveth his prince" (Barry, *A Discourse*, p. 8). No community, civil or military, can exist without the complete allegiance Michael displays. Both martial and social theorists concur when they discuss rightfully appointed substitutes: the leader and his surrogate require equal obedience. "[E]urie man," says Styward, "ought to followe and obeie the saide deputie, with no lesse care and diligence then they would the Captaine himselfe" (*Pathwaie*, p. 49). Michael realizes that God and the Son have equal authority over him since their goals for their retainers are identical.

Satan parodies certain aspects of an integrated group, but he routinely emphasizes only externals. His alignments appeal to

---

[1] *The True Church* (London, 1629), p. 860.

the eye of casual observers who assume precise formations like those in war texts mean stability. Although parade shapes like "Crosse . . . triangle, & . . . stars" (Smithe, *Instructions*, p. 97) or "Ring . . . Esse . . . Snaile" (Styward, *Pathwaie*, pp. 68-70) or "Rounds," "Diamonds" and "Wind-Mill" (Markham, *Grammar II*, pp. 60, 66) have positive political implications, these patterns lose their visual impact since they are arranged by creatures with little sense of stable personal identity. Satan's grasp of soldierly minutia earns some short-range credit. He is the kind of unphilosophical fact collector who would relish the chapter in John Robert's *Compleat Cannoniere* that tells "How to loade and fire a Peece of Ordnance like an Artist" (p. 26). Yet his *ad hoc* imitations of the songs in Heaven that everyone sings (3. 370-71) or the "Mystical dance" (5. 620) to which all contribute translate into drill field forgeries that only briefly control the basic antinomianism of his followers. When consulted, juniors like Moloch, Belial, and Mammon display rampant unconcern for *koinonia*. Community in Hell involves universal malevolence that remains unfocused unless Satan guides it. Once he leaves his soldiers to their own devices, they "Disband, and wand'ring, each his several way / Pursues, as inclination or sad choice / Leads him perplext, where he may likliest find / Truce to his restless thoughts, and entertain / The irksome hours, till this great Chief return" (2. 523-27). Their aimless deeds are less like vacation amusements (army camps were encouraged to imitate university campuses) than the confusion Ovid notes among bees when their king departs: "they often wander in bewilderment" (*Fasti* 3. 555-56). Satan's example teaches most of his troops not lasting discipline but merely temporary obedience that evaporates when he disappears from sight.

If Satan falsely presumes that he can achieve unity by positioning members who lack inner commitment, he also mistakes another rule for enduring fellowship. Unlike Michael, who dresses as a soldier because God has given him a mission and not because he copies his ruler's appearance, Satan habitually looks to others for guidance. The more he stresses autonomy, the more we can suspect that he compensates for its lack. Like the libertine talking of discipline or the fool of wisdom, he can only respond to someone else's value. Apparently Satan thinks of himself as the primitive Roman deity Vedjovis, a mirror image of Jove. Whereas God in *Paradise Lost* is pacific, just, and indescribable, Satan perversely contradicts these characteristics when he becomes a warrior. Instead of displaying independence, however, his decision proves that he takes his clues from others, preferring to react rather than create.

So many of the Fiend's traits have parallels in mythology that his martial identity may result from an urge to copy others. A few individuals in myth were given the chance to become immortal by being passed through fire. Thetis tried to guarantee Achilles by such a ritual as did Demeter for Demophon and Isis for the unnamed infant of King Malcander. After his immersion "in the fiery Gulf" (1. 52), Satan acts as if his life cannot end. He is wrong, of course, since a more complete memory of these legends would reveal that each fire-ceremony failed. Another mythological pattern that he tries to imitate also backfires Unlike deities in the form of serpents who fathered such illustrious children as Alexander the Great, Scipio Africanus, and Augustus, Satan can only sire Death. The other children killed as part of a plan for their nation; Death is thankless to his father when they meet and finally carries out the plan of Satan's enemy, God, thereby emphasizing Satan's inability to reproduce any notable gesture. The narrator hints that the Devil initiates less and imitates more than his infernal vanity admits. Satan rules over creatures who obey him although "Thir Glory [is] wither'd": "As when Heaven's Fire / Hath scath'd the Forest Oaks, or Mountain Pines" (1. 612-13). Perhaps Milton means that the fates of Satan's tree-soldiers depend on external objects and not their own will. Frazer's *Balder the Beautiful*, volume 2, recalls many myths in which the individual's life is linked to some tree's existence (esp. Chapter 10). If Milton alludes to common European beliefs about the soul's dependence upon another object, then his simile exactly captures the derivative nature of Hell's activities.

Some of Satan's projects seem to be adequate imitations of famous enterprises. Pandaemonium might raise him to the level of Augustus, who boasted he found Rome a city of brick and left it one of marble. Or the Fiend's military maneuvers, which often comply with high standards in war books, might win him some commendation. But Milton consistently speaks of these accomplishments in terms that underline evil's banality, or he treats them ironically, thereby lowering their seriousness. His devil restates and reacts. Satan's one assertion of independence, the war in Heaven, cuts him off from the only source of true creativity in the universe. By disobeying, he thought to eliminate servility. In fact, he enslaved himself to secondary sources of information that exist solely because God's wisdom eludes their authors. Like the aggressive "new men" in Rome who sought freedom from aristocratic *optimates*, Satan has ambivalent feeling toward the organization into which he is placed. He wants to be quit of it sometimes and othertimes he seeks only to recall it. He often speaks of Heaven's glories even while he plots to destroy them. Satan's uncomfortable duality reminds me of the great arch that Hadrian erected in Athens: on one side was engraved, "This city was once Theseus' "; the other side had, "This city is now Hadrian's." Satan looks backward and forward, vainly trying to discover some authority to replace the one he rejected, but still living in the same world.

The military traditions to which Satan turns help explain his curious reception by critics. Some of these traditions, those exemplified by Michael, for instance, claim war defends a civilized community against disorder; other moral traditions, however, equate Lucifer with the very forces of depravity that menace society. Since Satan adopts the form of warrior, he naturally partakes of the divided opinion that Milton's age held concerning two normally discrete activities. Satan does not merit a simple epithet like "hero" or "fool" because Milton involves the king of disruption with normally respectable activities peculiar to a soldier. *Paradise Lost* interweaves two traditions, one that praises warriors and a second that castigates the devil. Such melding must have startled early readers who were conditioned to respect (or at least excuse) military men. When Th[omas] Beard lists those evildoers whom God will punish, he includes heretics, hypocrites, conjurers, atheists, perjurers, Sabbath breakers, stubborn children, murderers, rapists, adulterers, drunkards, thieves, usurers, and "English traitors." But *The Theatre of Gods Judgements* has no room in its more than two hundred pages for any slurs upon soldiers.[2] Other moral commentators regularly blame the Devil for leading us astray. By identifying demonic actions as martial, Milton attacks the "double speak" of his time. He insists that his reader choose one standard for evaluation, not two. Like a modern liberal who wishes to prove that all "anti-communist" nations can not be called "free," Milton demonstrates how different are the bases for moral and military thought.

Paradise Lost tries to purify speech just as earnestly as Milton's *Grammar* or his *Logic*, but without any popular call for such renovation. Others who dreamed of sanctifying England accepted Rome as their ideal kingdom and assumed, as did Plutarch, that any lasting state must be military (*Roman Questions*, 84). Milton's colleagues were also convinced that war in the old world promoted law and commerce (*Aeneid* 6. 847-53; Livy 1. 16. 7; Ovid, *Fasti* 2. 508); why, they asked ingenuously, should war not be equally profitable in modern times? The epic answers that human strife always involves "slaughter and gigantic deeds" (11. 659). A zealot may romanticize "gigantic deeds," but no sane observer should forget the "slaughter." Although unconsulted, Milton attempts to heal what he considers a psychic rift in seventeenth-century Europeans who complacently parroted truisms about war. He knows that otherwise decent men believe, with gullible simplicity,

> *The end and fruits* [of war] . . . *is honour most high, flowing wealth, euerlasting fame, victorie and dominion without bounds.* (Styward, *Pathwaie*, Sig. A$_{ii}$^{v})

Paradise Lost opposes this dangerous bromide by locating warlike impulses inside the admittedly evil mind of Satan.

---

[2] *The Theatre of Gods Judgements* (London, 1597).

Whatever brilliance the Fiend generates in the epic usually results from his military actions. He commands his army competently, but his home is Hell, a dreary realm of "darkness visible" (1. 63), or (to use John Davies' words), a confused wasteland,

> Whose light is darke, which darke is palpable;
> Whose pleasur's paine, which pain no pen cā tell:
> Whose life is death, which death is damnable:
> Whose peace is strife, which strife is discords well:
> Whose ease is toile, which toile's vnthinkable:
> Where most obedience, learnes most to rebell:
> Where all confusion raignes in endless date,
> In a tumultuous State-disord'ring State.
> (*Humours Heav'n*, p. "153," misnumbered for p. 53)

Anything emerging from such a paradoxical wilderness must be tainted: polluted soil cannot bring forth healthy plants. With scrupulous logic, Milton advances from this genetic premise to a second belief that his audience also accepted: devils can change themselves into any size or shape at will. A translation by "J. F." of Agrippa's *Three Books of Occult Philosophy* restated what most people felt about the nine orders of infernal creatures: they went about "heightning themselves to the length of a Giants body, and again shrinking themselves up to the smalness of the Pigmies, and changing themselves into divers forms, [to] disturb men with vain fear."[3] Since this ability was taken for granted, Milton properly (and unexpectedly) allows his fallen angels to metamorphose into soldiers. When we have finished the epic, we can appreciate how Milton, not Satan, shows the greatest obedience to certain conventions and, simultaneously, the greatest freedom from them. Like Michael and our informed Parents, the author chooses to obey and thus retain his independence, giving the lie to any counterclaim for the virtue of worshipping war.

Milton's unprecedented way of conflating demon with soldier resembles the technique of Freud's dream censor. Both mecha-

---

[3] *Three Books of Occult Philosophy* (London, 1651), p. 400.

nisms neutralize frightful entities by picturing them as slightly ridiculous. The epic's ultimate consolation, however, is not some cartoon *alazon* who lurches up from Hell; rather, Milton implies that the communal nightmare of his age is the heroic vision of war allowed by centuries of lazy analysis had allowed to grow. Once Milton demonstrates that only a fallen creature idolizes war, a reader can free himself from its unwarranted fascination and concentrate upon some "better fortitude" (9. 31).

Paradise Lost anatomizes war so graphically that it stands almost alone in our literary tradition. In the years after its publication, most Englishmen, wearied by contention, longed to preserve domestic tranquility. They made large concessions to keep war away from their lives. The professional army grew, but Marlborough's victories could not save him from disgrace and the Jacobite troubles were ruthlessly suppressed on Scottish soil. Europeans, too, looked more to diplomacy than to thin red (or blue) lines. These retreats from wholesale conflict may be part of a disillusion with war that Milton's epic anticipates.

Since I began by comparing *Paradise Lost* to one work of plastic art, let me conclude by mentioning a second. The column of Marcus Aurelius in Rome rises nearly 150 feet above the Piazza Colonna. It records the emperor's campaigns among barbaric tribes who fought against southern dominion. With grim candor that only eyewitnesses could maintain, the sculptors create a mute illustration of Milton's poem. They depict real soldiers bowed under heavy packs, jostled in the chaos of sieges, resigned while forcing German prisoners to behead their own comrades. This, plead the sculptors, is how actual armies carry on the work of war. Both column and poem were superintended by men who resented battle. Yet neither Marcus nor Milton could ignore it. Each realized that his countrymen often saved themselves from national despair by monumentalizing the details of belligerency. Both philosopher and poet manage to remain faithful to their cultural heritages when they produce their memorials, but neither allows convention to smother his private estimate of combat. *Paradise Lost* speaks against war with such learning, complexity, and humaneness that it still towers over other statements in our long Western tradition.

APPENDIX

Some Additional Bee—War References

Source	Place / Disaster / Time
Varro, *De Re Rustica* 3. 16. 30	When bees swarm, they sound like soldiers breaking camp.
Livy 21. 46. 2-3	Ticinum: swarm over Scipio's tent precedes Roman defeat by Hannibal. 218 B.C.
—— 24. 10. 11-12	Roman Forum: prelude to panic when populace thinks Hannibal has seized Janiculum. 214 B.C.
—— 27. 23. 2	Casinum: warning that the Consuls are about to be ruined. 208 B.C.
Valerius Maximus, *De Dictis Factisque Memorabilibus* 1. 6. 12	Pharsalus: omen that Pompey will be defeated by Julius Caesar. 48 B.C.
Plutarch, *Brutus* 39 and 48	Philippi: sign that Brutus and Cassius will lose to Antony. 42 B.C.
—— *Dion*, 24	Soothsayer worries Dion that bees' presence indicates initial prosperity will be followed by ruin.
Tacitus, *Annals* 12. 64	Roman Capitol: prelude to Agrippina's poisoning of Claudius. 54 A.D.
Appian, *Civil Wars* 2. 10. 68	Pharsalus
—— 4. 17. 134	Philippi

Source	Place / Disaster / Time
Florus, *Epitomae* 1. 22. 14	Trasimene: prodigy before Roman defeat by Hannibal. 217 B.C.
—— 2. 13. 45	Pharsalus
Dio Cassius, *Roman History* 41. 61. 2	Pharsalus
—— 42. 26. 1	Roman Capitol: bees near Hercules' statue warn of year's disasters. 48 B.C.
—— 47. 2. 3	Aesculapius' shrine: portent of return to Rome by Antony, Lepidus, and Octavius. 43 B.C.
—— 47. 40. 7	Mt. Pangaeum in Macedonia: presage of Cassius' defeat and end of Republic. 42 B.C.
—— 54. 33. 2	Visurgis (Weser) River: warning to Drusus before Germans nearly annihilate Roman army. 11 B.C.
—— 56. 24. 4	Germany: token of Varus' defeat. 9 A.D.
—— 61. 35. 1	Roman Capitol: prelude to Agrippina's poisoning of Claudius. 54 A.D.
—— 79. 25. 1-2	Forum Boarium: harbinger of Macrinus' downfall. 217 A.D.
Ammianus Marcellinus 18. 3. 1	House of Barbatio, Commander of Infantry under Constantius II: "highly dangerous augury" precedes his involvement in treasonous correspondence with wife, both of whom are executed. 359 A.D.

BIBLIOGRAPHY

I. Editions of Milton

Bentley, Richard, ed. *Milton's Paradise Lost. A New Edition.* London, 1732.

Carey, John and Alastair Fowler, eds. *The Poems of John Milton.* London, 1968.

Hughes, Merritt Y., ed. *John Milton: Complete Poems and Major Prose.* New York, 1957.

Patterson, Frank Allen, gen. ed. *The Works of John Milton.* 23 vols. New York, 1931-40.

Tillyard, Phyllis B., tr. *John Milton: Private Correspondence and Academic Exercises.* Cambridge, 1932.

Wolfe, Don M., gen. ed. *Complete Prose Works of John Milton.* 8 vols. New Haven, Conn., 1953-

II. Bibliographies

Boswell, Jackson Campbell. *Milton's Library: A Catalogue of the Remains of John Milton's Library and an Annotated Reconstruction of Milton's Library and Ancillary Readings.* New York, 1975.

Cockle, Maurice J. D. *A Bibliography of Military Books up to 1642.* 2nd ed. London, 1957.

Higham, Robin, ed. *A Guide to the Sources of British Military History.* London, 1972.

Young, Peter and Richard Holmes. *The English Civil War. A Military History of the Three Civil Wars, 1642-1651.* London, 1974. (Sources listed on pp. 347-53)

III. Primary Authorities

[Abbot, George]. *A Briefe Description of the Whole Worlde. Wherein is Particularly Described All the Monarchies,*

Empires and Kingdomes of the Same, with their Academies. 3rd ed. London, 1608.

Achesone, James. *The Military Garden, or Instructions for All Young Souldiers, and Such who are Disposed to Learne, and have Knowledge of the Militarie Discipline*. Edinburgh, 1629.

Acontius, Jacobus. *Satans Stratagems, or The Devils Cabinet-Councel Discovered*. Anonymous tr. London, 1648.

Aelian. *On Animals*. Loeb Classical Library.

————. *The Art of Embattailing an Army. Or, the Second Part of Aelians Tacticks*. Tr. John Bingham. London, 1629.

————. *The Tactiks . . . Or Art of Embattailing an Army after ye Grecian Manner*. Tr. J[ohn] B[ingham]. London, 1616.

Aeneas Tacticus; Asclepiodotus; Onasander. Loeb Classical Library.

Aeschylus. *The Lyrical Dramas*. Tr. John Stuart Blackie. London, 1906.

Agricola, Georg. *De Animantibus Subterraneis*. Basle, 1548.

Agrippa, Henry Cornelius. *Three Books of Occult Philosophy*. Tr. J. F. London, 1651.

————. *The Vanity of Arts and Sciences*. London, 1676.

Ambrose. *Expositio in Lucam*. Patrologia Latina, vol. 15, col. 1899.

————. *Hexaemeron*. Patrologia Latina, vol. 14, cols. 249-50.

Ammianus Marcellinus. *Roman History*. Tr. C. D. Yonge. London, 1894.

Anonymous. *Machivells Dogge*. In *The Prince*. Tr. E. D[acres]. London, 1617.

————. "A True Relation of a Brave English Stratagem Practised Lately upon a Sea Town in Galicia . . . by One English Ship Alone . . . with No More than 35 Men in Her." London, 1626. In *Stuart Tracts: 1603-1693*, ed. Firth, pp. 299-308.

Apollodorus. *Library*. Loeb Classical Library.

Appian. *Roman History*. Loeb Classical Library.

Aquinas, Thomas. *The Summa Theologica*. 2nd ed. Tr. Fathers of the English Dominican Province. 22 vols. London, 1920.

Aristotle. *Works*. Loeb Classical Library.

Asclepiodotus; Aeneas Tacticus; Onasander. Loeb Classical Library.

Augustine. *De Doctrina Christiana*. Patrologia Latina, vol. 34, col. 2.

———. *The City of God*. Tr. Marcus Dods. New York, 1950.

Babington, John. *Pyrotechnia or, A Discourse of Artificiall Fire-Works*. London, 1635.

Bacon, Francis. *Essays*. Ed. W. A. Wright. London, 1862.

———. *The Moral and Historical Works*. Ed. Joseph Devey. London, 1890.

Ball, John. *A Treatise of Faith*. 3rd ed. London, 1637.

Bancroft, Thomas. *Time's Out of Tune; Plaid Upon However. In XX Satyres*. London, 1658.

Barret, Robert. *The Theorike and Practike of Moderne Warres, Discoursed in Dialogue wise. Wherein is Declared the Neglect of Martiall Discipline . . . the Fittest Weapons . . . the Parts of a Perfect Souldier . . . the Imbattailing of Men in Formes Now Most in Use*. London, 1598.

Barriff, William. *Mars, His Triumph. Or, the Description of an Exercise Performed the XVIII. of October, 1638. In Merchant-Taylors Hall by Certain Gentlemen of the Artillery Garden London*. London, 1639.

Barry, Gerat. *A Discourse of Military Discipline*. Bruxells, 1634.

Bartholomeus Anglicus. *De Proprietatibus Rerum*. Tr. John Trevisa. London, 1535.

Barwick, Humfrey. *A Breefe Discourse, Concerning the Force and Effect of All Manuall Weapons of Fire, and the Disability of the Long Bowe or Archery*. London, 1594?.

Basil the Great. *On the Hexameron*. Patrologia Graeca, vol. 27, col. 172.

Bateman, St[ephan]. *The Doome, Warning All Men*. London, 1582.

Bear, Edmond. "An Agreement of the People for a Firme and Present Peace, upon Grounds of Common-Right and Freedome." London, 1647. In *Freedom in Arms: A Selection of Leveller Writings*, ed. A. L. Morton. New York, 1975.

Beard, Th[omas]. *The Theatre of Gods Iudgements: or, A Collection of Histories . . . Concerning the Admirable Judgements of God upon the Transgressours of his Commandements*. London, 1597.

Becon, Thomas. *The Catechism*. Ed. John Ayre. Parker Society Reprint, vol. 3. Cambridge, 1844.

de Bellay, William. *Instructions for the Warres. Amply, Learnedly, and Politiquely Discoursing the Method of Militarie Discipline*. Tr. Paule Ive. London, 1589.

Bernard of Clairvaux. *Epistles*. Patrologia Latina, vol. 182, col. 360.

Bernard, Ric[hard]. *The Bible-Battells. Or the Sacred Art Military. For the Rightly Wageing of Warre According to Holy Writ. Compiled for the Use of All Such Valiant Worthies, and Vertuously Valorous Souldiers, as upon All Just Occasions be Ready to Affront the Enemies of God, our King, and Country*. London, 1629.

Bettenson, Henry, ed. *Documents of the Christian Church*. New York, 1947.

Boniface of Crediton. "Aenigmata de Virtutibus." Patrologia Latina, vol. 89, col. 890.

Bourne, William. *Inventions or Devises. Very Necessary for All Generalles and Captaines, or Leaders of Men, as well by Sea as by Land*. London, 1578.

Bradford, John. *The Writings*. Ed. Aubrey Townsend. Parker Society Reprint, vol. 5. Cambridge, 1848.

Bruno of Chartreuse. *Sententiae*. Patrologia Latina, vol. 165, cols. 922-25.

Burton, Robert. *The Anatomy of Melancholy*. Ed. Floyd Dell and Paul Jordan-Smith. New York, 1927.

Butler, Charles. *The Feminine Monarchie or a Treatise Con-*

cerning Bees, and the Due Ordering of Them. Oxford, 1609.

Butler, Samuel. *Hudibras.* Ed. Alfred Miles. London, 1895.

Caesar, Gaius Julius. *Commentarii.* London, 1585.

———. *Gallic War.* Loeb Classical Library.

Calvin, John. *Institutes of the Christian Religion.* Tr. Henry Beveridge. Vol. 3. Edinburgh, 1846.

Cassian, John. *On the Incarnation.* Patrologia Latina, vol. 50, col. 208.

Cassirer, E., et al., eds. *The Renaissance Philosophy of Man.* Chicago, 1963.

Castiglione, Baldesar. *The Book of the Courtier.* Tr. Charles S. Singleton. Garden City, N.Y., 1959.

Ceriol, Federico Furio. *A Very Briefe and Profitable Treatise Declaring How Many Counsells, and What Maner of Counselers a Prince that will Governe Well Ought to Have.* Tr. T[homas] Blundeville. London, 1570.

"Charles I." *Eikon Basilike. The Pourtraicture of His Sacred Majesty in His Solitudes and Sufferings.* London, 1649.

Chaucer, Geoffrey. *The Works.* Ed. F. N. Robinson. 2nd ed. Boston, 1957.

Chrysostom, John. *Concerning the Statues.* Patrologia Graeca, vol. 49, col. 129.

Cicero. *The Basic Works.* Ed. Moses Hadas. New York, 1951.

Clarke, Samuel. *The Marrow of Ecclesiastical History.* London, 1650.

Claudian. *De Bello Gothico.* Loeb Classical Library.

Columella. *De Re Rustica.* Loeb Classical Library.

C[ooke], E[dward]. *The Prospective Glasse of Warre.* London, 1639. Combines two earlier works: *The Character of Warre, or The Image of Martiall Discipline: Contayning many useful Directions for Musters & Armes* (London, 1626); *The Prospective Glasse of Warre. Shewing You a Glimps of Warre['s] Mystery, in her admirable Stratagems, Policie[s,] Wayes* (London, 1628).

Caecilius Cyprian. *The Treatises.* In *A Library of Fathers of the*

Holy Catholic Church Anterior to the Division of the East and West. Tr. Members of the English Church. Vol. 3. Oxford, 1839.

Daniel, Samuel. *The First Fowre Bookes of the Civile Wars.* London, 1595.

Dansie, John. *A Mathematicall Manuel: Wherein is Handled Arithmeticke, Planimetry, Stereometry, and the Embatteling of Armies.* London, 1627.

Dante. *Inferno. Purgatorio. Paradiso.* Tr. John D. Sinclair. 3 vols. Oxford, 1948.

Davies, Edw[ard]. *Military Directions, or The Art of Trayning; Plainely Demonstrating how Every Good Souldier Ought to Behave Himselfe in the Warres.* London, 1618.

[Davies of Hereford, John.] *Bien Venu. Greate Britaines Welcome to Hir Greate Friendes, and Deere Brethren the Danes.* London, 1606.

―――. *Humours Heav'n on Earth; With the Civile Warres of Death and Fortune; As also the Triumph of Death.* London, 1605.

Dekker, Thomas. *The Seven Deadlie Sinns of London.* London, 1606.

Digges, Leonard and Thomas. *A Geometrical Practise, Named Pantometria, Divided into Three Bookes.* 2nd ed. London, 1591.

Dillingham, William. "Continuation of the Siege of Ostend, from 25 July, 1601, as far as 7 Mar. 1602." In *Stuart Tracts: 1603-1693,* ed. Firth, pp. 175-80.

Dio Cassius. *Roman History.* Loeb Classical Library.

Diodorus Siculus. *Works.* Loeb Classical Library.

Earle, John. *Microcosmography.* Ed. Harold Osborne. London, n.d.

Edmonds [sic], Clement. *Observations upon Caesars Commentaries.* Enlarged ed. London, 1604.

Edmunds, Clement. *Observations upon Caesars Comentaries* [sic]. 2nd ed. London?, 1609.

―――. *Observations upon the First Five Bookes of Caesars*

Commentaries, Setting fourth the Practise of the Art Military, in the Time of the Roman Empire. . . . For the Better Direction of our Moderne Warres. London, 1600.

―――. *Observations upon the First Five Books of Caesars Commentaries*. London, 1604.

Erasmus, Desiderius. *The Complaint of Peace. Wryten in Latyn . . . And Nuely Translated . . . By Thomas Paynell*. n.p., 1559.

―――. *The Enchiridion*. Tr. Raymond Himelick. Bloomington, Ind., 1963.

Eustathius. *Hexaemeri Metaphrasis*. Patrologia Latina, vol. 53, col. 949.

Fairfax, Thomas, Lord. *Short Memorials*. Ed. Brian Fairfax. London, 1699.

Firth, C. H., ed. *Stuart Tracts: 1603-1691*. New York, n.d.; rpt. 1890.

Fowler, Edward. *Libertas Evangelica: or, A Discourse of Christian Liberty. Being a Farther Pursuance of the Argument of the Design of Christianity*. London, 1680.

Frontinus. *Strategems*. Loeb Classical Library.

Garrard, William and [Robert] Hichcock. *The Arte of Warre. Beeing the onely Rare Booke of Myllitarie Profession*. London, 1591.

[Gough, John.] *A Godly Boke wherein is Contayned Certayne Fruitefull, Godlye and Necessarye Rules, to bee Exercised & Put in Practise by All Christes Souldiers Lyvynge in the Campe of This World*. London, 1561.

"A Great Man in the State . . . of Sweden." *A Trumpet to Call Souldiers on to Noble Actions. By the Rare and New Examples of Two Christian Kings and a Prince . . . Viz. Gustavus the now-Present King of Sweden, Against Sigismond King of Poland, and the Prince his Sonne, in Removing of the Siege of Meve, a Towne in Poland . . .* [September 1616]. London, 1627.

Gregory Nazianzen. *Orations*. Patrologia Graeca, vol. 36, col. 59.

Grimald, Lawrence. *The Counsellor*. London, 1598.

Grimeston, Ed[ward]. *A Generall Historie of the Netherlands . . . 1608 . . . till . . . 1627*. London, 1627.

Grotius, Hugo. *De Jure Belli ac Pacis Libri Tres*. Ed. P. C. Molhuijsen. The Hague, 1919.

Herbert, Th[omas]. *A Description of the Persian Monarchy Now Beinge the Orientall Indyes*. London, 1634.

Herodotus. *Histories*. Tr. Aubrey de Selincourt. Baltimore, 1954.

Herring, [Francis]. *Mischeefes Mysterie: or, Treasons Master-Peece. The Powder-Plot*. Tr. John Vicars. London, 1617.

Hesiod. *Theogony*. Loeb Classical Library.

Heywood, Tho[mas]. *The Hierarchie of the Blessed Angells. Their Names, Orders and Offices. The Fall of Lucifer with His Angells*. London, 1635.

Hexham, Henry. "Account of the Assault on Ostend, 7th January, 1602." In *Stuart Tracts: 1603-1693*, ed. Firth, pp. 200-10.

————. *The Principles of the Art Militarie; Practised in the Warres of the United Netherlands*. London, 1637.

————. *The Second Part of the Principles, of the Art Militarie Practised in the Warres of United Provinces*. London, 1638.

Hill, Thomas. *A Profitable Instruction of the Perfect Ordering of Bees*. London, 1608.

Hincmar of Rheims. *Explanatio in Ferculum Salmonis*. Patrologia Latina, vol. 125, cols. 840-43.

Homer. *Iliad*. Loeb Classical Library.

————. *Odyssey*. Ed. W. B. Stanford. 2 vols. London, 1965.

Horace. *Complete Works*. Ed. C. E. Bennett and rev. John C. Rolfe. Boston, 1960.

Hugh of St. Victor. *De Bestiis*. Patrologia Latina, vol. 177, col. 13.

[Hugo, Herman.] *The Seige of Breda by the Armes of Phillip the Fourt under the Government of Isabella Atchived by the Conduct of Ambr. Spinola*. Tr. Gerat Barry. Louvain, 1627.

Isidore of Seville. *Etymologiae*. Patrologia Latina, vol. 82.

Ivo of Chartres. *Panormia*. Patrologia Latina, vol. 161, cols. 1307-18.

James I. ΒΑΣΙΛΙΚÒΝ ΔῶΡΟΝ. Or his *Maiesties Instructions to his Dearest Sonne, Henrie the Prince*. London, 1603.

———. "A Proclamation Prohibiting the Publishing of any Reports or Writings of Duels." 15 October 1613.

Jerome. *In Ezekiel*. Patrologia Latina, vol. 25, col. 15.

[Johnson, Richard.] *The Most Pleasant History of Tom ALincoln. The Renowned Souldier, the Red-Rose Knight, who for his Valour and Chivalry, was surnamed the Boast of England. Shewing his Honourable Victories in Forraigne Countries, with his Strange Fortunes in the Fayrie Land: and how he Married the Faire Angliotora, Daughter to Prester John, that Renowned Monarke of the World*. London, 1631.

Du Jon, Fr[ancis.] *The Apocalyps, or Revelation of S. John the Apostle and Evangelist of our Lord Jesus Christ. With a Briefe and Methodicall Exposition upon Every Chapter by Way of a Little Treatise, Applying the Words of S. John to our Last Times that are Full of Spirituall and Corporall Troubles and Divisions in Christendome*. Cambridge, 1596.

Jonson, Ben. *The Complete Poetry*. Ed. William B. Hunter, Jr. Garden City, N.Y., 1963.

Julius Obsequens. *De Prodigiis*. Ed. Car. Benedict. Haas. Paris, 1823.

Kelly, J.N.D., tr. *Early Christian Doctrines*. London, 1965.

[Kellie, Thomas.] *Pallas Armata, or, Militarie Instructions for the Learned: And All Generous Spirits Who Affect the Profession of Armes. The First Part*. Edinburgh, 1627.

Knolles, Richard. *The Generall Historie of the Turkes, from the First Beginning of that Nation to the Rising of the Othoman Familie*. London, 1603.

Lactantius. *De Ira Dei*. Patrologia Latina, vol. 7, col. 129.

———. *Divine Institutes*. Patrologia Latina, vol. 6, col. 708.

Lawrence, Henry. *An History of Angells, Being a Theologicall*

Treatise of our Communion and Warre with Them. London, 1649.

La3amon. *Brut*. Ed. G. L. Brook and R. F. Leslie. Vol. 2. Oxford, 1978.

[Leigh, William.] *Great Britaines, Great Deliverance, from the Great Danger of Popish Powder*. London, 1606.

——. *Queene Elizabeth, Paraleld in her Princely Vertues, with David, Josua, and Hezekia*. London, 1612.

L[eighton], A[lexander]. *Speculum Belli Sacri, or The Looking Glasse of the Holy War. Wherein is Discovered: the Evill of War. The Good of Warr: The Guide of War. In the Last of These I Give a Scantling of the Christian Tackticks*. n.p., 1624.

"Leo the Emperor." *De Bellico Apparatu Liber*. Tr. John Cheke. Basle, 1554.

Livy. Loeb Classical Library.

"Lords of His Maiesties . . . Privy Counsayle." *Instructions for Musters and Armes, and the Use Thereof*." London, 1623.

Lucan. *Pharsalia*. Loeb Classical Library.

Lucretius. *De Rerum Natura Libri Sex*. Ed. William E. Leonard and Stanley B. Smith. Madison, Wis., 1968.

Luther, Martin. *The Bondage of the Will*. Tr. J. I. Packer and O. R. Johnstone. Westwood, N.J., 1957.

Lyly, John. *Euphues*. Ed. E. Arber. London, 1868.

Lyndsey, David. *A Dialogue betweene Experience and a Courtier, of the Miserable Estate of the World, First Compiled in the Schottische Tongue*. London, 1566.

Machiavelli, Niccolò. *Il Principe*. Ed. L. Arthur Burd. Oxford, 1891.

——. *The Art of War*. Tr. Ellis Farneworth and rev. Neal Wood. Indianapolis, Ind., 1965.

——. *The Arte of Warre*. Tr. Peter Whitehorne. London, 1560.

Macrobius. *Saturnalia*. Teubner.

Malthus, F[rancis]. *A Treatise of Artificall Fireworkes both for Warres and Recreation*. London, 1629.

[Marcelline, George.] *Vox Militis: Foreshewing what Perils are*

Procured where the People of This, or any other Kingdome Live without Regard of Marshall Discipline. London, 1625.

Marcus Aurelius. *Meditations.* Loeb Classical Library.

Markham, Francis. *Five Decades of Epistles of Warre.* London, 1622.

———. *The Booke of Honour. Or, Five Decads of Epistles of Honour.* London, 1625.

[Markham, Gervase.] *Cheape and Good Husbandry for the Well-Ordering of all Beasts, and Fowles, and for the General Cure of their Diseases.* London, 1614.

———. *The Second Part of the Soldiers Grammar: or A Schoole for Young Soldiers.* London, 1627.

———. *The Souldiers Accidence. Or an Introduction into Military Discipline . . . A Worke fit for all Noble, Generous, and Good Spirits, that Love Honor, or Honorable Action.* London, 1625.

Raban Maur. *Commentario in Librum Judicum.* Patrologia Latina, vol. 108, col. 1124.

———. *Expositio super Jeremiam.* Patrologia Latina, vol. 111, col. 1227.

———. *De Universo.* Patrologia Latina, vol. 111, cols. 449-551.

M[ay], T[homas]. *A Continuation of Lucan's Historicall Poem till the Death of Julius Caesar.* London, 1630.

della Mirandola, Pico. "Oration on the Dignity of Man." In *The Renaissance Philosophy of Man,* ed. Cassirer et al., pp. 223-54.

[Monk], George, Duke of Albemarle. *Observations upon Military & Political Affairs.* London, 1671.

Monro, Robert. *Expedition with the Worthy Scots Regiment (called Mac-Keyes Regiment) levied in August 1626 . . . for the Use of All Worthie Cavaliers Favouring the Laudable Profession of Armes.* London, 1637.

More, Thomas. *Utopia.* Ed. Edward Surtz. New Haven, 1964.

Morton, A. L., ed. *Freedom in Arms: A Selection of Leveller Writings.* New York, 1975.

Mouffet, Thomas. *Insectorum sive Minimorum Animalium*

Theatrum. London, 1634. Tr. as *The Theater of Insects.* London, 1658.

Musculus, Wolfgangus. *Common Places of Christian Religion . . . for the Use of Such as Desire the Knowledge of Godly Truth.* Tr. John Man. London, 1578.

N[eade], W[illiam]. *The Double-armed Man, by the New Invention.* London, 1625.

Nepos, Cornelius; Florus. *Works.* Loeb Classical Library.

Norris, [John]. *A True Discourse of the late Battaile Fought betweene our Englishmen, and the Prince of Parma, on Monday the 15. of November 1585.* London, 1585.

Norton, Robert. *The Gunner Shewing the Whole Practice of Artillery: With all the Appurtenances thereunto Belonging. Together with the Making of Exrraordinarie Artificiall Fire-workes, as well for Pleasure and Triumphs, as for Warre and Service.* London, 1628.

Ogilby, John. *Aesopicks: or, A Second Collection of Fables.* 2nd ed. London, 1673.

Onasander; Aeneas Tacticus; Asclepiodotus. Loeb Classical Library.

Onosandro Platonico. *The Generall Captaine.* Tr. Peter Whytehorne. London, 1563.

Origen. *The Writings.* Tr. Frederick Crombie. Edinburgh, 1872.

Orrery, Roger Boyle, Earl of. *A Treatise of the Art of War: Dedicated to the Kings Most Excellent Majesty.* London, 1677.

[Osborne, Francis.] *Politicall Reflections upon the Government of the Turks.* Oxford, 1656.

Overbury, Sir Thomas. *Observations, in his Travels, upon the State of the Seventeen Provinces, as They Stood Anno Domini 1609; The Treaty of Peace Being Then on Foot.* London, 1626. In *Stuart Tracts: 1603-1693,* ed. Firth, pp. 211-32.

Ovid. *Fasti.* Tr. J. G. Frazer. 6 vols. London, 1929.

————. *Works.* Loeb Classical Library.

Patrizi, Francesco. *La militia romana di Polibio, di Tito Livio, e*

Dionigi Alicarnaseo . . . Ma ancora, in paragone, farà chiaro, quanto la moderna sia difettosa & imperfetta. Ferrara, 1583.

———. Paralleli militari . . . Né quali si fa paragone delle milizie antiche, in tutte le parti loro, con le moderne. Rome, 1594.

———. Paralleli militari. Parte II. Della militia riformata. Nella quale s'aprono, i modi, e l'ordinanze varie degli antichi. Accomodate a nostri fuochi . . . Rome, 1595.

Paynell, Thomas. The Complaint of Peace. London, 1559.

Peeke, R[ichard]. Three to One. Being an English-Spanish Combat Performed by a Western Gentleman of Tavistock in Devonshire, with an English Quarter-staff, against Three Spaniards . . . the 15th Day of November 1625. London, 1626. In Stuart Tracts: 1603-1693, ed. Firth, pp. 275-93.

Pepys, Samuel. Memoirs. Ed. Richard Lord Braybrooke. London, n.d.

"Philanactophil" [Edmund Bolton]. Nero Caesar, or Monarchie Depraved. An Historicall Worke. London, 1624.

Philip of Harveng. De Institutione Clericorum. Patrologia Latina, vol. 203, cols. 924-26.

Phillips, Edward. "The Life of Milton." In John Milton: Complete Poetry and Selected Prose, ed. Hughes, pp. 1025-37.

Pliny. Letters. Loeb Classical Library.

———. Natural History. Loeb Classical Library.

Plutarch. Works. Loeb Classical Library.

Polyaenus. Stratagems of War. Tr. R. Shepherd. London, 1793.

Polybius. The Histories. Loeb Classical Library.

di Porcia, Count Giacomo. The Preceptes of Warre. Tr. Peter Betham. London, 1544.

Praissac, Lord of. The Art of Warre, or Militarie Discourses of Leavying, Marching, Encamping; and Embattailing an Armie . . . Tr. J[ohn] C[ruso]. Cambridge, 1639.

Quintilian. Institutio Oratoria. Loeb Classical Library.

Rawlins, John. The Famous and Wonderful Recovery of a Ship

of Bristol, called the Exchange, from the Turkish Pirates of Argier. London, 1622. In *Stuart Tracts: 1603-1693*, ed. Firth, pp. 247-74.

Rich, Barnaby. *A Path-Way to Military Practise. Containinge Offices, Lawes, Disciplines and Orders to be Observed in an Army, with sundry Stratagems.* London, 1587.

Roberts, John. *The Compleat Cannoniere: or, The Gunners Guide . . . With Divers Excellent Conclusions, both Arithmeticall and Geometricall belonging thereunto: As Also Sundry Serviceable Fireworkes.* London, 1639.

Roberts, Lewes. *Warre-Fare Epitomized, in a Century, of Military Observations: Confirming by Antient Principles the Moderne Practise of Armes.* London, 1640.

Rohan, Henry, Duke of. *The Complete Captain, or, An Abbridgement of Caesars Warres, with Observations upon Them.* Cambridge, 1640.

―――. *A Treatise of Modern War.* Tr. J[ohn] C[ruso]. Cambridge, 1640.

Rufus, Quintus Curtius. *De Rebus Alexandri Magni.* Ed. Samuel Pitisk. Utrecht, 1685.

Salkeld, John. *A Treatise of Angels. Of the Nature, Essence, Place, Power, Science, Will, Apparitions, Grace, Sinne, and all other Proprieties of Angels.* London, 1613.

Sallust. *Conspiracy of Catiline.* Loeb Classical Library.

Scriptores Historiae Augustae. Loeb Classical Library.

[Segar, Sir William.] *The Booke of Honor and Armes.* London, 1590.

Selden, John. *The Table Talk.* Ed. Samuel Harvey Reynolds. Oxford, 1892.

Servius. *Commentarii.* Teubner.

Silius Italicus. *Punica.* Loeb Classical Library.

Smaragdus of Anaine. *Diadema Monachorum.* Patrologia Latina, vol. 102, col. 609.

Smith, John. *The Generall Historie of Virginia, New-England, and the Summer Isles: with the Names of the Adventurers, Planters, and Govenours from their first Beginning .Añ: 1584. To this Present 1626.* London, 1631.

————. *The True Travels, Adventures, and Observations . . . In Europe, Asia, Affrica, and America, from Anno Domini 1593. to 1629.* London, 1630.

Smithe, John. *Instructions, Observations, and Orders Mylitarie.* London, 1595.

————. *Certain Discourses . . . Concerning the Formes and Effects of Divers Sorts of Weapons, and Other Very Important Matters Military.* London, 1590. Modernized version, ed. J. R. Hale. Ithaca, N.Y., 1964.

Soranzo, Lazaro. *The Ottoman . . . Wherein is Delivered a Full and Perfect Report of the Might and Power of Mahamet the Third . . .* Tr. Abraham Hartwell. London, 1603.

Spencer, Edmund, *The Complete Poetical Works.* Ed. R. E. Neil Dodge. Cambridge, Mass., 1936.

Sprat, Thomas. *The History of the Royal Society of London.* London, 1667.

Sprigge, Joshua. *Anglia Rediviva; Englands Recovery: Being the History of the Motions, Actions, and Successes of the Army under . . . Sr. Thomas Fairfax.* London, 1647.

[Stafford, Thomas.] *Pacata Hibernia, Ireland Appeased and Reduced. or, An Historie of the Late Warres of Ireland, Especially within the Province of Mounster, under the Government of Sir George Carew.* London, 1633.

Statius. *Thebaid.* Loeb Classical Library.

Styward, Thomas. *The Pathwaie to Martiall Discipline, Devided into two Bookes, verie Necessarie for young Souldiers, or for all such as Loveth the Profession of Armes.* London, 1581.

Suetonius. Loeb Classical Library.

Sutcliffe, Matthew. *The Practice, Proceedings, and Lawes of Armes, Described out of the Doings of Most Valiant and Expert Captaines, and Confirmed Both by Ancient, and Moderne Examples, and Praecedents.* London, 1593.

Symmons, Edward. *A Loyall Subjects Beliefe, Expressed in a Letter to Master Stephen Marshall.* Oxford, 1643.

Tacitus. *Annals.* Loeb Classical Library.

————. *Histories.* Loeb Classical Library.

Tasso, Torquato. *Jerusalem Delivered*. Tr. Edward Fairfax. London, 1600.

Tertullian. *Adversus Judaeos*. Patrologia Latina, vol. 2, cols. 660-61.

———. *Apology*. Loeb Classical Library.

———. *The Writings*. Ed. Alexander Roberts and James Donaldson. Vol. 1. Edinburgh, 1869.

Topsell, Edward. *The History of Serpents*. London, 1608.

Trussell, Thomas. *The Souldier, Pleading his Owne Cause*. 3rd imp. London, 1626.

Valerius Flaccus. *Argonautica*. Loeb Classical Library.

"Signior Valesco." *Newes from Rome. Of Two Mightie Armies, as well Footemen as Horsemen: The First of the Great Sophy, the Other of an Hebrew People. . . . Also Certaine Prophecies of a Jew . . . Called Caleb Shilocke*. Tr. "W. W." London, 1606?

Varro. *De Re Rustica*. In *Roman Farm Management*. Tr. "A Virginia Farmer." New York, 1913.

Vegetius Renatus, Flavius. *The Foure Bookes*. Tr. John Sadler. London, 1572.

———. *Military Institutions . . . in Five Books*. Tr. John Clarke. London, 1767.

Vere, Francis. *The Commentaries*. Ed. William Dillingham. Cambridge, 1657.

Vergil, Polydore. *Anglica Historia*. London, 1534.

Vincent, [Philip]. *The Lamentations of Germany. Wherein, as in a Glasse, We May Behold Ther [sic] Miserable Condition, and Reade the Woefull Effects of Sinne*. London, 1638.

da Vinci, Leonardo. *The Notebooks*. Ed. Jean Paul Richter. 2 vols. 1884; rpt. New York, 1970.

Viret, Peter. *The Schoole of Beastes; Intituled, the Good Housholder, or the Oeconomickes*. London, 1585.

Virgil. *Works*. Loeb Classical Library.

Vives, Juan. "A Fable about Man." In *The Renaissance Philosophy of Man*, ed. Cassirer et al., pp. 387-93. Chicago, 1963.

de Voragine, Jacobus. *The Golden Legend*. Tr. Granger Ryan and Helmut Ripperger. New York, 1941.

Ward, Robert. *Anima'dversions of Warre; or, A Militarie Magazine of the Truest Rules, and Ablest Instructions, for the Managing of Warre*. London, 1639.

———. *Anima'dversions of Warre. The Second Book*. London, 1639.

[Watts, William.] *The Swedish Discipline, Religious, Civile, and Military*. London, 1632.

White, T. H., tr. *The Bestiary*. New York, 1960.

Whitelock, Bulstrode. *Memorials*. London, 1682.

Williams, Griffith. *Jura Majestatis, the Rights of Kings both in Church and State: . . . and, the Wickednesses of the Faction of this Pretended Parliament at Westminster*. Oxford, 1644.

———. *The True Church*. London, 1629.

Williams, Roger. *A Briefe Discourse of Warre*. London, 1590.

———. *The Actions of the Low Countries*. 1618. Ed. D. W. Davies. Ithaca, N.Y., 1964.

Wither, George. *The Hymnes and Songs of the Church*. London, 1623.

Xenophon. *Works*. Loeb Classical Library.

Zanchy, Jerome. *Confession of Christian Religion*. Anonymous Tr. Cambridge, 1599.

———. *Operum Theologicorum*. Geneva, 1613.

IV. Secondary Authorities

A. BOOKS

Adams, Robert P. *The Better Part of Valor: More, Erasmus, Colet, and Vives, on Humanism. War, and Peace*. Seattle, 1962.

Allen, Don Cameron. *The Harmonious Vision: Studies in Milton's Poetry*. Baltimore, 1954.

Armstrong, John. *The Paradise Myth*. London, 1969.

Bainton, Roland. *Christian Attitudes Toward War and Peace.* New York, 1960.

Bamberger, J. *Fallen Angels.* Philadelphia, 1952.

Boynton, Lindsay. *The Elizabethan Militia: 1558-1638.* London, 1967.

Broadbent, J. B. *Some Graver Subject.* London, 1960.

Carus, Paul. *The History of the Devil and the Idea of Evil from the Earliest Times to the Present Day.* 1900; rpt. New York, 1969.

Cope, Jackson I. *The Metaphoric Structure of Paradise Lost.* Baltimore, 1962.

Coughlan, Robert. *The World of Michelangelo, 1475-1564.* New York, 1966.

Cruickshank, C. G. *Elizabeth's Army.* 2nd ed. Oxford, 1966.

Curtius, Ernst Robert. *European Literature and the Latin Middle Ages.* Tr. Willard R. Trask. New York, 1963.

Daiches, David. *Milton.* New York, 1966.

Department of the Army. *Guerilla Warfare and Special Forces Operations.* Field Manual 31-21. Washington, D.C., 1958.

Department of Defense. *The Armed Forces Officer.* Pamphlet I-20. Washington, D.C., 1965.

Dorian, Donald C. *A Study of Milton's Ideas of War.* Columbia University M.A. Thesis, 1929.

Duncan, Joseph E. *Milton's Earthly Paradise: A Historical Study of Eden.* Minneapolis, 1972.

Emerson, Everett H. *English Puritanism from John Hooper to John Milton.* Durham, N.C. 1968.

Fallon, Robert Thomas. *Milton's Military Imagery: Its Growth and Function in his Art.* Columbia University Dissertation, 1964.

Firth, Charles H. *Cromwell's Army.* 3rd ed. London, 1921.

Frank, Joseph. *Hobbled Pegasus: A Descriptive Bibliography of Minor English Poetry, 1641-1660.* Albuquerque, N.M., 1968.

——. *The Levellers.* Cambridge, Mass., 1955.

Frazer, J. G. *Balder the Beautiful*. 2 vols. London, 1923.

French, J. Milton. *The Life Records of John Milton*. 5 vols. New Brunswick, N.J., 1949-1958.

Frye, Roland Mushat. *Milton's Imagery and the Visual Arts: Iconographic Tradition in the Epic Poems*. Princeton, 1978.

Gardiner, Samuel R. *History of the Great Civil War, 1642-1649*. 4 vols. London, 1893.

Giamatti, A. Bartlett. *The Earthly Paradise and the Renaissance Epic*. Princeton, 1966.

Haller, William. *The Rise of Puritanism*. New York, 1938.

Hanford, James Holly. *A Milton Handbook*. 4th ed. New York, 1946.

Hill, Christopher. *Milton and the English Revolution*. New York, 1977.

Hughes, Merritt Y., gen. ed. *A Variorum Commentary on the Poems of John Milton*. 4 vols. in 5. London and New York, 1970-75.

Jebb, R. C. *Homer*. London, 1887.

Johnson, Samuel. *Selections from Lives of the Poets*. Ed. Edmund Fuller. New York, 1965.

Jung, Leo. *Fallen Angels in Jewish, Christian and Mohammedan Literature*. New York, 1926; rpt. New York, 1974.

Ketchum, Richard M., ed. *The Horizon Book of the Renaissance*. New York, 1961.

Kluger, Rivkah Schärf. *Satan in the Old Testament*. Tr. Hildegard Nagel. Evanston, Ill., 1967.

Kranidas, Thomas. *The Fierce Equation: A Study of Milton's Decorum*. The Hague, 1965.

Landor, Walter Savage. *The Complete Works*. ed. T. Earle Welby. Vol. 7. London, 1938.

Langsam, G. Geoffrey. *Martial Books and Tudor Verse*. New York, 1951.

Lawry, Jon S. *The Shadow of Heaven*. Ithaca, N.Y., 1968.

Levin, Harry. *The Myth of the Golden Age in the Renaissance*. Bloomington, Ind., 1969.

Lewis, C. S. *A Preface to Paradise Lost*. London, 1942.

Lieb, Michael. *The Dialectics of Creation: Patterns of Birth and Regeneration in Paradise Lost*. Amherst, Mass., 1970.

Masson, David. *The Life of John Milton: Narrated in Connection with the Political, Ecclesiastical, and Literary History of His Time*. 7 vols. Cambridge, 1859-94.

Mohl, Ruth. *John Milton and His Commonplace Book*. New York, 1969.

Montaigne. *The Complete Essays*. Tr. Donald M. Frame. 3 vols. Garden City, N.Y., 1960.

Olson, Marilynn Strasser. *Nil Medium: Noble Soldiers in the Drama in English, 1625-1660*. Duke University Dissertation, 1975.

Panofsky, Dora and Erwin. *Pandora's Box*. 2nd ed. New York, 1962.

Parker, Geoffrey and Angela. *European Soldiers 1550-1650*. Cambridge, 1977.

Parker, William Riley. *Milton: A Biography*. 2 vols. Oxford, 1968.

Parry, R. H., ed. *The English Civil War and After: 1642-1658*. Berkeley, 1970.

Patch, Howard Rollin. *The Other World*. Cambridge, Mass., 1950.

Paulson, Ronald, ed. *Hogarth's Graphic Works*. 2 vols. Rev. ed. New Haven, 1970.

Peter, John. *A Critique of Paradise Lost*. New York, 1960.

Pointon, Marcia R. *Milton and English Art*. Manchester, 1970.

Purce, Stella Hill. *The War in Heaven: A Study of the Tradition and Paradise Lost*. Yale University Dissertation, 1960.

Radford, E. and M. *Encyclopedia of Superstitions*. New York, 1949.

Schwoerer, Lois. *"No Standing Armies!" The Antiarmy Ideology in Seventeenth-Century England*. Baltimore, 1974.

Shawcross, John T., ed. *Milton: The Critical Heritage*. New York, 1970.

Steadman, John M. *Milton and the Renaissance Hero*. Oxford, 1967.

Stein, Arnold. *Answerable Style*. Minneapolis, 1953.

Taine, H. A. *History of English Literature*. Tr. H. Van Laun. Vol. 1. New York, 1872.

Tillyard, E.M.W. *Studies in Milton*. London, 1951.

Waldock, A.J.A. *Paradise Lost and its Critics*. Cambridge, 1947.

Walzer, Michael. *The Revolution of the Saints*. Cambridge, Mass., 1965.

Watson, G. R. *The Roman Soldier*. Ithaca, 1969.

Webb, Henry J. *Elizabethan Military Science: The Books and the Practice*. Madison, Wis., 1965.

Webster, Graham. *The Roman Army*. Chester, Eng., 1973.

———. *The Roman Imperial Army of the First and Second Centuries A.D.* London, 1969.

Wedgwood, C. V. *The World of Rubens, 1577-1640*. New York, 1967.

West, Robert H. *Milton and the Angels*. Athens, Ga., 1955.

Woodring, Carl R., ed. *Prose of the Romantic Period*. Boston, 1961.

Wright, B. A. *Milton's 'Paradise Lost.'* London, 1962.

Young, Peter. *The English Civil War Armies*. Reading, Eng., 1973.

B. ARTICLES

Adamson, J. H. "The War in Heaven: Milton's Version of the Merkabah." *JEGP*, 57 (1958), 690-703.

Addison, Joseph. *Spectator*, No. 297 (9 February 1712).

Baldwin, E. C. "An Instance of Milton's Debt to Vergil." *JEGP*, 7 (1908), 85-86.

Barry, Boyd M. "Puritan Soldiers in *Paradise Lost*." *MLQ*, 35 (1974), 376-402.

Bawcutt, N. W. "Policy, Machiavellianism, and the Early Tudor Drama." *ELR*, 1 (1971), 195-209.

Beller, E. A. "The Military Expedition of Sir Charles Morgan to Germany, 1627-9." *The English Historical Review*, 43 (1928), 528-39.

Blissett, William. "Caesar and Satan." *JHI*, 18 (1957), 221-32.

Cassirer, E. "Giovanni Pico Della Mirandola." *JHI*, 3 (1942), 123-44, 319-46.

Crosman, Robert. "Some Doubts about 'The Reader of Paradise Lost.' " *CE*, 37 (1975), 372-82.

Daniels, Edgar F. "Milton's 'Doubtful Conflict' and the Seventeenth-Century Tradition." *N & Q*, 206 (1961), 430-32.

Dickerman, Sherwood Owen. "Some Stock Illustrations of Animal Intelligence in Greek Psychology." *TAPA*, 42 (1911), 123-30.

Emerson, Everett H. "Milton's War in Heaven: Some Problems." *MLN*, 69 (1954), 399-402.

Fallon, Robert T. "John Milton and the Honorable Artillery Company." *MQ*, 9 (1975), 49-51.

Freeman, James A. "Satan, Bentley, and 'The Din of War.' " *MQ*, 7 (1973), 1-4.

———. "The Roof Was Fretted Gold." *Comparative Literature*, 27 (1975), 254-66.

Hale, J. R. "Incitement to Violence? English Divines on the Theme of War, 1578 to 1631." In *Florilegium Historiale: Essays Presented to Wallace K. Ferguson*, ed. J. G. Rowe and W. H. Stockdale, pp. 368-99. Toronto, 1971.

Hanford, James Holly. "Milton and the Art of War." *SP*, 18 (1921), 232-66.

Hunter, William B., Jr. "Milton on the Exaltation of the Son: The War in Heaven in *Paradise Lost*." *ELH*, 36 (1969), 215-31.

———. "Satan as Comet: *Paradise Lost* II. 708-711." *ELN*, 5 (1967), 17-21.

Kastor, Frank S. "By Force or Guile Eternal War: *Paradise Lost*, IV 776-1015." *JEGP*, 70 (1971), 269-78.

———. " 'In His Own Shape:' The Stature of Satan in *Paradise Lost*." *ELN*, 5 (1968), 264-69.

MacCracken, Henry N. "Vegetius in English: Notes on the

Early Translations." In *Anniversary Papers by Colleagues and Pupils of George Lyman Kittredge*, ed. Fred Norris Robinson et al., pp. 389-403. Boston, 1913.

McQueen, William. *"Paradise Lost* V, VI: The War in Heaven." *SP*, 71 (1974), 89-104.

Momigliano, Arnaldo. "Some Observations on Causes of War in Ancient Historiography." In his *Studies in Historiography*, pp. 112-26. New York, 1966.

Ong, Walter J. "The Writer's Audience is Always a Fiction." *PMLA*, 90 (1975), 9-21.

Parsons, Coleman O. "The Classical and Humanist Context of *Paradise Lost*, II, 496-505." *JHI*, 29 (1968), 33-52.

Patrides, C. A. " 'The Bloody and Cruell Turke': The Background of a Renaissance Commonplace." *Studies in the Renaissance*, 10 (1963), 126-35.

Raimondi, Ezio. "Machiavelli and the Rhetoric of the Warrior." *MLN*, 92 (1977), 1-16.

Revard, Stella P. "Milton's Critique of Heroic Warfare in *Paradise Lost* V and VI." *SEL*, 7 (1967), 119-39.

―――. "Milton's Gunpowder Poems and Satan's Conspiracy." *MS*, 4 (1972), 63-77.

―――. "The Warring Saints and the Dragon: A Commentary Upon Revelation 12:7-9 and Milton's War in Heaven." *PQ*, 53 (1974), 181-94.

Ridden, Geoffrey. *"Paradise Lost*, IX. 119-22." *MQ*, 7 (1973), 109-10.

Rosenblatt, Jason P. "Milton's Bee-lines." *TSLL*, 18 (1977), 609-23.

Scudder, H. H. "Satan's Artillery." *N & Q*, 195 (1950), 334-47.

St. George, Priscilla P. "Psychomachia in Books V and VI of *Paradise Lost*." *MLQ*, 27 (1966), 185-96.

Steadman, John M. "The Quantum Mutatus Theme and the Fall." *American Notes and Queries*, 2 (1964), 83.

Taylor, George Coffin. "Milton on Mining." *MLN*, 45 (1930), 24-27.

Weidhorn, Manfred. "Satan's Persian Expedition." *N & Q*, 103 (1958), 389-92.

Weismiller, Edward. "Materials Dark and Crude: A Partial Genealogy for Milton's Satan." *HLQ*, 31 (1967), 75-93.

Whaler, James. "Animal Simile in *Paradise Lost*." *PMLA*, 47 (1932), 534-53.

Winn, James A. "Milton on Heroic Warfare." *Yale Review*, 66 (1976), 70-86.

INDEX

Library of Congress Cataloging in Publication Data

Freeman, James A   1935-
   Milton and the martial muse.

   Bibliography: p.
   Includes index.
   1. Milton, John, 1608-1674. Paradise lost.
   2. Milton, John, 1608-1674—Knowledge—Military sciences.
   3. War in literature.   I. Title.
   PR3562.F66   821'.4   80-7519
   ISBN 0-691-06435-0